MIRRORED LIVES

MIRRORED LIVES

AGING CHILDREN AND ELDERLY PARENTS

TOM KOCH

PRAEGER

New York
Westport, Connecticut
London

Library of Congress Cataloging-in-Publication Data

Koch, Tom.
    Mirrored lives : aging children and elderly parents / Tom Koch.
        p.   cm.
    Includes bibliographical references.
    ISBN 0–275–93671–6 (lib. bdg. : alk. paper)
    1. Parents, Aged—United States—Psychology.   2. Adult children—
United States—Psychology.   3. Parents, Aged—Health and hygiene—
United States.   4. Aging—United States.   5. Koch, Norman.
    I. Title.
    HQ1063.6.K63   1990
    306.874—dc20   90–7457

British Library Cataloguing in Publication Data is available.

Library of Congress Catalog Card Number: 90–7457
ISBN: 0–275–93671–6

First published in 1990

Praeger Publishers, One Madison Avenue, New York, NY 10010
An imprint of Greenwood Publishing Group, Inc.

Printed in the United States of America

The paper used in this book complies with the
Permanent Paper Standard issued by the National
Information Standards Organization (Z39.48–1984).

10 9 8 7 6 5 4 3 2

For Rebecca Elniski, Lucy Tarquin, and
Don Clark, who helped; for Ruth K.
Astmann, who insisted; for Ruth
Burnhardt, who supported; and for
Robert Warner, who always understood.

"Let us recognize ourselves in this old man or in that old woman."
Simone de Beauvoir, *The Coming of Age*

"They live more by memory than by hope."
Aristotle

"We must deepen a case history to a narrative or tale: only then do we have a 'who' as well as a 'what'; a real person, a real patient, in relation to disease, in relation to the physical."
Oliver Sacks, *The Man Who Mistook His Wife for a Hat*

Contents

Preface: A Who as Well as a What   ix

1. A Simple Operation   1

2. Time and Chance   27

3. Nothing Fails Like Success   48

4. Paradoxical Existences   76

5. Ceaseless Deprivation   97

6. Incessant Mourning   144

7. The Deprived Time   168

Afterword: What We Learned   184

Select Bibliography   213

Preface
A Who as Well as a What

> At the end, the space of illusion narrows to solitude and we become at best, a presence in the memories of others.
> Murry M. Schwartz, *Memory and Desire*

It would be nice if we could learn from the trials of others. Literature is dedicated to the proposition that by describing one life, even a fictional one, universal or at least cultural truths can be revealed. But writers of fiction have the luxury of creating their cases to fit the moral each hopes to present. Those with the temerity to craft history into narrative do not have a similar freedom. They must walk the thin, tight, high wire of specific fact and general relevance, and most who try this balancing act ultimately fall. Case studies, the intense description of an individual or group's single, specific experience, are a peculiar category of literary enterprise. Potential insight promised by a story's very specificity is usually lost in the flood of reminiscence and detail. If they are to be of more value than catharsis for the author, such works face an almost impossible chore. Each must not simply describe personal triumphs and traumas but also imbed within those stories principles and issues of wider, social import. Somewhere in the minutiae of each clinician's chart may lie a human tale of general applicability. The problem is digging it out.

This is a case history and thus must fit the rigors of descriptive truth while searching for the human values underlying the reportage of a single man's geriatric decline and the effects of that process on his and his family's world. Its topic is the way age and illness progressively the life of one man, Norman Koch, and through that process affected those closest to him. I am its narrator and his son. The text is built from notebooks, workbooks, and letters written during my father's years of progressive distress. The intent has been to furnish a cautionary tale for others caught in age between active hope and geriatric illness.

The resulting book is not dramatic in the usual sense. There is no single crisis, no clear resolution, and no dramatic moment of climax or sublime revelation. Norman Koch is not bankrupted by his illness, ill treated by his physicians, or violated by his children. In fact, he was generally well served by the communities—professional and familial—that worked so hard to maintain his life. There is no violence here and the main subject is not tragic, at least not in the Aristotelian sense. This book's central figure was until his retirement a contented businessman and family provider who appears to have possessed the normal allotment of human frailties and strengths. Finally, this story is one of trial without clear resolution and thus devoid of literature's traditional convention of narrative suspense ultimately resolved. Norman Koch's life extends beyond this tale's completion, and he is neither miraculously healed nor sublimely reconciled to the facts of his decline. The whole of this book describes the frustration of a family whose central member's life is progressively diminished by physical and mental impairment. Thus its value must lie elsewhere than in narrative suspense and the uniqueness of an exceptional, heroic, or tragic male.

DISABILITY AND DEPENDENCE

This book describes in detail the symptoms of a progressive, geriatric decline in which specific illnesses combine to create a systemic failure in an elderly individual. But what is of wider moment than the mundane daily progress of Norman Koch's hepatitis, osteoporosis, leukemia, ambulatory problems, and creeping senility is the battle he fought with the corrosive effect they all had on his perception of life and on the bedrock of his self-esteem. This was the real battleground both for him and for those who cared for him. It was not simply that Norm was sick but that he was old as well. Illnesses were fought with modern pharmacologies and the protocols physicians today can wield. But it was age that first isolated and then, finally, defeated the man. It was not simply that he was ill but that, ultimately, the illness's etiology was, at base, geriatric. It deprived him of mobility while truncating his hope for a future in which new friends and alliances could be formed. Caught between how he was in extremity and how he believed life should be, my father experienced his world shrinking from an encompassing circle to the single point of his sick room.

Like many people, he insisted that to be alive meant to be active. To be able to drive a car, write a check, work, read, or travel were, for him, acts that made of existence a worthwhile adventure. My father believed, as do most North Americans, that life means independence and that to be so bounded by infirmity that the simplest act requires another's help would make of continuance a loathsome burden. His values, then, were those most of us hold, and the drama of this story lies in the effect of his illness on the emotional world Norman Koch had constructed across the seventy-four years of his existence and not simply in the inexorable progress of the diseases themselves.

But this man was not independent, or at least no more so than anyone can be who has lived for decades in a specific place. He stood at the center of a world based in Buffalo, New York, existing within a complex of associations spread across life's time and space. In his home town were acquaintances known since the days of earliest youth and a sister whom he saw with frequency. That "circle," as he called it, also linked him to friendships formed in his former, happily married life. Finally, Norman was a father who fashioned four sons as independents in his own image. He took some pride in the fact that by 1984, when this story begins, they had long been dispersed across North America. That distance assured, he insisted, they would be forever free of his care. "I don't ever want to be a burden to you," he had cautioned them in their youth. "Move away from here when you grow up. You have your own lives to live." He tried to visit his sons each year and they, when life was not too busy, visited him. But then, when he was seventy-four years old, this carefully constructed aura of self-sufficient existence began to unravel. A "routine" operation led to progressive complications, and Norman Koch could no longer, in his own words, "do for myself."

Perhaps the most important issue his story raises is the degree to which anyone should aspire to lead an independent life. That supreme American value—self-sufficiency—is at the center of much that happens here. We are trained from youth to "stand on our own two feet," to "be adults" and "get on with our lives." And as each child learns in time to take those steps, the parent usually swells with pride. But what Norman found, much to his chagrin, was that living alone and being independent, even when money is not the limiting factor, is not always possible. The most galling thing to him was not excruciating pain or simple disability but that illness forced him to rely on others at the end of a life whose boast had been that others came to him for help. He became dependent both on his sister and on a son, a fact that my father found humiliating and frustrating in turn.

If independence was the issue for the patient, that same theme reverberated through the world of his family and friends. Each of Norm's four sons had to decide the degree to which he would sacrifice his time and disrupt his life to assist and comfort an ailing parent or, conversely, had to choose to continue what had become a distant association. For them all, the increasing dependence of their father and the waning of his power forced them to examine both their common past and separate, practical futures as Norman's mobility and sentience declined. His sister and their friends in Buffalo were faced with similar choices made all the more difficult by Norm's unfocused anger over the increasingly strict limits illness imposed on his world. Like most who suffer a disability, he did so neither in silence nor with excessive grace. That made him a hard man to be with through much of this time and provided a convenient excuse for individuals who chose to be elsewhere. Simply, there was little pleasure in visiting my father, whose world had shrunk to a rage at his infirmities, and most people found good reason to stay away.

A number of people have debated the degree to which an elderly individual's personality may change with age and the extent to which some nasty, long-buried self may surface during a geriatric decline. The case studied here suggests that what happens is something more complex and, at the same time, more mundane. Norm's periodic unpleasantness was not simply the manifestation of long-buried madness or the psychiatric transformation of a once social man, but rather his reaction to an increasingly dependent life. What others see as the nastiness of the elderly is at least in part a reflection or, perhaps, refraction of their distaste at the erosion of another's once self-sufficient world. In this there is more than a small measure of fear; insistence on the unpleasantness of the aged is how we, who are still able, distance ourselves from the elderly infirm. Certainly this occurred within my father's world. His context suggested that we whose lives were based on values similar to his had banked our futures upon the fragile proposition of the virtues of personal independence. What to others seemed to be his intransigent and unreasonable behavior was, in the end, a manifestation of their own fears of reliance and not simply my father's secret self coming to the fore. In short, we changed in relation to his progressive diminution. His increasing dependence accentuated the fears of those closest to him that their self-sufficiency was a chimera and not the base on which lives can be built.

Norm and his world, in short, fight simultaneously on two fronts. To the extent that he faced, at any one time, a specific medical crisis with a known etiology and accepted protocol, he was seen as an unchanging individual suffering the specifics of a single, invading organism. In this he was like all modern patients for whom illness and self are supposed to be corporate and distinct. One could identify and separately treat his osteoporotic hip, his degenerative osteoarthritis, his postoperative hepatitis, his hematologic dysfunctions, gastric bleeds and surgical complications. But to the degree he was old and sick, to the extent that his illnesses were geriatric and the etiology one of dependent age for which there is no cure, he was isolated from his world. Rather than accept limitations, he pulled back from the potentials still available and, to our shame, most of us who associated with him were glad to let this elderly changeling go.

THE LANGUAGE OF DESPAIR

This theme of independence is not played out analytically or by inference but in very specific ways. The issue, typically, was transposed from self-esteem to financial cost, and each time the issue of money was raised, it was a cipher for independence. "I'm not rich," Norm insisted, but he was, in his own words, at least "comfortable." A member of the upper echelons of North America's vast middle class, he had invested and saved for almost fifty years against a time of need, but when it arrived, begrudged using those resources to make of life a more tolerable event. Money was independence to him and to spend it even when in extremis was as hard for my father as admitting that he no longer could drive a car. More important, perhaps, was that money became synonymous to him with the idea of legacy, and each time the issue of cost arose, it spoke to Norman Koch's desire for a future, attacking with each bill his hope to leave enough behind so that, even after death, he would be remembered as a potent provider. To spend in his present was to truncate that future by diminishing his carefully accumulated, accountable worth. Finally, to pay nurses and home care aides was, for him, a final and humiliatingly expensive signal that he was in fact an aged and helpless man.

Since he was not particularly introspective, Norman could not voice the fears and frustrations geriatric illness brought to him except to insist, almost daily, that he was "getting better" and to express the hope that, sooner or later, he would "do for himself" again. So the cost of illness in financial terms, of everything from doctor's bills to the price of a favorite food, is what he chose to protest. The tension between a specific, treatable illness and isolate age was voiced continually by him in the language of money. The poor-houses of his youth and modern "homes for the elderly" were a single metaphor for an isolating social and psychological impoverishment whose overt manifestation he was determined to avoid even as, bit by bit, the reality of his proscribed and enfeebled condition was made clear. Father's stated fear was not that his health would not improve but that we, his profligate caretakers, would bankrupt him in the interim. Issues of cost were, in fact, a language Norm's sons and sister spoke as well. Thus financial matters become, in this manuscript, social issues transposed into a minor key. The libretto of Norman Koch's despair was not that of an elegaic Greek chorus or elegant quatrain but the transformed facts from his accounting ledger propelled by the beat of medical bills that came daily to his door.

Like his physicians, Norman separated the specific complaint from its general context. The issue to him was the care of his leg, his spleen, his stomach, his blood or bones but never one of debilitating age. "As soon as this hip gets better," he continually promised himself, "I'll be able to drive to work again." The problems of age itself, the diminution of life's scale and the proscription of mobility that come with geriatric decline were facts neither he, his family, nor his physicians were willing to discuss or accept. To be old, for Norman Koch, was by definition to be isolated, segregated, and diminished just as, in his youth, to be poor meant a life that would end in the solitary ignominy of a poorhouse. The chimera of independence meant, for him, not only self-esteem but security. As long as he remained in his own house he was empowered and in control. With his savings he could direct his life in some way and thus forestall a personal and progressive isolation of self from his formerly active world.

GERIATRIC VS. GENERAL DISABILITY

To some extent, the trials of Norman Koch that began in his seventy-fourth year are little different from those all of us go through when faced at any age with a disability. While he was in rehabilitation at General Taylor Hospital, for example, there was another patient usually present, a young man who had lost his left leg in an automobile accident. The therapists tried for hours to get him out of his wheelchair and involved in a program of prosthesis and exercise, but for weeks the amputee refused their threats and entreaties. A nursing aide would roll him to therapy each day, and there he would sit, imprisoned in his wheelchair, watching other, mostly elderly clients as they relearned to ambulate with walker or cane. This man said nothing and did nothing. Like Norman, he was angry with his body and indignant to the point of immobility at those trials that a random universe had imposed. Eventually my father's silent compatriot did participate in the assigned therapies because, I think, he became bored watching others and refused the specter of a life whose years might be spent observing from the corner of an exercise room.

It took me a long time to understand the difference between my father's angst and this man's rage, between the one's reaction to geriatric decline and the other's to a type of traumatic or systemic disorder that younger people must sometimes face. The quotes that precede this text are clues, and perhaps that is all we who are younger can have until the day our lives have been largely spent and only the spare change of a few years is left. Quite simply, the man had a future to fashion that sitting obstinately in a wheelchair in General's therapy room could not mold. The difference between enfeebled them and empowered us, in short, is time.

Those handicapped from birth often make what seem to others to be amazing adaptations to a physically limited world. To be born without a leg, an arm, or a sense of sight means the excitement of movement is defined from the start by that body's specific, physical realities. The experiential world of those blind since birth is still rich with sounds, smells, and potential to be carried into maturity. But adults whose accustomed physical powers or senses have been revoked often feel cheated of their future. To become sight-impaired in one's thirties, for example, means that what had been commonplace will forever after be only memory. "We die a little so many times and in so many ways," a Buffalo gerontologist said to me one day. "Each time, we go through the steps of grief, through denial, anger, rejection and—if we're lucky—end up with acceptance and hope." For the mature adult that passage is, if one is not simply to give up, a triumph critical in and of itself. But this progression rests on the assumption that time is available that must be spent and, for we who reside between adolescence and senility, there is still a life to pursue, a future to create. Most people accommodate to specific handicaps because there are decades still to be lived and, despite the physical truncation of a sensory, mobile world, we want them to be as full as possible.

For the elderly, however, time itself is different. There will be no new families to raise, businesses to create, or excesses of abundant energy to expend. Time itself becomes a retrospective, and the future by definition stands limited. This is a physical as well as psychological change. With the curtailment of progressive time comes the fact that an individual's physical abilities are diminished and the geriatric's body is defined, in part, by lost tone and suppleness that can never be regained. Within these changes the individual stands bewildered and at increasing risk from activities that a few years before would have seemed both safe and easy. An uncle says in this book that for him age means doing half as much in twice the time as he accomplished before retirement. For the elderly, geriatric decline emphasizes life's inevitable truncation, and any decrease in abilities means not only a loss of independence but a more clearly proscribed future as well. Time is short, and a life's work has been largely completed.

Whatever the geriatric individual loses is lost forever and will not be regained.

The blind child often develops an extraordinary auditory acuity, gaining freedom through the use of aids like braille and a seeing eye dog. The newly blind young or middle-aged adult accommodates, learning what he or she can while adapting a new stance before the future world. One learns less intuitively, perhaps, than a child but makes of life the best that it can be. But to go blind in one's seventies is a different experience entirely. Few at that age have the force of will to learn braille. Typically, they are too frail to undergo the rigors of seeing-eye-dog obedience school. They are too old to persevere as masters in the rigors of that bonding. Further, that blindness is more likely to be systemic, the result of diabetes or other diseases, and thus only a part of the patient's adjustment problem. For the elderly, disability before a truncated future means to be wounded in one's self-esteem and to have only in memory what daily reality in fact denies. To go blind in one's dotage means, for most, fighting a rear-guard action to maintain old habits and entrenched lifestyles, because few elderly believe they have the time or energy to learn new modes. The past is where most geriatric patients live, and the sicker they are the more they tend to inhabit a world of memories. Thus those nearing life's end have little hope of anything better, and for them the promise of physical ailments becomes with each birthday catastrophically worse. Time itself is the villain here and, for the geriatric, what is most proscribed.

GERONTOLOGY AND MEDICINE

Thus the elderly do not face illnesses attacking from outside so much as an erosion from within. It is not the insinuation of bacteria, retrovirus, or accidental injury that so limits their lives, but the body's systemic degeneration, which makes recovery difficult in the face of otherwise mundane medical events. Each illness or specific complaint becomes tied to other, progressive ailments because the elderly's immune and physiologic systems are frail. To the degree this case history details medical issues, the treatment and views of medical personnel involved in Norman Koch's care are given substantial attention. The heartening thing is the degree to which some individuals—nurses and aides especially—could make of professional expertise a human concern. If life is, as Norman was fond of saying, "for the living," then physicians may have made continuance possible, but it was the nurses and caretakers who, for him, made it livable. They insisted that life itself, even in reduced circumstances, remained worthwhile.

Most doctors saw my father as a frail old man with, in their jargon, "unremarkable" ailments that were expected to be fatal in the short course of time. They treated him because that was their job, and when a crisis occurred, worked with finesse and enthusiasm. But few were concerned with the quality of life their patient was left to when that specific, clinical event had passed. The bare fact of continuance was the arena in which most of his physicians worked. Nurses, home aides, therapists, and friends, on the other hand, were specifically concerned with helping Norm to regain control of his progressively restricted environment. They were by definition involved in his world and not simply in the orchestrated and clinical treatment of a specific medical event. Thus they became a part of his home care and life, individuals who by their very presence stood for a vision of life's richness within the limits of a geriatric decline. A patient's will to be is crucial, and is based, ultimately, on social perceptions and self-perceptions. Home care allowed this man to hold to the twin chimeras of independence and self-esteem rather than to abdicate his individuality to a nursing home's impersonal regimes.

THE CASE HISTORY OF NORMAN KOCH

These are the issues that this case history raises, the themes that run like a strong undertow beneath the minutiae of Norman Koch's geriatric decline: independence versus need, existence versus living, future scrutiny versus immediate want, solitude and pride weighed against family necessity, past regret balanced against future hope. They also are the poles most younger people bounce between but rarely consider before crisis strikes. Perhaps the most remarkable thing about the elderly is the degree to which each resembles us, who are indeed their younger selves. They are we who have subsumed the lessons and visions forced upon us as children a generation or two ago. So the themes of this book are played out not only through Norman Koch's actions and words but also through those of his family and friends. They are not abstract concepts but, from within this case history, the principles on which a family's complex of lives was first built and then challenged in a single geriatric crisis. Thus the smallest and most mundane thing—a pack of cigarettes or silver table setting—becomes a mnemonic and, as time's aid, sets a fulcrum to balance individual power against memory's regret. All things are related through the past, combining into discordant harmonies surfacing sometimes in unusual ways.

The details chosen for inclusion in this book attempt a balance between narrative necessity, the basic descriptive record, and illustrations of these themes. Myriad incidents are excluded and much is summarized to meet the necessity of the manuscript's appropriate length. The fear of aging most of us manifest and the power held by the issues this book attempts to raise can be measured by the fact that, as a condition of publication, it was deemed necessary to change most of the names of the actors in this book. Even at this remove, years after the events this tale chronicles have ended, the incidents described still carry the power to anger and wound. So Norman Koch keeps his own name and history, as do I, his son. But relatives, doctors, nurses, friends, and the hospital itself have been given a soothing cloak of anonymity in the dress of fictitious names. My father never lived on East Street in Buffalo, and one would search that city in vain for a General Taylor Hospital. It is not simply that physicians, nurses, and other relatives involved in the case of Norman Koch might have perceived the whole in ways far different from me but, as the publishers insisted, that this tale goes beyond interpretation and to the heart of how we all see ourselves, into the mirrored lives of aging children and elderly parents, and that is an arena fraught with peril.

Changing names does not, however, make of this a fictional tale. The whole is fashioned from letters and journal entries made by me throughout the period of Norman Koch's care. Care has been taken to be as accurate as possible, and to give each actor in the narrative a chance to state his own case. Thus this book's first chapters are its most exhaustive; it was in the early stages of this story that the crucial figure, Norman Koch, was best able to state his own case. Later sections focus more on our relations and context, because as the tensions of the issues described here corroded aspects of my father's social and familial worlds, he became physically and mentally less able to act on his own behalf or speak in his own defense. As my father's decline extended in time, the issues of money, independence, loyalty, and love became dilemmas for those who surrounded him as well as focal points for the frustration that he daily fought and felt. The issues that make of this case history a greater life are a chorus we all know and must sing throughout our lives. It is just that at an earlier age and with a future still stretching forward, those of us who are younger sing not in the aged's minor key but with stronger, dominant chords.

The degree and method through which theme and event, memory and an immediate reality are combined can be made clear by a diary entry not included in the text but relevant to all the issues discussed here. It is dated November 26, 1988, a night in which aides were absent and Norm was in my care:

The first, the oldest memory I hold of my father is of an early Sunday morning when he placed me on the blue shag throw rug in the tiled, upstairs bathroom. Memory shows an open safety pin dangling like a cigarette from his lower lip and in his eyes there is tiredness and impatience as he looms over me on hands and knees—a position which a few years later would be used when we played "horsey."

He is grabbing for a clean diaper as I watch and, with practiced hands (I was the youngest of four), strips the soiled cloth from my body. "I hope you grow out of this soon," he sighs and, perhaps for the first time ever, I learn what it means to be dependent and a burden. With him and from that day I begin to hunger for independence.

I know it was early because he wears in memory a hastily tied robe and his face is rough, unshaven. Further, his hair is uncombed and stringy; a state, I learned later, he would remedy each day after his first cup of coffee. In those early years time for me was a seamless, endless thread which joined feeding, changing, and sleeping into the whole, but I'm sure in retrospect that it was a Sunday morning because only on that day did he care for us, allowing Mother an extra hour or two of sleep.

When finally I was toilet trained it was liberation for us both. Norm was freed both from the tyranny of my bowels and the monthly bills of Dyee Dee Diaper Service, Inc., which had serviced his house for years. I, in turn, gained a measure of control and that first taste of independence that meant I need not call for his or Mother's help for these basic, bodily functions. In memory it was then, upon this liberation, that I earned my first weekly allowance—a nickel to spend or save as caprice or caution moved. Maybe it was later, but the memory of a diaper's changing is linked, somehow, to that of Norm handing me a nickel with the caution that if I saved it for a week, I then would have a whole dime to call my own.

Shit and money are the measures of our life, the points of an individual's control on the world which holds us all.

Yesterday he called me into his room and he was crying quietly. All in all, our roles are almost exactly reversed from the postures assumed that early Sunday morning thirty-six years ago. I am now my father's keeper, at least part-time. I work now and he stays home, a fact he sometimes finds hard to forgive.

"What am I going to do with this?" he asked in tears, holding up for my inspection the edge of his badly soiled hospital gown. They are all he wears, now, unless we dress him to go out. "I'm so embarrassed," he sobbed, and I stroked his hair, telling him it was alright and a problem simply resolved. "I'll change it," I said. Bending over him, rolling his body to the side so I could change his clothes and clean his "mess," the memory of that diapered Sunday morning returned.

To the extent one can, as Oliver Sacks enjoins, deepen a case history into a human portrait, that life's story can take on specific importance to us all. But that portrayal must be a communal affair in which life takes on the dimension of time and the characters involved assume the depth of past relations. There are practical aspects of geriatric care, specific things individuals or families can do both before the onset of a crisis and in media res. Based in part on my family's experiences, a concluding section presents a paradigm that suggests how the worst aspects of familial geriatric crises can be, if not tamed, then at least somewhat better handled. It is offered in the hope that it (like this book) may be of assistance to others—care givers and patients—now facing similar crises of their own. In that chapter I've drawn on the case histories of other care givers and reviewed the writing of professionals in the field in an attempt to define a general set of acts and principles that can guide others through this mire. Most of the suggestions offered involve a modicum of planning, minimal expense, and a good deal of common sense.

But practical ideas will be of little use if the social and personal issues Norman fought so bitterly and for so long are not first resolved. In understanding the critical human and social elements of this story I am indebted to a number of people whose actions and postures are chronicled in this book. The therapists at General Taylor Hospital and the home care aides who helped us through the years taught both my father and me a great deal about gerontology and the mechanics of caring for an elderly human being. The nurses who maintained my father in his home are the heroes of this book, expending both skills built up across a professional lifetime and humanistic perspectives gained during those careers. To them all my gratitude is enduring.

I was assisted as well in the crafting of this work by the time and understanding of Dr. William McArthur of Vancouver, Canada, and Dr. Robert Warner of Buffalo, New York. Both provided information and perspectives on the issues of gerontology, rehabilitation, and the relation of the disabled to the world at large. Psychologists Elliot Gale and Ben Herman also offered their professional understanding and personal assistance as I attempted to come to grips not only with the facts of my father's decline but also with the greater issues that decline seemed to stand for. As well, I am indebted to a number of friends who read and criticized drafts of this book as it slowly matured from personal record to public tale. Those who performed this sometimes thankless but ultimately crucial task include: Neal Gallaford, Heather McNeil, John Daley, Anders Richter, Denis Wood, and Ingrid Hanson Wood. To all of them I am indebted, although I reserve, of course, the blame for any errors or inconsistencies as my own.

1

A Simple Operation

Age creeps up on us when we are not looking, when we are doing a lot of things that are a lot of miserable foolishness such as . . . working all day and being too tired in the evening to do anything but argue. . . . When you look at yourself in the mirror as you arrange your curly locks with an Ace pocket comb you realize that you are old, and mean as hell, and you wonder where the years went to so sudden.

Richard Bissel, *High Water*

We are told, over and over, that age equals weakness. The warranty is good for fifty thousand miles or five years, whichever comes first. Unfortunately, there is some wisdom—or at least accuracy—in this verdict.

David P. Barash, *Aging: An Exploration*

Death has gone from an event, a fact, to a long drawn-out process of years. It was once a telegram from the war, delivered by a Western Union messenger boy riding a one-speed bicycle; a chill that became fever and then pneumonia lasting at most, two weeks. Death was once the tightened, suffocating pain of a coronary artery's sudden bursting in the night. Now it is a series of battles in which ground is lost with each skirmish, with each partial defeat leading to greater fears. Progressively disabled and exhausted, the old ones linger a little weaker, a bit more afraid, and with greater confusion at the failing powers that remain after the doctor cheerfully congratulates himself for once again holding on, abetting survival, and "pulling the patient through."

To be more than seventy years old, to be in the "fullness of age" past the biblical limit of three-score-and-ten has changed, during my father's lifetime, from a rare occurrence to being the statistical norm. This is a new situation born of modern medicines and procedures. Past generations died early deaths of childhood diseases now half-forgotten or they succumbed later to some adult illness ranging from the prosaic pneumonia and once common tuberculosis to more painful but certainly more rapid cardiovascular and gastroenterologic conditions. Within his lifetime, the former have been neutered by a class of drugs beginning with penicillin, the later by surgical techniques ranging from the now routine coronary bypass to the colostomy.

No one is prepared. The march of medical miracles over the last seventy years has given today's elderly the not unreasonable expectations that for whatever ails them there will be a cure. They had expected to die at a younger age, to follow the example of parents and friends but, survivors, live on with the intense belief that somewhere there is a pill, a protocol, a surgical procedure that will make it all go away. At the same time, physicians who were once family friends have become technicians and members of medical corporations utterly divorced from their patients' lives and hopes. So when the elderly are told, as was my father, that an illness is traditional, one to be charted and watched to its inevitable crisis but left inviolate to "take its course," the result is bewilderment. Not only have they been betrayed by their bodies but by the very medical science that has kept them alive past their greatest expectations.

The barrier separating vigorous senior citizens and the gentle elderly from the querulous old is serious, nonfatal illness, a rite of passage tumbling the patient through a bewildering maze of medical reports, emotional terrors, and diminished expectations. Whatever the cause or prognosis, illness for one past seventy years promises a future of decreased mobility and independence, the end of a cherished vision each has of him- or herself as mobile, vibrant, giving, and able. Illness is the real finish line of that race to retirement whose public rewards are bus, cinema, and travel discounts. It is the reality that makes medical insurance a necessity for those who have come of age. For those of us who accompany others through the hospital corridors, doctors' waiting rooms, and sleepless nights of worry and pain, infirm age is a first death, the demise of memories of another's strength, and the failure of lifelong expectations.

Debilitating age is a new disease and one for which we can conceive no cure, a gradual but pervasive condition that affects us all. Those who have yet to catch the contagion know it at second hand through the symptoms and suffering of those who are afflicted and yet still known and loved. If it is not my parent, aunt, or neighbor, then the patient is your cousin, lover, former teacher, or uncle. But despite its ubiquity and the importance of this complex to our world as a whole, physicians and patients alike spend their time with the symptoms of each isolated illness while ignoring the social and personal facts of the disease itself. Because we insist that the cardiac, gastric, or hematologic problem is divorced from the sufferer's general condition, we isolate the etiology from the illness. Thus a geriatric crisis too often leads to isolation and denial. It creates a firm insistence on the part of all that whatever is wrong, it is based not on dreaded progressive time but rather on a simple and treatable medical problem. To the extent one can pretend, the diminishment is deferred even though the cost of that pretense is a refusal that makes the social effects of geriatric illness worse.

Terminal illness has its own regime and a different emotional protocol. It is, somehow, a known quantity around which all can plan; a release at the end of a disease's trial. As well, terminal illness has its own timetable sloping towards a specific and discussable finish through those preparations that can describe the completion but not necessarily the destruction of memories and life's relations. Nonfatal but debilitating illnesses, those that offer the potential of hope, follow a different and often more disastrous course that is destructive to the patient in a way death is not. This is the fulcrum, the balance line. On one side people live by Dylan Thomas's injunction and "rage, rage against the dying of the light," refusing to go gently into the night. On the other, they wait and hope for release. With Kierkegaard, their last words are not of anger at work yet undone but of dissolution already past. "Sweep me up" were the last words he uttered. Illness already had reduced him to living dust.

It sounds so simple in retrospect, so clear a progression. It should be such a natural thing. But in the living, age and illness become confused when physical disability turns existence and life itself—

another day or week or hour—into something of a dreaded goal simultaneously feared and hoped for. Follow its course through a single run and tell me, please, when the tale is finished, exactly what you would have done. This siege began, as do most things these days, with a telephone call. For those beginning a marathon, it happened, appropriately enough, in Los Angeles's Olympic year.

When my father telephoned it was with a studied nonchalance, a "by-the-way-perhaps-I-should-mention" bravado perched upon and peeking from beneath the chitchat of his words. He never called without a reason, without some piece of information or a pertinent question because "calling across all these states is expensive, as you know." The very idea of long distance still meant to him an increased cost and, as he was fond of saying, "stamps are cheaper than the phone." In recent years I had visited him in Buffalo once every six months or so, and every other year he would fly first to Denver where my older brother Walter lived and then to me in Vancouver. Mostly we existed to each other in weekly letters (typed by me and penned by him), regular as the progression of our native Buffalo's seasons and as constant as his prejudices. Telephones were reserved for immediate information, like the telegrams of his youth, when Western Union boys on bicycles were virtually synonymous with bad news, themselves messages presaging some specific doom. I would have preferred that—a short news bulletin crisp and unequivocal in counted words—to these rare calls across three time zones and 2,800 miles in which the addition of voice and cadence told me as nothing else could that my father was filled with fear.

Buffalo's summer was progressing nicely, he said by way of introduction. This was a necessary preamble to what he had called to say, part of the ritual of our shared life. It was a signal that whatever else was wrong, his sense of courtesy and form remained intact. It meant the days of his city were hot and the evenings a bit muggy but that, like others born and raised in the Great Lake's climatic extremes, my father took pride in an ability to live equitably within them. By mid-January of each year he would complain of the snows—"I've had enough of winter"—but by late August he would dream of a whitened world in which the very idea of summer was again a distant hope. After seventy-four years lived within the region's confines he was still the last of his friends to haul out a winter coat each November and the last to take down storm windows in the spring. Life for him was to be lived in expectation of yet one more Indian summer and in fear of unusually late snowstorms in April or May.

I sat impatiently in my Los Angeles hotel room, waiting distrustfully for his news. This was, after all, my triumphant month, the period I'd worked towards for years, and anything that impinged upon its glory would be something to resent. It was 1984, the city's Olympic year, and I was a correspondent to those games. A foreign correspondent for Canadian Broadcasting Corporation, I was working in my native land and broadcasting to an adopted one. If the contract was only for five weeks, it would lead, I knew, to better and more permanent things. A family trauma during the games would be, I thought, a personal tragedy for me as well. Maybe he's merely lonely, I hoped. I told him I had an interview to do and asked what, exactly, was crucial enough to justify a long-distance call during the daytime hours, which, I reminded him that he always reminded me, was the most expensive time of the day in which to place a call.

Nothing major, my father said, simply that he thought I should know he had been scheduled for surgery. "No big thing," he assured me as the flare of match to his new cigarette hissed across the wires. The smell of it, Tempo brand, came unbidden from memory and somehow made his presence more real. "Surgery?" I asked, and with the mnemonic of his tobacco sounds as aid, in my mind's eye I could see him shrug. Just a new hip to be implanted, he replied, a bit of bionic improvement replacing the pin that patched the head of a femur cracked in a fall while on safari in Africa in 1977. I breathed a sigh of relief. For a man born in 1910 who had lived through four wars, four sons, one marriage, and a Great Depression, it did not sound like anything to worry about. This was, after all, Norman Koch, a man who had buried his wife and survived two ulcers into his seventy-fourth year with a permanently dislocated shoulder, osteoarthritis, a cracked femur, chronic leukemia controlled by medication, and an underactive thyroid gland that had required daily medication for fifty years. Minus his prostate gland but with four gallstones in reserve, my father continued to work five days a week bolstered by a misanthropic view of the world and, more recently, a growing desire to turn the clock back to what he remembered as a better, more civil age.

The operation would be July 31 in Buffalo, New York, he said, adding that he was fine and didn't want me flying back to attend him during this siege. I had no intention of flying back, of leaving the assignment that to me justified years of daily police reportage and the picky flotsam of work in half a dozen city newsrooms. To be on an international assignment—with the promise of future work—meant that I had arrived, and, while irritated at the inconvenience his operation had promised for me, I was cheered by its timing. Assured that my father did not need me and that his sense of independence remained intact, I promised to visit when the games had ended and assured him as if reciting a litany that "if you need me, Pops, I'll be there." Much later I was to ponder those words, but now he simply thanked me, as we agreed it would be neither sensible nor economical for me to leave my work. Nurses would care for him in the hospital, and I would visit while he recuperated at home—after the games—before heading off (filial obligations fulfilled) to whatever my next assignment would be.

"You'll be back at work in no time," I told him by phone that day in early July. He was a volunteer at the hospital where, nine years before, my mother had shriveled with cancer and died. For five hours a day, five days a week, fifty weeks a year, he sat tallying in the purchasing and billing departments, filling out forms and scrutinizing the statements of lifelong friends and relatives who, for one or another reason, had rolled through General Taylor. His letters were filled with brief comments on the medical ills of old family friends who were figures in my childhood but unvisited by me for years. The job provided his raison d'être, and at least once a month he told me how grateful he was for the way it filled his otherwise empty days. The hospital gave him purpose and proved to my father that, a businessman, he could ply his skills after retirement and the dispersal of his family into other geographic regions and new, nuclear homes. It was, he said firmly, his salvation, proof that he was a senior citizen both active and needed, not a drain on those who knew and loved him. That had always been his greatest fear. "I'm old but not decrepit," he told me that day. "I can take care of myself."

I encouraged him over the phone with tales of the routine nature of his impending operation, telling him what the doctors had already said and what he, in his turn, had first reported to me. Hip replacement has become a standard procedure; the new teflon and titanium joint would be better than the old one, patched as it was with a metal pin then receding from osteoporotic bone. About 80,000 Americans receive new hip joints each year, and most become spry, active individuals again, walking with nary a limp to show they carry a bionic miracle imbedded in their increasingly fragile skeletons. Remember Jack Risotto, I said, naming a man younger than my father, an arthritic friend who had received two knee replacements several years before. There was a pause. "He had to have them removed," my father said. "Some problem." There was silence while he lit another cigarette, and I could hear him inhale over our long-distance line. I said I'd be back in Buffalo when he came home from the hospital in mid-August, after the games had ended. He said it was something to look forward to.

The first warnings came on August 6, a few days after the operation. First there was a confused telephone call in which my father complained about the hospital's food, and later that day a letter from him arrived at my hotel. It was written the day before his surgery and said, in a tremulous hand, how scared he was of what was to occur and how alone he felt in it all. The letter said he knew it was necessary but that he was getting no younger and had begun to worry whenever a part of his body failed. I remembered a line from one of T. H. White's letters in which he said, "As I get older myself, bits keep falling off, like an old car, but one can't do much about it. In some ways it will be a relief to be dead—no more spare parts to fuss about, and think what a rest, too!" A year or two before, I'd sent it to my father, who had replied that wry submission and patience were not enough. The time to die, my father believed, was before age imploded and the future shrank to a series of progressively smaller steps. Before driving his car became an impossibility and freedom shrank to the size of a walking stick, he had assured his sons for years, he would end it all while time still stood as more than a progression of old memories stacked against some present regret.

What worried me was that he would keep his vow and lunch on the bottles of prescription pills he had banked in his home like the triple-A bonds he also had purchased against an uncertain future. His pills were stored not in the vault, however, but in his night table and in kitchen drawers, and buried under a pin-striped shirt in his dresser bureau, hidden beneath his underwear. Each morning one or more bottles of pills would peep out at Father as he dressed, promising death should his body falter or his will give out. Like a miser with dollars stuffed beneath his bed, Norm for years had kept his stash against the eventuality of physical bankruptcy, determined to forestall the hobbled existence he believed was all life held for the decrepit old.

I had promised to return to his house when the Olympic marathon had been run and worried sporadically over the next few days that this time, perhaps, he would not beat the odds, that recovery would not be a simple matter of rehabilitation and physical return. Part of me had always believed his threats of suicide were posturing, and mostly I thought my father still brash and foolish enough to believe life could be lived on dictated terms. He was due home in mid-August, and I would be in Buffalo to ease him through his recuperation after the Olympics ended on August 12. It seemed the least I could do, or perhaps it was simply that I had no compelling reason not to go. His orthopedic surgeon, Donald Stryon, had predicted a two- to three-week postoperative stay in the hospital as the minimum, and probably the necessary, recovery period. My brothers and I had argued by telephone about who would be in Buffalo—and when—to care for Father at his house, rescheduling our lives to makehis rehabilitation as easy as possible both for him and for ourselves.

But the man who we, his sons, called "that stubborn old kraut" had other plans. On August 8 my father telephoned his oldest son, Walter, to say that he was fed up with the hospital and its regimes. The food was abysmal, the nurses tyrannical, and, since he could maneuver on an ambulatory walker, Father was determined to return home that weekend. He then suggested it would be nice if Walter could be there too. My brother telephoned me and I called Father to argue along with Walter against our father's insistance on a too rapid discharge. Father was adamant, however, insisting he could be alone if necessary and did not need anyone to look after his health. Walter finally agreed to fly from his home in Colorado to Buffalo and promised he would be with our father within hours of his hospital discharge. "Fine," Father said smugly. A nurse would drive him to the house we had grown up in, and assisted by his walker, he would receive Walter when the latter arrived that afternoon.

On Saturday night Walt telephoned me in Los Angeles from Buffalo. "Are you coming tomorrow?" he asked. I said it would be Monday morning before I would arrive. "Don't change your plans," he said. "But be prepared. There are, ah, complications." Not serious, he continued, but difficult. He would explain when he met my plane. Do not rush, he urged, but, please, do not dally in Los Angeles. I did not. The cab carried me from Wilshire Boulevard to the airport while firecrackers resounded and skyrockets soared above the city in an ostentatious finale to the games. Throughout the ride and then on the airplane, ensconced in my seat, I thought about Buffalo and how much it resembled my father. He was born there and had lived his whole life within its confines. Through childhood, war, marriage, depression, family business, and retirement he had been rooted in that city. For forty years he had lived in the same house, which stands three miles from the one in which he and his sister, Janice, were born. Sons and friends had moved away, but he remained, adamant in his defense of the region, constant in his praise of its virtues. Father would hear no complaints about Buffalo's weather, whose severity, he insisted, was vastly overrated. Nor would he entertain thoughts of moving, as had others we knew, to sunnier climates.

In the weekly letters we had exchanged for years, he would praise his home and constantly look forward to the blitzkrieg of Buffalo's changing seasons. Sometimes he would describe concerts at the financially troubled local symphony to which he subscribed each season, or at other times, would lament the financial problems of Buffalo's zoo, where for a decade he had served as docent. His letters described visits to the homes of remaining friends and said he would never leave his house or his city. This is where he lived, Father wrote, where his memories were rooted. To drive through Buffalo in my father's company was to watch history roll by as he pointed out the coordinates of long memory. Here was the house his parents had almost purchased just before the Great Depression began; there had stood his Uncle Izzie's office, now a half-filled parking lot. Over there, near Delaware Park, stood a company he once had worked for, and on Lancaster Avenue had lived his childhood friend so-and-so who then married another schoolmate whose children I had known. His city had become a chronology, a map in time with each block overlaid by a personal past.

Buffalo and my father had aged together, and both found the going difficult. From 1960 to 1970, when my father managed the three furniture floors of a local department store, it was among the fastest shrinking cities in the United States. Major manufacturers of long tenure fled one by one to escape high taxes, aged machinery, and northern labor costs. From 1970 to 1980, the period of his retirement and solitude, the exodus continued. My mother died a year or two before the department store where father had labored was torn down to make way for a parking lot. More companies fled the area, and Buffalo became a place to be from; its people scattered across the country and around the world. In Mexico, Honolulu, Ecuador, and Hong Kong I have met former residents, Buffalonians eager for any news I could bring of the place they had once believed was home. They were refugees, proud of their escape but nostalgic for ancestral, geographic roots. In Kwaloon, Hong Kong, I once had lunch with "young Bobby Hirsh," then in his fifties, a brother of my father's oldest friend. Bobby was filled with stories of my father's youth and curious about the metamorphosis Buffalo was engaged in. "And how is Norm?" he asked. He had stayed and endured, my father. Bobby Hirsh and I were both in awe and slightly contemptuous of that.

As Buffalo shrank in population, my father's circle also drew back, the victim of age, infirmity, and disease as well as an exodus to Florida retirement homes. The city was plagued through this period by insurance fires that dissolved what had been immigrant neighborhoods in my grandfather's day but, after World War II, were transformed into black ghettos. Houses where none would live were cindered first into rubble heaps, and finally, when nobody would build on the site, transformed into parks. But what was left was treasured all the more, both by my father and city officials. For him there was continuity and memory, the comfort of lifelong association. For the mayor and his staff there was the "housing stock" and "green space" as well as a "core population" to give the city hope. In truth, both my father and the city had trouble coming to grips with this general decline. All expected a renewal of vigor, a return to the prominence of earlier days, and, expecting, seemed to wait in vain. Buffalo and my father, I thought beneath the airplane engine's drone—both waiting now in an eternal February for last year's Indian summer.

Walter met my flight and said that for him Buffalo's greatest virtue was its airport parking. So few people arrived at any one time that curbside spaces metered at fifteen cents were virtually guaranteed. To someone from Denver, with its overcrowded Stapleton Airport, this was a miracle indeed. Collecting my bags, we walked to my father's car, which waited directly in front of the baggage area, twenty feet from the terminal doors. He drove through light traffic to North Buffalo, smoking one cigarette after another, and described the situation.

"There are two problems now, the worst being his fall. Dad was alone on his walker when I arrived, opened the door for me and was doing very well. A little later, when we were in the bedroom, he bent down to get something from a low bureau drawer and fell. He banged his back and couldn't move. I lifted him onto the bed and called Paula Debillio, his nurse, the one who brought him home. She came right back, looked Father over, and said it would be sore for a few days, his back, but that the new hip was okay. He's supposed to walk, but since the fall Father says it hurts too much, and he won't get out of bed." The second problem, my brother continued, involved tape burns created in the hospital when they removed the bandage covering Father's new surgical scars. Because of his leukemia, he had very dry, tender skin which had developed an allergy to surgical tape. Ripping off the bandages had pulled off the skin as well, leaving two long, large open wounds. They had not healed and required a painful baking soda and water paste treatment, Walt continued. Normally that would have been bearable, but added to the agony of walking after the fall, it had transformed our father into a pitiful invalid.

"He can't get up without help. I slept on the second floor last night and gave him the bell to ring if he needed to get up in the night. But, you know me, I sleep soundly and didn't hear him ring for minutes. So tonight one of us will have to sleep downstairs on the couch." The bell was a memory of our childhood buried until that moment. During those childhood illnesses when mumps, chicken pox, or measles laid us low in turn, an old, silver servant's bell would be placed by our beds against the event of needing help we were too tired or weak to shout for. With six people in the house a weak child's shout could go unheard, but the sound of that bell was sure to bring assistance (and comfort) to the one in need.

I knew that I would be the one to sleep downstairs that night. When we had been young and lived as a family it had been my job to wake Walter in the morning, to pound on his door, turn on the radio, and force him to get up for school. Even as a teenager he had slept so soundly that only with progressively greater efforts could he be aroused. I laughed as I reminded him of the times he had thrown pillows, clocks, or heavy books at me while I stood grinning in safety from behind his bedroom door. I remembered, too, the era when I had been an adolescent and he would visit from college and both of us would bring dates home at night. The question then had also been who would get the couch, I said, but Walter did not seem amused by the memories.

We were home in twenty minutes, and I wondered, as I have at each return, that it seems never to change. With its three stories and twelve rooms, the house has been a constant throughout my life. In thirty-five years the living room has seen two carpet changes, three sofas, and a few new wall decorations, but in essence it remains forever the same. My room on the second floor is always as I last left it, pictures from my teenage years still in place; the kitchen spice rack, pots, and pans are where they have always been. This place is a shrine, I thought that day, a testament to our youth and the days when its rooms were filled with children and friends and life.

The only radical change the house had ever undergone was the addition twenty-five years before of a family room designed to accommodate the then new world of television and high fidelity stereos. It began as a place where children could congregate while adults relaxed in the living room, but by the end of that decade my parents had transformed the family room into their bedroom and added a bathroom to what had been the laundry area adjacent to their new abode. This was "just in case we can't get up the stairs someday," my mother explained to us all. Before, my parents had slept upstairs in the master bedroom, and as we had moved away from Buffalo one by one, they had signaled a change in their lives by "moving down" as if to take control of the house that, as children, we had dominated for so long. With the move they had retaken possession of their house and, installing an invalid's toilet with an elevated base, had completed preparations for the possibility of their old age or other infirmity. Now, I thought inanely, the plan would be put to the test.

Entering the house, I dropped my bags and went immediately into the old family room—the new master bedroom—where my father lay unshaven, arms stretched towards me, head shrunk against the pillow. He was dressed in a hospital gown and thinner than I had ever seen him. "Tommy, boy," he cried as I rushed to his side. The muscles of his arms had atrophied and the skin hung like a long sleeve or a carrying bag that had been emptied of its contents. He thanked me for coming, and I asked, "What did you expect? That I would forget you when you needed me? Of course I came." He told me all my brother had described, making the fall sound like an act of God, another trial like a Buffalo winter storm that had to be endured. My brother said it was time to change the dressings and I moved out of his way but stayed to watch.

"This is the worst," my father explained, rolling a bit more to his side to make the procedure easier. The burns on hip and back were open, slightly suppurating wounds, the largest more than nine inches long. They were not healing, despite a week of treatment, and each time the baking soda paste was applied it was a painful ordeal. I turned away, unable to watch. This was my father, and his skin had the consistency of tissue paper. He had been strong, but now his blood had so thinned it would not carry the necessary proteins to close a surface wound. A man of utmost modesty, he lay with his gown open, exposing legs, genitals, and pubic hair. He smelled of stale sweat and disease. His voice had a whining, self-pitying tone.

Then it was lunchtime, and I quickly discovered that my father had no appetite at all. A small dish of yogurt and a single piece of dry toast had become for him a major midday meal. When Walter later insisted Father get up and try to walk, it was torture for us all. Each move in the process of standing erect was agony for Father, who complained incessantly. Walking was, step by step, a triathlon of endurance, and getting him to shuffle twenty feet an exhausting accomplishment for the three of us. Afterwards, my father took an afternoon nap. "He is worse than he was yesterday," Walter said. "It seems that each day he loses ground. I don't see how he can stay here, in the house, unless there is some radical improvement."

That was the specter that haunted us, Father most of all. Without improvement he would need constant attention and thus be unable to stay alone at home, and yet our father had always said life would not be worth living without independence in the house that had always been the center of his world. "Doing for myself" was his favorite phrase, but if he could not even walk twelve steps to the dining room, what could anyone do? Walter could not stay in Buffalo for long—he had work to return to—and I had no intention of making Buffalo my home again or gerontology my profession. The doctors had said that if Norm wished to recover full mobility, he would have to walk fifteen times a day to stretch and exercise the newly implanted hip. That day he walked, with great difficulty, twice.

That night was my first of many on the sofa in the living room. Unlike my brother, I awake easily and at the sound of my father's bell was up three times to bring water, to carry his urinal, and when he was unable to sleep, simply to chat with him in the late night hours. The next day was worse, Father walking with even more effort and less result. By Wednesday we were frantic and discussed the idea of a nursing home. Walter called the nurse who had cared for our father in the hospital, "his nurse" Paula, who the week before had driven Father home. We asked her to come back and advise us. To Father, Walt just said Paula would be dropping by, and for his part, our father did not ask when or why. The idea seemed to give him comfort.

She entered Norm's bedroom later that day with energy and determination. "What are you doing in bed?" she demanded of Father, patting him on the shoulder. "You look like an invalid." He told Paula it hurt, that he was uncomfortably constipated, and that any movement was extremely difficult. She began to examine the tape burns, carefully peeling away the surgical gauze my brother had gingerly placed on the wounds. "Of course you hurt," she chuckled. "I warned you not to bend and get things from low drawers while on the walker, but you just wouldn't listen. So you fell and bruised yourself, and because you're not walking, now you've stiffened up. It's your own fault. Constipation is usual after an operation, especially if you don't eat enough." She covered him and straightened up, examination completed. "Those aren't getting any better. I'm going to call your doctor and we're going to see a dermatologist."

Then she was on the phone, talking to Norm's physician, Mike Pangless, and demanding a referral to a specialist who could treat "the worst tape burns I've seen in forty years." Hanging up, she returned to Norm's room with satisfaction and informed my father he had to get dressed because they were to visit a Dr. Norbert. When I asked how, if he could barely stand, she would get him to the doctor, Paula answered, "I'll take him in my car. That's how I got him home from the hospital, and he can do it going back." But even she was amazed at how fragile he had become, at how hard it was to get her patient out of bed. Reconsidering, Paula instructed me to call an ambulance service and order a wheelchair vehicle to the house in "say, a half hour."

"Get up now, honey," she commanded Father. "We're going to get you dressed and into the living room." He obeyed, complaining of the pain at each stage of the dressing, and each time she replied that it served him right because he had disobeyed her orders and had not continued to exercise after his fall. Why hire her at all, Paula asked, if he insisted on violating her directions? She made his pain her insult and, magically, when he was dressed, they walked past the most distant point Walter and I had managed with him in two days and entered the living room as he screamed at her in pain. "Getting mad, are you?" she chortled. "It's about time. That's good. Get mad." Neither my brother or I nor the two of us together had been able to make him move, but under Paula's bullying, he was compliant. What game was this, I asked myself, that he would respond only to nurses who knew his limits, and did that mean he should be in a nursing home after all? Angry at the changes disease and infirmity had caused, I was angry with him. Certainly Paula was not the only person who could be strict, I vowed, and if his recovery was to be my responsibility, I would learn to speak as she did in commanding, declarative sentences.

He rode the ambulance to the medical office building, and I rode with Paula in her car. For her, patients were all vexing if interesting creatures to be chided, coaxed, and bullied as needed. Norm, she said, was doing all things wrong. He had fallen because he refused to accept his infirmity, bending in a way that was proscribed, and then had refused to walk because of the pain despite the knowledge that exercise was necessary. He had become an invalid seeking somebody's care. He needed firm attention and love, Paula said, not warehousing in a nursing home. I promised he would get it.

In the physician's office building, Father seemed to straighten up and be aware, for the first time, of his appearance. A public arena, even this one, reaffirmed him, and he became once again the man I knew, my father, and not the wreck who had wallowed in his sickbed, cringing. While we waited, his orthopedic surgeon wandered by. "What are you doing here?" he asked testily of my father.

"Your hip is in as solid as a rock." Paula explained about the tape burns, and the surgeon shrugged as if offended at the suggestion that any problem could arise after he had so handily cemented in a teflon hip. Without another word he turned and walked away.

Then the dermatologist's secretary called, and Paula and I wheeled Norm into the examining room. Dr. Norbert took a quick look at Norm, who stood pants down with hands on his walker like a character out of Marquise de Sade, prescribed some topical medicines (three times daily), and sighed politely when told of Stryon's hoary cure of a baking soda paste. Paula and I stopped at a surgical supply store on the way home to fill prescriptions and to purchase a huge stock of surgical compresses, gauze, and rolls of hypoallergenic tape. She warned me that I must forget the patient was my father, that he must be treated as a client whose whims never take precedence over necessary protocols. Then she suggested I call the county's Visiting Nurses Association (which offers free physiotherapy), promised to work with me, and drew up to the door of the house, timing her lecture to end as I carried our supplies into the sickroom.

The ambulance had preceded us, and my father was already ensconced in his bedroom chair with a glass of iced tea by his side. I immediately called the Visiting Nurses and made arrangements for visits to begin the following week. My father was relieved when informed it was a free service because, he said, when we were later alone, his medical bills and Paula's hourly charge of eleven dollars would be onerous. My presence, he suggested, was as much an economic necessity as a personal comfort. I asked Paula to join us, and when she was present, offered my father two alternatives. He could, I said, go to a medium-care nursing facility costing at least $150 per day, or he could stay at home with me in charge of his care. But if I were to undertake responsibility for his recovery, I insisted on total control with no arguments about what he thought he could, should, or wanted to do. I did not mind, I said, changing from my role as an Olympic commentator earning $1,000 a week to the new position of unpaid nurse's aide and attendant. But if I was to do this, I insisted, no discussion of prohibitive costs would be allowed. I would be reasonable, of course, but the final decisions would be mine. If Father was to be my charge, then I would have to be free of the normal restrictions fathers presume with dutiful sons.

Paula sat nodding and smiling as Norm agreed because, really, he had no other choice. The idea of a nursing home was not only unnecessary but expensive. Further, it would place him again within the hospital-like regime of nurses and strangers that he had so detested during his hospital convalescence. When I was young he had mastered the art of offering me choices that answered themselves, and no clearer signal of my ascendancy could have been displayed than this use of his techniques, those of my childhood, against him. But he seemed to resent it not at all and, indeed, was delighted to relinquish responsibility for his rehabilitation and recovery. When family friends stopped by later that afternoon they were impressed, each said, with how much better Norm looked. He informed them that it was because I was in charge of his recovery and that he had promised to accept my judgment on all matters relating to his convalescence. Questions about what he could or could not do, Norm said, would for the time being be cleared through me.

The next day Walter made ready to return to Denver but before he left suggested a bed be brought downstairs for me. I insisted my nightly vigils were to be a temporary post and that the living room should remain, as ever, a public space without bedrolls chunked into the corner. He argued, sensible man, that we did not know how temporary the situation would be and that whatever strength and rest I could get would be needed. But I was adamant, and it was, after all, I who was sleeping on the couch. When he left we were convinced the worst was over. In a few weeks, we assumed, all would be as it had been before. In the interim, the house settled down to a routine of daily physical exercises that I supervised, weekly bouts of physiotherapy with the visiting nurses, and visits by Paula— to help with showering and other complexities—two or three times a week. The early squeamishness I had felt in looking at my father and his wounds quickly disappeared under the pressure of constant proximity. They became, those miserable burns, a matter of clinical interest as I mentally divorced myself from the knowledge that they were a part of this man I had always known.

I slept on the sofa in the living room and rose, each night, at the apologetic sound of my father's bell. During those late night hours as we talked he seemed to be searching for a posture, for some stance to take before the world. Some nights he was self-pitying and would complain that his life was over and its future had shrunk to a foreshortened and flat perspective. At other times, he was determined to return to his volunteer work and promised to do whatever was necessary to regain his strength and mobility. Work was more than a hobby in retirement, but the essential armor of his identity. Finally, he worried about taking me from my career to nurse him—even briefly—in his dotage. It seemed in those talks as if he first had tried on the mask of helpless and aged invalid but, when Paula's presence ordered an end to that, had taken on the role of a loyal and valued hospital employee who would do whatever was necessary to return to his job. Finally, he was the parent who worried about but gloried in the presence of a youngest son.

Tiring though it was for me, I enjoyed those early weeks. The loyalty and love I felt for Father, emotions that had never been expressed before, now had a focus and outlet. He had always insisted on being in charge, the one who offered aid but would accept nothing in return. This was my chance to repay that debt by bringing him back to a strength and purpose he once had given me. "He needs me now," I told my friends by phone. "This is what being a son is all about." For his part, Norm reveled in my care and the constant presence of a son. He and my mother had lived for years towards the day when, children grown, they could enjoy themselves, but she had, he said often, died too soon. For the first time since her death he had someone to cook, clean, and fuss over him. If physical exercises and therapies were the price, he seemed to accept it gladly.

His problems became my own and, experienced vicariously, they were fascinating. Food, for example, became a major battleground as constipation remained a minor one. Father virtually refused to eat, a fact that slowed his healing while foiling the regime of suppositories prescribed by Paula, who continued to visit twice a week. He did not digest enough to "become regular," she said although he insisted he ate each day "until ready to burst." His constipation was a source of endless worry, and I came to dread the inevitable nightly television commercials dealing with "the problem." My father was rapt with interest as each thirty-second case was resolved and then would ask me if I thought the featured product might help. When the show these advertisements supported returned, Father settled back in bed and closed his eyes. Dramatic plots did not interest him at all. He identified with the commercials.

The real difficulty, I soon discovered, was that Father had become a senile anorexic, believing himself gross but eating in reality no more than 800 calories a day. He was, he told me, "fat" and needed to lose weight. His friends and sister said that in the months preceeding his operation they'd noticed he ate less and less. As a result his stomach gradually shrank as his appetite decreased, but determined to become no fatter, he always had eaten less than hunger demanded. Like most elderly men who have not exercised in years, he had lost muscle tone, and that created a bulge, a pot over his abdomen that he would rub like a talisman before pushing his plate away. When I urged him to eat more, Father would grab the skin of his flaccid abdomen, roll it towards me, and state it was proof that, indeed, he was seriously overweight. The problem was solved after I noticed he never looked at the large bathroom mirror except when he was fully dressed. One day, as I helped him to the shower while he was naked, I suddenly shouted, "Look up." Tricked, he saw his own reflection but was unable, at first, to recognize its reality as the person of his memory. "Who's that?" he cried, looking away, but steadying him with one hand, I turned his head back with the other. "That's you," I said quietly. "Look fat, do you?" He said he looked like an inmate of Dachau on his way to be gassed. "But you're the guy who won't eat because he is overweight," I pressed, insisting he count his ribs, each distinct in the mirror's image. After that, Father began to eat voraciously, and with larger meals, the constipation ended.

Wounded in his self-esteem like any adolescent girl, he had starved himself to sustain a comfortable image acceptable, he believed, to the world. I had robbed him of that and forced my father to see the face Juvenal described when he lamented the changes age can bring: "To begin with, this deformed, hideous, unrecognizable face; this vile leather instead of skin; these pendulous cheeks; these wrinkles like those around the mouth of an old she-ape as she sits scratching in the shady Thabarcan woods." No wonder my father was surprised. What faced him in the mirror that day was not simply the mask behind which hope and strong convictions beat but a signal and cipher of infirmity, the Tenth Satire's "train of woes—and such woes—as come with a prolonged old age."

In the following months he told me again and again what a shock that moment had been. "I didn't recognize the old man in the mirror," he would say on sleepless nights. "Somehow, I knew it couldn't be me." For years Norm had shaved, washed, and brushed his teeth before that mirror seeing, he said, not the progressive changes of age, but "me, the same as I've always been." Preparing for work at the hospital each day he had seen staring back in reflection a man of responsibility and uncertain years combing his hair, a pastiche of memories and vanity in which age was a muted but not a conscious concern. Dressed each morning in his uniform of sport coat and tie, ready for his volunteer work, my father had held before the world and the bathroom mirror alike an image of the capable businessman. Then, deprived of the activity that gave him identity and without the clothes that complemented it, he had known for the first time, I think, not simply the present, written in a bold surgical line along the hip, but the vision of an infirm future, which he was determined to dispel. First he avoided the mirror's image, preferring to see himself reflected in memory. But when I insisted, he was so frightened that he began to eat whatever I cooked and then to ask for more, like a concentration camp survivor finally convinced that the war was over and there in fact might be a future to live for.

We became a nuclear family, with him the nucleus. He was my life, eighteen hours a day. I slept waiting for the ringing bell of his need or the sound of the television to signal that he could not sleep. Awake, I was free only when Paula came, and that time was used up by the household chores—shopping, banking, cleaning, and cooking—that are a part of every life. Despite the pain and inconvenience, the loss of independence, I understood that in large part Father loved this time. During this period I wrote to a friend that

Father revels in the constant attention and my presence. For a man who never learned to live happily by himself, it is a treat to have a son at beck and call 24 hours a day. He creates problems when none in truth exists, of course, or magnifies minor pains into major aggravations. Since my mother died nine years ago he has lived in limbo, rarely cooking, eating out, hating to be alone but refusing to do the things necessary if one is to live with others. And now I return, the prodigal son turned nurse.

In his insomniac's nights when we would talk at three, four, or five o'clock, Norm would tell me with pride of past doctors' predictions that he would die in middle age of a heart attack, dropping onto a sofa he was selling at the department store or slumping into cardiac arrest while driving his car on a highway. He had smoked two packs of cigarettes a day for over fifty years, had drunk steadily, had eaten rich foods, and had not exercised since high school. At Walter's graduation from university, Norm laughed one night, he had sent a postcard saying, "Hah. Made it" to the doctor who had predicted that if Norm didn't slow down he would never see that day. Now Norm rued the fortune that card had signaled with such glee. "That would have been the way to die," he sighed to me: under full steam and in the midst of life, not at its end and by pieces.

"Don't you think it a bit selfish to be sorry now that you couldn't check out when, in retrospect, it would have been high water?" I asked. "If you had died then it would have been hard on us, your sons, and on Mother, too." I said. He admitted the point but added he was glad that she did not have to meet age's errors on her own. "At least I spared her that," he said, as if it were something he had done. Theirs had been one of those rare, romantic loves that began with a single meeting, a telepathic glance that never lost its intensity. I had never heard them argue, and even their friends had commented on the almost neurotic completion—Norm and Sue, Sue and Norm— each had given the other. Since her death almost a decade before he had transformed his grief into a profession, made of mourning an occupation to complete his retirement years. He had turned his house and life into a shrine to the memory of my mother. Everything was as it had been. Her bed, beside his, had been left intact and inviolate in the years of his solitude, and when we visited, no one was allowed to sit upon it or even ruffle the coverlet. Now that bed was heaped with spare blankets, bandages, and medical supplies used to dress his burns.

Since her death he had refused to cook more than the occasional scrambled egg, proclaiming his ignorance in culinary arts but, I think, secretly insisting that it was still his wife's responsibility, and death did not free her from it or give him the right to intrude. Each pot and pan remained as she had left it. Each jar, still half-filled with now stale spices, was where Mother last had set it nine years before. He worked as a volunteer at the hospital because that is where he had last seen her, the one great love of his life. It was, he said, his "salvation," but in truth it was his penance. She had died and he had lived. That was not as it should have been, he believed, so he spent his days in atonement.

I told him that bereavement had become a neurotic obsession, a second job to fill his time when the hospital didn't need him, and that he should have married again, at least for convenience, rather than turning away from the world and future love. Maybe, he would reply when the topic had become old terrain we covered at least once a week. But, he would insist, I didn't understand. How could I when, a bachelor in my thirties, I'd built no life or family or home—none of the perspectives that would have given me a vantage point like his from which to see? It was the argument he had used against me since infancy, the unassailable position that youth cannot know what maturity has learned through the years.

During this period Father was visited and telephoned daily by the loyal remains of my parents' inner circle, Buffalonians with whom they had grown up and who had known my father since all were children together. Mrs. Bee, Mrs. Jakonoski, the Greens, Mrs. Kuhn, and Mrs. Brocken—names from my past kept coming forward by telephone or appearing at the door for permission to visit their friend Norm. Once I had visited their homes and asked if their children Bonnie, Rick, or Ray could play. Now they came and petitioned at my door. The strangeness was not only a reverse of roles from my youth to this maturity, but that it was occurring in Buffalo at all. It was as if the eighteen years of my distant domiciles, the period since my departure, had evaporated. Although I no longer considered myself of Buffalo or a member of my father's community, participation in his world had gained me a temporary membership—or one renewed—in his communal world. Most important, perhaps, was his sister, Janice, who came almost daily with gifts of food she had prepared for him. Rice pudding, apple sauce and lamb, roast beef, or squash—all paraded through in a procession of plastic containers, each gift designed to appeal to his palate and to assist in the recovery of his appetite. Each meal was a tie to their history, something he had liked as a child or that their mother had taught her to prepare years before I was born.

My aunt was hard of hearing and had fought her disability for years, refusing to buy a hearing aid until the world had diminished from shout past speech to a dimly heard whisper. During my adolescent years my mother, her best friend, always sat on Aunt Janice's right, and I was relegated to the deafness of her left. Like any child who speaks to an adult who will not respond, I had presumed it was indifference to me and only understood much later that it was her refusal to acknowledge a handicap that had made her seem so aloof. For years she had fought the quieting world, holding out against accepting infirmity just as Norm had embraced his grief or, later, fought the strictures his operation had imposed, bending to get a letter from a bureau drawer and falling as a consequence. Both were of that quality and time that believed intransigence was a posture with which to face the world and that if one did not dignify handicaps with recognition, perhaps they would disappear. But by this time she had bowed and wore a hearing aid outside her house and would tell me when I spoke too softly or too fast for her to understand.

Her example allowed me to believe that the problems my father faced, physical and emotional, were not something incomprehensible until I, too, received golden age discounts. They were disabilities, pure and simple. It seemed to me then that the elderly face the same obstacles as any handicapped individual. If one is thirty-five or seventy-five years of age, a wheelchair still remakes the world; the sudden inability to drive a car forces the environment's restructuring. The world does not necessarily shrink with age. Senior citizens and handicapped individuals of all ages and both sexes travel the world. Disability is no necessary barrier to scope—a cerebral palsy or multiple sclerosis victim can listen to Bach, read Mailer, and live in the cosmos as easily as can we who are not infirm. The true withdrawal of the elderly, I decided, is in time: a rejection of the future and an insistence upon the more comfortable past. In a letter to friends I wrote:

My father does his living, in great part, out of present time but in place, hauling himself to a temporal location of personal history where he is loved and useful and strong. It is bewildering to watch, and confusing. Sometimes he is there, heart and soul, fighting and striving for immediacy. But often his attention wanders and he is elsewhere, back in a time when legs were never given a second thought and daily life was filled with energy and interest. When life was filled with joy.

I want to return him to my present, to insist he can find the world—as it is—worth his constant attention. But to do that, he has to change, to accept this current reality. My greatest fear is that unless this happens he will lose both past and present—lose friends and sympathy, support and hope until the day when there is nothing left but to stop remembering and fighting together. On that day he will stop breathing, too, like an elderly, forgotten M. F. K. Fisher character.

By early September, Father was working out on a sporty, four-pronged orthopedic cane, preparing to shed the large, cumbersome walker that had been his mobility and support. His therapist from Visiting Nurses was pleased with the progress we had made, as was I, who had begun to sleep again in my old room on the second floor. I took Norm to visit his general physician, Dr. Pangless, who had been a camper more than fifty years before when Norm was a counselor at Camp Lakeland. Although his weight was still below pre-operative levels, Pangless assured me that there was nothing to worry about and that my father would be fine. I asked about the tape burns that had caused us such difficulty. Why, I asked, had a dermatologist not immediately been called, and what other problems could we expect? Dr. Pangless said surgery wasn't his responsibility and if I had questions, to take them up with Dr. Stryon, whom we were scheduled to visit next. But on our way to the orthopedic surgeon's office, Norm told me not to "make waves" because, he said, "I have to live with these guys, so do me a favor and please, be quiet." Stryon rotated Norm's hip with a few quick jerks and declared his progress satisfactory. He said that Norm's bruised back and days of immobility had retarded the healing but that soon Norm would be able to drive again and that he had no postoperative worries.

Then I began to make plans for my departure, and this meant making sure others would be present to take over my functions in Buffalo. Norm's friends told me that he had been terribly depressed the previous spring and that they believed his dietary problems had begun during that period. For years I had urged him to accept counseling. Now I was adamant, reminding him that he had given me the right to make these decisions. And so Ed Sterman, a pleasant, ascetic-looking psychologist, began weekly home visits. Father, despite his objections, at first seemed in some way perversely pleased. "I'm seeing a shrink," he told a friend, "because I'm all screwed up." "Good," the friend shrugged politely, and the conversation moved on to other things.

I also began to call homemaker services to find someone who could help Father in the house. Most agencies had long waiting lists and would not even consider adding a new name to their rolls. Finally, one, Homemakers, Inc., admitted they had available personnel and promised to send someone out for an interview. Telling Father what I had done, I explained that when I left Buffalo and until he could drive again, he would need someone to cook, assist in his exercises, and, I thought, to function as a home companion. Forget the expense, I urged. "I can't," he said, insisting that I was going to "bankrupt" him but agreeing, finally, that a few hours of help a day made sense.

That week Julia Shea entered our lives from 10 a.m. to 1 p.m. several days a week. The agency received $6.25 for each hour worked, and she in turn received $3.50 of that amount. During those three hours she made sure Father had lunch and prepared a dinner that he could warm up at his leisure. She supervised his exercises, cleaned the house where I had not, and became adept at jollying Norm into accepting help with everything from putting on his socks to preparing weekly grocery lists. About thirty years old, with a son and a husband, she had the perfect attitude of quiet assistance and professionalism. Julia had an innate respect for both his person and his property and, somewhere, had developed the special talent of being always present but never intrusive. That, perhaps, was her greatest strength, a sense of propriety and belief in the necessity of home care. Julia's son had been born with a serious hearing deficiency requiring constant attention and expensive, special education. To her, Norm's transient problems were merely another type of deficit, simply a handicap that should be viewed with neither fear nor shame. It mattered little to her if the patient was, like her son, pediatric or geriatric like Norm.

My father quickly became so fond of Julia that his concern over the money paid each fortnight to the agency was silenced. Norm told me privately that she needed help because of her deaf son. It was as if he saw her employ as a gift to the handicapped child, charity disguised within the context of his own particular needs. Thus he maintained to himself the fiction that he did not need care while gladly accepting Julia's help. Father complained bitterly, however, about the $45 an hour his psychologist Sterman charged (in truth a bargain rate), the cost of his hip replacement (fully covered by Medicare), the phone bill I ran up, and the money Paula's visits had cost. Julia would leave the room when Norm and I argued these things, carrying on a debate that had no resolution. He would end the fight each time, saying, "There is only so much [money], and when it's gone, that's it." I had no idea how much he had; I knew only that he had saved for years against the specter of future illness or incapacity. Arguing the point seemed futile, and finally, six weeks after my arrival, I was ready to depart. His strength was returning and every day he could walk a little farther. No longer necessary to my father's survival, I was eager to return to my world.

Before leaving, I sat in at their request on a session between Sterman and Father, listening with amazement as he told the therapist how alone he was, how his circle of friends had moved away or died. He said there was little left for him to look forward to—his sons had all moved away and rarely had time to visit him. His days, he said, were a minimal existence spent husbanding meager resources. Here, Father concluded, was a spent man petering out at the end of a working life. I could have strangled him, and later, in private, tried to convince my father that none of it was objectively true. He was neither impoverished nor alone. Where I saw a man with good friends offering enormous reservoirs of support, he saw himself as bereft, dull, and alone. I saw a man with sons who loved him and work he insisted he loved to do. He saw a man in solitude, dribbling away his days. It was as if the mirror's image had transfixed him, and now instead of an ageless self he saw in reflection a destitute, solitary beggar tottering to the alms house. But this was Sterman's domain, I told myself. It was nothing I could cure.

2

Time and Chance

What a train of woes—and such woes—comes with a prolonged old age. To begin with, this deformed, hideous, unrecognizable face; this vile leather instead of skin; these pendulous cheeks; these wrinkles like those around the mouth of an old she-ape as she sits scratching in the shady Thabarcan woods.

Juvenal, *Tenth Satire*

I left for Toronto, New York, Washington, D.C., and finally Raleigh, North Carolina. For twelve days I returned to my professional and personal world where everyone said how wonderful it was that I had chosen to help my father and how unusual it was for a son to take the time, to take over in this fashion. At each stop I heard a new tale of aging parents and the problems they presented, and discussed with others the complexities of home-care services as our grandparents had once, I presume, discussed their difficulties with household servants. Each night I would awaken at about three o'clock to what I was sure was the ringing of my father's bell. Most of those I visited, a mix of editors and old friends, saw themselves as creeping along the cusp of middle age while engaging at one remove in the problems of gerontology, bracing for two life crises at once. There has to be an article here, one editor said. I promised to think about writing one.

Father and I were linked by the telephone, and he reported with pride when he began to take walks up and down the block each day with Julia at his side. Neighbors whom he had not seen in weeks greeted him and said how nice it was to know he was "on the mend." These slow, limping excursions were, in my father's eyes, a coming out—a return to his environment—and not simply mandated exercise performed under a caretaker's cautious eye. Julia, who at his request wore no uniform, watched my father carefully, however, stopping him when he would bend forgetfully to pick up something. "He's always trying to stoop down," Julia told me one day. "If I weren't here he would have fallen and injured himself any number of times." Norm dismissed this as "women's worries," although I had no doubt it was true. "She won't even let me take out the garbage," he complained, as if he could lug his old, metal trash cans while simultaneously balancing on the walker. Both agreed that Norm's appetite was good, thanks to Julia's cooking. "I'm stuffing myself," he said proudly, and promised to be fattened before my return. I agreed to come back to Buffalo for a few days so we could "enjoy each other" in his convalescence without the trauma of rehabilitation. Then I would fly to the South Pacific and a story I had long wanted to do, a six-week sail from Hawaii to the islands of Kiribati at seven degrees north latitude.

The last Saturday of September I returned to the house in Buffalo where Norm met me at the door. "Watch," he said happily as I dropped my bags in the hall. As the cab drifted down the street my father first limped up and then down, back up and then down the house's front stoop with no support other than a regular cane. Its tip steadied his weight while the good leg climbed or sank a step, holding until the operated side could follow in its turn. All the while his face was set in that look of proud concentration a child displays while mastering a two-wheeled bicycle. This was, he said, a little gift to me, a demonstration of determination to match the time I'd spent when he had been unable to do for himself. "I did everything you said," Norm insisted like a promise, intimating he had been worthy of my confidence and the time I had invested in his recovery. I complimented him extravagantly and suggested we sit down because, in truth, he looked terrible. Father's skin had taken on the color of a faded, dirty tan and the sclera, the whites surrounding the pupil of his eyes, were jaundiced yellow. He admitted to a touch of diarrhea but insisted that "otherwise everything is swell."

Sunday morning when she arrived Julia said that his appetite had fallen off and that she was worried, too. At her insistence he had called his doctor on Friday morning, reaching instead a substitute physician because Pangless was away for a long weekend. My father had told the man about the recent surgery and the more recent symptoms that worried Julia at the time: skin discoloration; tiredness; loose bowels with a loose yellow, ashlike stool; and a urine now darkish red. The unseen physician had prescribed for the diarrhea and suggested to my father that if things did not improve, they should call Dr. Pangless on Monday. Father grew worse, and when we called Pangless, he agreed to a visit the next day. That Tuesday he glanced at my father's color, palpated his abdomen, and ordered a barrage of tests—from blood levels to a sonogram—which resulted in Norm being assigned a private room in a semi-isolation wing of General Taylor.

Father seemed delighted to be back in the hospital. He praised the food, chatted with the nurses, and pointed with pride to one or another implement that he had ordered while working there. Friends of his from the volunteer and business offices dropped by to chat and each asked if he needed anything, a courtesy that told my father he was still a part of the "hospital team," and to each he said, "Just hold my job open for me, so when I'm ready, I can return." His supervisor told me how valuable Norm was and my father beamed modestly—as if someone had just given him a raise. He glanced at me as if to say, "You see. I'm appreciated here and able to perform a service others really need." By phone he told his friends he was "just in for tests" and then gave me a list of things to do at home.

At first I wondered why he was so happy to be again in the hospital when after the hip operation he had been so eager to leave. Then I realized he had known something was wrong but had refused to admit it to himself or to me. His marching up and down the stairs was both demonstration and mask, pride in accomplishment and a cover for the fear he must have felt as his stool and urine changed. The illness surely affected him, but he had set its symptoms aside to spare me on that weekend. In the hospital, finally, he could stop pretending and be content to give in to its power. Relieved, free of my expectations and the responsibilities of rehabilitation, he reclined on his bed and said, simply, Let it come.

Another and welcome bonus of this admission for Father was his inability to keep his scheduled appointment with the psychologist

Sterman. My father preferred unhappiness to the rigors of emotional counseling with a psychologist whose job was to get him to talk about himself. "I tell him the same thing every time, and that takes maybe five minutes," Father had complained the day I returned to Buffalo. "Then he asks, 'What else?' and I say, 'That's it,' and we sit for the rest of the half hour in silence. I try to make conversation, but for what?" Unwilling to open up, to discuss his feelings, he had deeply resented my insistence on therapy. It had been, for him, a humiliating admission of failure, to speak of his life to a young stranger. Hospital was, among other things, a refuge from that ordeal where he had been caught between the role of host ("the man is, after all, in my house") and client, a posture he had no stomach for. Perhaps it had been naive of me to expect my father to unburden to others when he had spent a lifetime refusing to admit to himself. For a man trained—as were most born early in the century—to deny self-doubt and to distrust emotion, it would have taken problems far more severe than his for Norm to accept a counselor or therapist. Sterman had been the counter in our battle of wills, a bet by me that Father had to cover in a game he did not want to play. That was the last we saw of the therapist. I gave up on the campaign, and it would be months, in the end, before Norm was able to see anyone at all.

Within days he was spectacularly ill. Virtually unable to eat, drifting in and out of sentience; his liver had almost shut down. Terribly weakened, he walked only with great difficulty, and aged before my eyes. Because he was in semi-isolation, his friends were afraid to visit, and I spent several hours a day on the phone delivering progress reports to our immediate relatives and members of his circle. My brothers all insisted I call them with frequent medical updates, and each in turn voiced his concern for our father's future. I tried to keep them informed, sometimes asking one to call the other in a linked chain of information. It was difficult, really, because none of the doctors would say with certainty what Father's problem was, and thus there was no real prognosis I could offer in hope or in despair.

All we knew was that his condition was adversely affecting his liver. The physicians would not discuss the probable causes of this disease, but nurses said to me that non-A, non-B, hepatitis resulting from contaminated blood was what everyone assumed he was suffering from. There was no proof, however. Although it was a differential diagnosis, an educated guess remaining after all other problems were ruled out, Norm fit the hepatic profile perfectly. Non-A, non-B hepatitis develops six to eight weeks after a patient receives contaminated blood, and following his hip operation Norm had received three pints. Those who suffer from other, prior blood problems—Norm's geriatric leukemia, for example—stood at particular risk to the disease and, Paula said, when he had been transfused everyone had worried about "something like this."

"If they were so worried, why didn't someone warn us?" I asked. Had Julia or I known what to look for we could have been alert for symptoms and certainly been able to insist to Pangless's substitute that my father needed care. "Why did Father have to wait five days—Friday to Tuesday—before a doctor would see him," I asked.

Paula was silent for a moment and then said that as a nurse, it wasn't her place to criticize irresponsible doctors.

Aunt Janice visited her brother in the hospital, and when she left his room that first day was beside herself with fear. Their mother had died of leukemia, and she believed her brother was dying of that same disease. The jaundice, physical wasting, a constant demand for sweets, and his other symptoms were also common in terminal leukemic episodes, so she was cheered but not entirely convinced when I assured her the tests showed categorically his problem was caused by something else. I saw my aunt daily at the hospital and, promoted to her right side and good ear, spent an increasing amount of time with her. She talked about both my father and what it was like to see the last human link to a chain of the past prepare to break away. They were the last of their generation and the final survivors of a once large German family visited by my father and his sister only twice in their youth, both times before the Great Depression. Aunts and uncles were all killed in Germany's concentration camps, and if there were cousins in America, I never heard either speak of them. When and if my father died it would be the dissolution of her own last link to another's memories stretching back from Buffalo to Germany. At that moment, a world would disappear for her along with whatever childhood reservoirs they carried together of shared, early years.

Memories, I realized, are rarely solo affairs. They are ensemble pieces amplified by the presence of others who have shared a past reality. As those others die or drift away, the memories fade as well.

Her brother's illness attacked her own worldview and, for my aunt, her brother's now sick and aged appearance forced a congruence with their shared memories of past deaths. I remembered a quote from Simone de Beauvoir: "The past is not a peaceful landscape lying there behind me, a country in which I can stroll wherever I please, and which will gradually show me all its secret hills and dales. As I was moving forward, so it was crumbling." That, my aunt said, was it exactly. "Moving forward and crumbling. Yeah."

My father also believed he was dying, although he would not admit it to his sister. In the first days following his admission he told me when we were alone that his sister was, after all, "only a girl" and should not be troubled unduly. That she was then over seventy years of age did not change the fact that, in his mind, she remained an adolescent needing to be protected as he remembered his parents protecting them. The lessons of their youth had endured, and women, he believed, were a weaker sex in need of care and cajoling. By saying nothing to her of his fears he remained, at least in his own mind, the active male whose job it was to handle hard truths. That in fact she was more aware than he of the extremities to which illness had laid us bare was, of course, irrelevant. His life had been lived within its own fictions, and the reality of intelligent, able women (mother, wife, and sister) who handled childbirth, death, disease, injury, business depressions, and war with equanimity was not a truth he had ever wished to know. Flat on his back and poisoned by his liver, he still was the elder brother watching out for his sister— "only a girl"—whose solicitations he could rebuff with the bravado of a firstborn son.

"Don't tell Janice, of course," he insisted to me, confiding that he was ready and almost eager to die. If the choice was between a rapid death and years of infirmity, he thought the former preferable. "I've loved my life and, really, what more is there to look forward to?" I tried to tell him there was his volunteer job, sons, and grandchildren, books to read and his neighborhood to enjoy, but he said no, "everybody goes and if it's my time, I'm ready." This was Noble Norm, I wrote in my journal. I did not believe he wanted to die, but the image of a man at peace with his world was better to him than that of an old man scared of disease and disability. He mentioned as we talked a novel that had impressed him in his youth, one where consumptives died a drawn-out but beautiful, wasting death. "I'd just as soon go quickly," he said, but was preparing, I suspected, for an elegant decline in the pattern of a nineteenth-century gentleman consumptive who lingered with elegance and died, finally, in quiet civility.

Already weakened by the operation and postoperative burns, Father's condition grew daily more serious. Within a week of his admission he was sleeping twenty hours a day, and when awake, barely aware of my presence in his room. He was verging on a hepatic coma: "one of the dreaded complications of liver disease and a manifestation of profound liver failure. The earliest symptoms of hepatic coma, i.e. the manifestations of impending coma, include minor mental aberrations and motor disturbances. The patient appears to be slightly confused; he becomes untidy, there is a far-away look in his eye; he tends to drowse during the day and to wander at night. . . . In a more advanced stage there are gross disturbances of consciousness and the patient is completely disoriented with respect to time and place."

That described his condition perfectly. I read it in the *Textbook of Medical-Surgical Nursing* which, with other nursing guides, became my bedtime reading. I tried the physician's guides but found they told me a great deal about the technical course of the disease but nothing about what the patient would feel or how to make my father comfortable. The nursing texts gave me all the information that I might need, explaining the blood tests and various scores which almost daily filled a voluminous chart kept in my father's room. It explained to me, as it is supposed to explain to nurses, what each test meant and provided tables explaining the relation of one test to another. As importantly, it warned me about potential medical complications that Father could face and focused the whole of this knowledge on not simply the disease itself but what it meant for the patient, for my patient, my father, Norm. I needed this help because my father's physician, Dr. Pangless, seemed determined to avoid me and would, when cornered, discuss my father's condition only in vague terms. He began daily hospital rounds, as do many doctors, before eight o'clock in the morning. This allowed the physicians to see their patients before office hours but also, one nurse said, "to assure they don't have to see the family." The floor nurses who cared for Father were more willing to explain what was happening and to admit the seriousness of his condition. They were efficient if brusque in the essentials, capable and even kind when his bed required changing or if a sweat-soaked gown needed to be replaced with a fresh one. There was nothing else they could do but wait and watch, hope he would not go into a terminal coma or, perhaps, hope that he would.

My brother Brian called from Atlanta to ask if he should come up, and when I said he should do what he wanted, replied, "Come on, you know what I mean." When I churlishly refused to speak in code he asked almost angrily, "Well, is he dying?" I denied it categorically with a certainty I did not feel. "He's a tough old kraut," I insisted. "He'll pull through. This is harder on me, I think, than on him." Reassured, Brian told me that were Norm dying of course he would come to Buffalo, but since there was nothing he could do for our father while we waited, he would continue to work.

I told everybody Norm would survive because I was unable to admit to others what a part of me thought to be true. He was dying and I only hoped it would be speedy and painless. Norm had declared his life ended, his remaining days a waiting. At least that is what, weeks before, he had told the psychologist Ed Sterman. And yet there was a tenacious intransigence, a core at the center of my father's being at odds with the face he presented to himself and to the world. This core could not die, I told him softly as he slept one day; it must not perish while holding Aunt Janice's memories intact and not while there was still the pride that had sent him walking up and down, up and down the stairs of his front stoop on the day of my return. The core, a central, ageless part of him, was clinging, fighting, hoping for something different, for a reversal, a new lease on life and another chance. It was the part of Father I believed in. For his part, my father maintained a faith in Pangless and the miracles of modern medicine. One day when Father woke from his almost constant doze he said, "Mike won't leave me like this. There has to be some pill." Then he drifted off again, and slept.

Each morning I would bring him containers of iced tea, one of the two things he seemed to enjoy. The other was ice cream. Every afternoon before I left the hospital, he would ask me to get from the cafeteria another drink—"For later," he would explain—and bring it to his room. But it was not the simple taste of tea (or even the coolness of ice cream) that he craved so much as the power of command and the sight of me coming through his door again. I discovered this one day when the hospital cafeteria's supplies ran low and

I told him they were out of both tea and ice cream and that I was going home. "Well then," he shrugged, "bring anything." It was as if without a specific task or necessity he did not think he could impose upon my time. The tea had become a necessary prop to bring me back onto his stage and, perhaps, to confirm his ability to command someone in a task. Afterwards I brought neither iced tea nor ice cream on my visits, waiting instead for him to ask me to fetch him a container of tea from the cafeteria. Thus at least once each visit I would return to his room both with a drink and the power of requests that will be neither questioned or denied.

His memory played very strange tricks throughout this time. Usually Father knew my name but would forget, day to day, what had happened the night before. The hip operation and its aftermath disappeared from his consciousness, which was a haphazard series of early memories peopled by aunts, uncles, friends, and relatives who had all died before I was born. It was as if he lived beside time and saw old worlds again, which he described to me, a voyeur in my father's past life. I listened because there was neither time nor strength for either of us to do anything else. In a notebook I kept to relieve the frustration of those days I recorded a diary of impressions. Some I later included in letters to friends, rewriting as a release from the intolerable inactivity of waiting. What I wrote on a day in mid-November stands as memory for this whole time:

Sitting crumpled in a hospital chair, his color jaundiced, yellow-brown, face filled with wrinkles and seams, my father looks like a pale leaf curled against the autumn wind; holding tenaciously to some small tether as the rain beats down. His face asks, Where has the summer gone? while his voice asks if I know what day it is for he, of course, does not. That is the image which my mind holds as I make the daily trek to his hospital room to comfort him and interpret, when he is sentient, the results of blood tests done by the doctor who cheerfully breezes through on early rounds. That is the vision I ponder, wondering if the transformation happened suddenly or, as with autumn's leaves, I just never saw the first hints of change and simply awoke one morning to find him a different man.

My father has been forbidden the right to leave his bed unassisted, relegated to impatient waiting when he needs or wants the simplest and most necessary things. They are right, of course, these nurses, for his new hip is weak and the illness has both fogged his mind and sapped what strength he had, earlier, in convalescence. Moving from his hospital bed to a commode eight steps away has become a long and dangerous trek through the obstacle course of table, bureau, and chair on dark green, linoleum floor. The bathroom, a fifteen-step journey from his bed, is impossibly distant and in its solitude offers other, more complex dangers. I helped him to the commode chair yesterday and then left the room to preserve his shreds of dignity and my memory of a self-sufficient man. "Call," I ordered, as the door to his room swung shut on a glimpse of hospital gown flapping as he sat down.

"Wait for me before you try to return to bed and we'll make the trip together," I said, leaving him for the hospital corridor where I walked, wondering whose dignity was more offended, his in infirmity or mine in memory of other nights past when he carried me to the bathroom door. Returning, I saw him tottering erect, pulling himself from the commode's back to the bureau, swinging hand over hand from dresser to table to headboard to bed like some grotesque child playing Tarzan on a playground's gym. He stumbled, finally, collapsing on the bed exhausted but triumphant at this first solo victory in days.

The weight loss, which has been sudden and extreme, accounts for the new folds of pendulous skin which hang so loose upon him now. That, I know, comes from the hepatitis which followed eight weeks after his surgery. The hepatitis is a result of postoperative blood transfusions made necessary by his leukemia. I know his sickly coloration is born in the liver, whose inflammation has allowed impurities to pour into his skin, sclera, and brain. That rerouting has transformed, in turn, his sentience into senility. Knowing all this, one always asks when did it happen, and how does it feel to stare out of those yellowed eyes and see oneself in the mirror, to find a stranger where once stared back a face as familiar as memory. I asked him and he told me. It feels lousy.

A nurse was behind me as I rushed to his side that day, and together we hustled his legs beneath the spread. "I told you not to get around alone," she scolded, and slammed into place the metal sides of the bed, transforming it into a crib. She walked away to other duties, and he beckoned me closer, pleading in a whisper—his loudest voice—that I lower the bars. "You've already fallen three times," I said, refusing what he wanted most. He called me once again and turned towards the window where a light breeze crawled through, "Tom," he said as tears routed through the stubble of his chin, "don't ever grow old."

Much to everyone's surprise, the crisis passed, and three weeks after his admission Father was returned to our house, considerably weakened and with test scores of his liver enzymes that, while high, appeared to be coming down. He had again lost weight, and his skin hung looser than ever on his frame, like a father's summer suit tried on by a small but growing preadolescent boy. We were given no directions for home care and I took the precaution of engaging Julia full-time from the agency. I knew Father would worry about the expense, but by then I did not care, needing the help almost as much as he. Waiting, watching the erosion of his body and his acuity had become almost more than I could bear.

His first few days went well. During his last week in the hospital some physiotherapy had been ordered, and at home he began again the quadriceps exercises his illness had curtailed. We called the county therapist and were assigned an appointment for the following week. Take it easy, I urged, but Father was determined to regain the strength already lost to this new disease, once again to move from the large walker he now required to his lighter, four-pronged cane. "If I can't walk, how can I return to work?" he asked, and since that goal was what drove him on, there was nothing I could say. My father was not a man to live with illness or disability. "Tell me what to do to get better," he had insisted in the hospital, "and I'll do it." When I reminded him of his age and his need to rest he would challenge me to a race around the block "just as soon as my hip is able." Father returned to his home on Monday, but by the following Saturday all the symptoms again were present and he could barely sit up in his bed. The jaundiced skin, yellowish stool, dark urine, flatulence, and a craving for sweets all reappeared, along with a wandering, vague mental laxity—the most frightening aspect of all to me. "Oh no, not again," he wailed. "I don't want to go back to the hospital." He saw the possibility of another admission as a further barrier to his hip's improvement because it would mean he could not exercise. Watching his dissolution, the relapse becoming more marked by the hour, I wanted him off my hands. It was clear that, whatever else was going on, he had passed beyond any hope of my home care.

In a panic, I called Dr. Pangless on Sunday morning only to be told by his answering service that he was unavailable. A Dr. Mogaldo was taking Pangless's emergencies and did I need help, the service asked politely. I did, I said, as soon as possible. Please ask Dr. Mogaldo to telephone at once. Frantic by then, I was furious when, more than two hours later, he finally returned the call. I described my father's history and symptoms and my fears of a relapse or recurrence. My aunt's worries had infected me, and I thought of a leukemic episode. Dr. Mogaldo suggested I do nothing and wait for Dr. Pangless's return the next day. But the last time an associate of Pangless's had said Norm should wait, his treatment had been delayed a week, and this time I did not think Father could afford to wait. I demanded tests be done and insisted my father receive immediate attention. Dr. Mogaldo said speed wasn't critical and I suggested he visit the house and see this patient for himself. Finally, the man reluctantly agreed to order some tests "to set my mind at ease." Silently I cursed him for a complacent, pompous oaf and vowed to kill Dr. Pangless on his next day off, but on the phone, humbly thanked Dr. Mogaldo for his time. Soon a cheerful technician came to the door and departed, five minutes later, with Father's blood in vials and his medicare number on the order sheet.

Father was awake while I talked to the doctor, napped until the technician came, and then fell asleep again. Despite his sickness and his fear of it, he criticized my handling of the physician. "You're going to get me into trouble," he said wearily. "These guys need to be treated with respect." In brief bouts of wakefulness that day, he also worried about money. If he had to return to the hospital it would be, he said, too expensive, and why didn't he just stay at home, with Julia and me to care for him. When I explained we didn't know how and that he was too sick to stay at home he predicted that in his absence I would spend a fortune on household expenses. "You never did know how to handle money," he said and then fell again into his drowsy, comatic sleep.

Then he rambled on in a monologue about the poorhouses that had been a feature of his youth. On Sunday drives long before, in the days of his family's Pierce Arrow, they would pass the county poorhouse and Norm's father would warn (sly glances to this son from the corner of his eye) that such would be the final home of all profligate and weak-willed boys. The feeling of fear and certainty of shame impressed upon Norm by those drives had remained, half-buried, until the day liver disease brought back the memories and made them live again. I promised he would not be sent away and then he slept some more, like a child assured the bogeyman won't come as long as a parent is in the house. Concerns about money, I began to understand, were also the language in which he framed emotional concerns. Fears of incipient poverty were a code in which he could speak around the terror of physical disability and the in-capacities of a lengthy and potentially terminal illness. Just as his volunteer job had been transmuted into "work," the theme that had given his life meaning, so too was the cost of hospitalization a code for the discouragement and fear that accompanied his decline. Per-haps money was a legitimate worry—I didn't know at the time. What became clear was the degree to which it was the language in which he spoke of other things like hope and self-esteem.

Monday Dr. Pangless called at 9:30 in the morning, furious at my temerity. Who was I, he asked sharply, to order doctors around? By what right did I demand that tests be done? If it had been an emer-gency, Pangless continued, he should have been called at home, and since it obviously was not an emergency, his very busy associate (who, the answering service had told me, took four other calls all Sunday morning) should not have been bothered at all. Just who, exactly, did I think I was, Dr. Pangless demanded. I began to apol-ogize, hating myself with every stumbling word. The service would not ring me through to your house, I protested, and the symptoms were so acute I was scared. He said he would call when the results of my "unnecessary" tests were available. He did not ask to speak with my father or inquire about his condition. Father, who overheard a part of the conversation, took some satisfaction in having been proved correct. "I told you there would be trouble."

That night I called my Uncle Jules, a pediatrician whom I had not yet seen during this period of my Buffalo tenure. We had talked a few times on the telephone, but in the beginning I could not leave my father alone, and later the exigencies of our shared life had kept me from visiting anyone. I called from the phone near my father's bed and spoke with caution because Norm, already terrified by an illness he did not understand, did not want to be left alone. My uncle asked why I'd not been by and when I said I'd been too busy he asked if anything was wrong. I did not answer, asking instead if he would be free the next day. "Norm is near the phone?" he asked. Yes, I said with a sigh, and he invited me for coffee the next morning when Julia would be on duty. As a child, I had extravagantly admired this uncle, trusting him as children will those rare grown-ups who treat them as sentient beings. He had been loud, boisterous, and argumentative, an amateur cook who swam and sailed. To my child-hood eye, Uncle Jules had been everything my quiet, cautious, and unathletic father was not. Where Norm had warned me about the effects of alcohol, Uncle Jules had offered me my first beer. If anyone could help us with Dr. Pangless, I decided, it would be this man. Sitting with Norm after the conversation, I already felt less alone.

Tuesday Julia arrived at 9 A.M. while my father slept, unable to eat and virtually unable to rise. I drove to Uncle Jules's in a rage. Angry at my continued residence in Buffalo, livid with the injustice of Dr. Pangless's rebukes, and discouraged over the futility of all that had been done so far, I was furious at the beauty of that late autumn day when all else in my life seemed so dismal. "You sounded upset on the phone," Uncle Jules said at the door, and as he turned to lead me to his study, I broke into a torrent of tears and sobs. He helped me to a chair and waited, patting my knee for several minutes until I could gasp, "I wasn't ready for this."

Then I cried some more. It was the first time I had wept in twenty years, and the force and power of the crying was terrifying. Men in my family never cried, not at funerals or at weddings. My father had sobbed briefly after my mother's death but then had quickly left the room and hid himself until self-control could be reasserted. Tears, we had been taught, were evidence of, at best, a lamentably childish lack of control and, at worst, a shoddy sentimentality of which both my parents disapproved. But here, in frustration and fear, I had no choice, and my Uncle simply waited it out, nodding like a mathematician who sees the expected sums appear at the end of a complex equation. He brought me coffee, and when I could speak again, he talked to me about Norm.

First Uncle Jules handed me an article on hepatitis and suggested I read it while the coffee brewed. It explained that the disease came from contaminated blood and that of 10,000 cases contracted in the United States in the previous year, some were cured, a few were fatal, and perhaps 10 percent developed into a chronic condition. After he returned with the coffee ("How do you take it, Tommy? I forget.") he asked why I had not visited him before, why I had waited until the whole complex overwhelmed me. I thought a minute and said I didn't know, that somehow there had been no time for anything but Norm's needs and concerns. Then we talked about Dr. Pangless, the immediate dilemma that I faced. Uncle Jules agreed to speak with him both as a family member and as a physician concerned with but not active on the case, adding that I, not Norm, was at greatest risk. Illness becomes a progressively closed world, a compact between the patient and medical personnel, with the family too often caught in the middle. It had sucked me in, he suggested, and was a strain no single individual could carry for long. He said I was to call him daily if I could not visit and insisted I go away at least for a few days, because "you'll do your father no good if you get sick as well."

Early that afternoon Dr. Pangless called to say that he had the test results at his desk and that an ambulance had been dispatched to bring Father back to General Taylor. Despite his sickness, Norm was distraught at the idea of another admittance. "I don't want to live like this," he wailed when I told him. "This is no way to end." He asked me to help him up from the bed. On my arm he shuffled to the bathroom where he glanced in the mirror and began to comb his hair. It was hard not to cry at this trace of his vanity, this insistence on some form of presentability when facing, in extremes, the world again. His hair had always been very fine and a source of some pride, preened by constant combing. Now it was a final reflex, and in the mirror I suspect he saw only an afterimage, a memory of the personas who had for years been there in reflection to greet him. He had passed the point of fear or concern and now used the comb as a talisman or, perhaps, a mnemonic whose power failed to evoke the sense of independent self it had always called forth in the past. That is how we stood, before a mirror neither truly dared to use, when the ambulance attendants arrived. I shouted towards the front door left open for them to come in that we were ready. Father was so insistent on his ability to walk that they watched him assay a step and then quickly picked him up, carrying his body over the stoop and down to a waiting stretcher. He never knew the difference and later told his sister that he had walked the whole way and that the ambulance ride had been a needless extravagance on my part.

I followed them to hospital and from there called his sister, who insisted I come to dinner. At Aunt Janice's I started to relate the day's events, but our conversation was constantly interrupted by the telephone as friends and relatives in Buffalo called her to ask about Norm. The local grapevine was alive and well. Someone had seen the ambulance and called the rest of their Buffalo circle. As she talked into the telephone (whose bell was magnified to a 120-decibel roar, which to her was a faint tinkle) I began to understand that she, too, had become totally involved in Father's maintenance. "How long will you stay?" she asked after Uncle Jules had called her for an update. "As long as needed," I replied. Like my uncle, she worried that my life was in abeyance, but that seemed to me to be the most minor of our problems. At least, it seemed so at that time, when anger at the physicians and frustration with the situation were all that I could feel.

She was furious with her brother for his concerns about money and his insistence on trying to walk to the ambulance. He had more than enough money to meet any emergency, his sister insisted, arguing that income had become his talisman against the solitude of widowerhood and the low self-image that retirement entailed. It had, she continued, become an excuse so he would not have to accommodate to the changes encroaching age and a deteriorating physical condition demanded. It was as if she blamed him for both his illness and for aspects of his personality that had secretly frustrated her for years. Norm had always been a rigid man, my aunt said to me, unable to bend or change. As proof she talked about his inability to adapt to the great injury of his youth. A superb high-school athlete, his shoulder had been permanently dislocated in a football game when he was seventeen. He had not searched for other sports that his injury would allow him to do but had simply "given up" athletics for life, a decision she had never understood. "He could have learned to use his left hand," she continued. "Your mother loved to bowl but he wouldn't go with her, you know. He could at least have done that left-handed, but oh no, not Norm! It's his way or not at all." Then she complained about his continued inability, after almost a decade, to adjust to my mother's death, just as in the years before retirement, he had found it hard to accept. Of course he would try and walk to the ambulance, his sister said. It is just what she would have expected of him. It was his vanity and pride, his spoiled intransigence, that had brought him to this enfeebled state. Illness became, in her analysis, not the intrusion of a retrovirus but cosmic retribution for his failure to live a better life.

I tried to suggest that a part of age, which differentiates it from other stages of life, is in fact precisely a decreased ability to change. How Norm dealt with the disabilities of his youth was one thing but, I said, in his present state any change would be by definition a virtual impossibility. The very body becomes inelastic as the bones grow brittle and the skin hangs from muscles that no longer hold their tone. I tried to tell my aunt that it was almost impossible for him to change—physically or mentally—and that his inflexibility was a result of illness and raw age. Perhaps he had been rigid in youth, but now something else was occurring. It was as if when future diminished to the span of a few short years, the whole individual—physical, emotional, and spiritual—became inflexible, clinging to "what has been" because the prospect of "what will be" is so limited.

That night I called my brothers to bring them up to date. Walter and Brian had called me regularly to ask after Father's status. Mark, my other brother, I called more infrequently and often asked Walter to talk to him in my stead. Partly it was because of the difference in time zones. I did not relish staying up until midnight to talk to Mark at 9 p.m. So I asked Walter to call Mark for me and then left town for a three-day weekend. That brief trip helped, although my mind constantly turned to Father in his new hospital room and I called each morning for a report on his condition. Returning to Buffalo, I visited the hospital daily, watching as bed rest brought Norm back to if not health at least a hope of survival. Pangless, Dr. Stryon, and a gaggle of hospital residents debated the case among themselves, I was told, although none of them talked readily to me. Chronic hepatitis was a continued and dangerous possibility, Pangless said one day in a hurried telephone interview. But then so, in theory, was complete recovery. It was as if Norm had become his property and my questions an intrusion.

After a fortnight the ambulance returned Father to our home with lower test levels than at the time of his first discharge but with scores that indicated he was still quite ill. Dr. Pangless made an appointment for us to visit his office in two weeks and seemed confident that "this time" the disease was under control. Uncle Jules had told me that in the 1940s hepatitis victims were given complete bed rest and warned me Norm should not be excited or allowed to exercise until the test scores returned to normal. I urged Father to simply stay in bed, but he insisted on starting his exercises again. So we called the physiotherapist and began on our own to exercise his hip. Father said he would prefer to die in bed than enter the hospital and "go through it all again."

I began to relax after the first week passed and Thanksgiving rolled around. My brothers called to chat, and each said to me, after talking with Father, that our father seemed to be on the mend, to show in flashes of humor and chatty strength his prehepatic self. A friend of his, a coworker at the hospital, sent in dinner for us both, and it promised to be a wonderful respite, for even I had begun to tire of my own cooking. It was, Norm said, a dinner "like Mother used to make," with turkey, stuffing, potato, gravy, vegetables, and a lemon pie for dessert. He talked that night about Thanksgiving dinners in the long past, when my mother and Aunt Janice had cooked for fifteen, and our Buffalo family would congregate throughout the house. It was as if that dinner signaled some reprise while holding, for Norm, a promise that some part of the past could be regained in a more healthy if still uncertain future we now shared.

When the date of our next appointment with Dr. Pangless rolled around, I drove Father to the medical building. He was very proud of his ability to arrive by car, not by ambulance, and believed this a sign of returning strength. "Next time," he said confidently, "I'll drive myself." But the jaundice was increasing and all other signs of active hepatitis had begun to manifest again. So Pangless insisted my father go immediately to the hospital, summoning a wheelchair to carry him one block down the street and into the admitting area of General. "What are you doing?" my father asked. "I thought I was doing so well." Dr. Pangless said, with rare honesty, he did not know what was occurring medically and then, with false assurance, insisted "we're going to get you better, kid." Father was returned to a new room on his recently vacated hospital floor before he had time to consider and refuse.

A whole new battery of tests was ordered to insure no other disease had been overlooked. More X rays, a CAT scan and sonogram were done. More blood was taken. Uncle Jules asked that a friend of his, a liver specialist, be called to the case. All agreed that hepatitis was the problem, a bad transfusion the cause of it all. When I asked about the specialist's report, Pangless said it advised against any exercise until the billirubin test levels dropped to near normal. Father had not listened to Uncle Jules, but now I insisted he follow the specialist's recommendation.

When he again was discharged in December, I forbade my father any exercise at all, allowing him to leave bed only for trips to the bathroom and to sit for meals in a chair placed beside his bed. He accepted this as, indeed, he accepted everything. Having surrendered control over his life to others, his only demand was that he not be returned to General Taylor again. Even a nursing home would be preferable, he insisted, to this constant shuttling between hospital and house. Death, my father said, would be kinder than a future of perpetual sickness, and he debated suicide with me as if the very act that would end life could affirm it as well. By telling me he might kill himself, Norm was telling himself as well that he had the power to order his life despite the abdication of choice to his medical masters and to me. I did not understand this at the time and lived nightly with the certainty that I would wake to find he had taken a handful of the prescription pills stashed in his room. I was relieved each morning, when I brought him his breakfast, to discover that he had not.

Gradually he grew stronger, beginning again to complain about the cost of things and to worry about his finances. While he was in the hospital I had visited his accountant to find out if I should continue to pay his bills myself. An old family friend, Leo Stein, said I did not need to support my father, who was in fact "quite comfortable" and could afford whatever he needed with no trouble at all. He was Norm's age, a dapper man who loved the ledger as carpenters do their levels, as my father had loved the furniture business's tricks and trade. Accounts and investments made Leo's life worth living, and he urged me to "tell Norm to spend for whatever he needs and if he balks, I'll make him do it myself."

It angered me that for all those months of long days and longer nights—especially before Julia's arrival—we could indeed have afforded help. My marathon vigils, weeks spent sleeping on the sofa and rising with Norm each night, in fact had not been necessary. "Why did you put me through this?" I shouted at Norm. "Why make me work so hard when help would have been better for us both?" He answered that "I needed to keep some family here and thought that otherwise you wouldn't stay." That, I decided, was at best a very partial truth. Maybe he was concerned that if we had hired more help I would have left, but time and again I had promised to stay as long as he needed or wanted my presence. In my youth he had struggled financially—I remember him carefully counting his pocket change each night—but now I deposited the dividend checks the mailman brought to his house most weeks and knew he could afford what he needed while in extremes.

The truth, I decided, was more complex, and I tried to work it out in a letter to old friends. Personal correspondence was for me the glue which held a distanced world together. Letters were a way in which I could live my life twice over: once in action, and secondly in its telling. Through letters I would fight for perspective on the events that built my days, a habit I had learned from Norm who, from my first experience at summer camp through college and into more recent years, had been my best and most faithful correspondent. Now I wrote of him and not to him, trying to understand us all.

Money had always been my father's greatest fetish and principal concern. In his youth, Norm's father would take the family for a drive in the country and point out the poorhouse as they motored by. It was a ritual which became, for my father, a symbol of destitute endings and remained his eternal fear. He had started college in the affluent 1920s, when his father was a financial success, but graduated after the market's crash and worked his last years of school as a waiter in a fraternity house. He had vowed his sons would not have to work their way through school and had spent years denying his wife and himself to make that promise come true.

Except for that brief period in university, he never worked for himself, for his own hobbies and pleasure. After graduation he became a traveling salesman, a job he despised, to help support his parents. When his sister married, my father paid for the wedding. Later, his income and energies were directed to wife and sons. Everything he had done and built was for us. Now we were living in distant cities, and his house had become a memorial to the memory of his wife.

Money is the foundation on which he built his life. It was to be, he always believed, one of continual building. Now he can add no more rooms to the structure and worries that without the sound of construction, the whole will dissolve. For those of his generation and upbringing, money is a reward for action, a compact with existence born of work. While a volunteer at the hospital he was contributing to society, and that act made him feel productive and thus richer, financially comfortable, although it brought in not a dime. Now he is adding nothing and the money must be spent. But for him, money is not for simple use but for banks; not for personal comfort but for the future, which is precisely what he now believes he does not have. Maybe there will be a few more years whose quality of life is uncertain, but nothing more. He makes a future of the past, when he was working and productive, a future with memories decades old of a world which has changed around him. His securities today are honored relics of those days—trophies—a legacy for his sons and a whisper of immortality.

Work is all he ever allowed himself to know and, retired, Father saw himself with back against the financial wall because there would be no future coups, no new and more lucrative jobs to move towards. That his investment income remained greater than mine from work was not, to him, the point. I had a future and he did not. Investments slowly built up over fifty years were a security blanket adding substance to his identity, and the idea of converting any of that solid equity into cash struck him as a treachery. "After all, I might need it for a serious illness," he said without a hint of humor. Really, it was legacy, something to leave "the boys"; to use it for any reason whatsoever would diminish his total estate, that final act of productivity in which he measured his final worth. So it all became sacrosanct, and in his mind he has moved from being a man with a net worth so comfortable he can afford anything he desires to a man with nothing but a checking account whose balance was dwindling daily.

All this is bad enough, but I have come to believe that he also suffers from a more general disease than these eccentricities alone. His complaints are geriatric ones, his story that of a whole generation. The elderly often see themselves as useless, as outlived tools maintained by pity and upon sufferance—but for what? They can build no futures and were taught in youth to give and care but never to expect and never to take. It is a perversion of noblesse oblige, where those who happily shouldered responsibilities find themselves not only uncomfortably free of obligations but foisting them elsewhere. Their frailty is underlined by the very products through which existence is maintained. The small type on pharmaceutical labels is too small to be read by eyes blurred with cataracts. Arthritic fingers can not turn the knobs or dials on child tamperproof bottle caps. Heavy pots, pans, and coffee mugs are easily dropped by the aged and infirm. With each failure, the ability to be independent is diminished; each failure shouts of impotence and that no one and nothing cares at all. Defeated by the very items which support them, the elderly complain instead about the price. It is an isobar of injustices ranging across every aspect of their lives.

3

Nothing Fails Like Success

More than fifty years ago I could perceive for myself that the race is not always to the swift nor the battle to the strong, but that time and chance happen to us all.

Joseph Heller, *God Knows*

People always say that from a worm there comes a butterfly: with mankind, it is the butterfly that turns into a worm.

Henry Montherland, *La Reine Mort*

December came and as the first, wet snows of an early Buffalo winter began to fall, Norm's health slowly improved. With complete bed rest and Julia's care his deep yellow skin color gradually faded into the semblance of a dirty tan. It looked, in early twilight, as if he had been in Florida for several weeks perhaps a month before. The pallor that characterizes Buffalonians in winter became a hoped-for sign of health. His color evoked false memories of days long gone when, after a winter vacation, my parents would cheerfully lament the daily demise of their tropical tans. In the harsh light of the clouded daylight that drizzled through his bedroom window, however, it was clear that my father had been ill. Norm's eyes still held a yellowish tint, and his skin was translucent and fragile underneath its still strange hues.

Father's weight had dropped so drastically that when Julia tried to dress him one day, the pants he wore simply slipped off his hips to crumple accusingly at the ankles as he walked with baby steps, hands set firmly on the walker. He called me from the kitchen to watch as Julia pulled his pants up and tightened the belt to its last notch. "Watch me walk," Norm commanded, and as he shuffled across the carpet, pushing the walker before him, his pants rode lower with each step before falling on the third shuffle like the prop of a vaudeville comedian. He repeated the act again and again, laughing each time his pants dropped, until we tired of the display and told him to stop, to sit down and rest. For years his doctors had ordered a diet, which was followed halfheartedly by my father but broken daily by the purchase of chocolate bars that gave him the necessary "energy," he would insist, to return to work. Now he had surpassed the weight reduction goal Pangless had ordered decades before. Indeed, Father's weight was that of his adolescent years, the time when he was a varsity football hero, and I remembered a line from Marcel Proust that tied these Norms together across those sixty years. "Adolescents who last long enough," Proust said, "are what life makes old men of."

In maturity his pants had sported a 40-inch waist, but now Julia ordered me to buy size 36 pants, which were, we discovered, still loose but serviceable with a belt cinched tight. His height had decreased in recent years almost as much as his weight. Norm had returned to the stature that had been his in high school's freshman year. As a senior with full growth he had been a tall six feet, an uncommon height in those days. Osteoporosis had withered him, however—physicians called it a "spontaneous cervical collapse." As his bones became brittle, the weight of his own body pulled him down, compressing or, perhaps, condensing his frame. The effect was accentuated, now, by a general weakness. His muscles were too flaccid for him to stand erect, and even with the walker for support, he shuffled along virtually doubled over as if carrying an enormous weight. The shortened spine had dropped his height two inches, but he seemed even shorter as he stood, curved like a question mark, hunched across the walker or four-pronged cane. His posture and stature looked as if gravity itself had become too great a weight for his body to bear.

Christmas was coming, and my father worried that he had done no shopping at all. He desperately wanted to make sure his sons, grandchildren, and friends had something from him in this of all years. It was important, he said, that gifts go out so that people would know he was sick and not crippled, poor but not impoverished. One day we sat down with a stack of mail-order catalogues and spent an hour choosing presents from companies that ship by mail. It was a practical solution, but one that gave him no pleasure. In past years he had taken pride in the search for gifts, and the purchase of Christmas presents had become a hobby that for Father lasted through much of the year. He would find this or that object in July or October and then place it carefully in the closet, labeled, lest he forget, with the eventual recipient's name. In weekly letters—as early as May and never later than November—he would casually mention the wrapping of my Christmas gift or the discovery of something "just perfect" for a brother. But this year illness had come too early, and he was unprepared. "I'm an old man, now," he sighed as we searched through the catalogues. "When I can't even shop it's time to give up."

It seemed strange to me that he would talk of giving up when his body had fought so desperately to survive the hepatitis. He had been determined to strengthen his leg to relative health in September and was anxious to return to volunteer work throughout the fall. To me these attitudes signaled a refusal to see the world as finished, but it slowly became clear the degree to which age and illness had combined to frustrate my father. The problem was, I came to understand, less a matter of "giving up" than of coming to grips with his infirmities and the isolation those deficits brought. Gifts were continuity and future, a way in which throughout the year he would plan for December's holidays. Since my mother's death he had spent most Christmases in Atlanta, Georgia, where Brian lived, returning to Buffalo for New Year's Eve with old friends. Now he would be unable to travel, and Christmas, too, would be a Buffalo affair. Whether he would even be able to make the annual New Year's Eve party was also uncertain. Norm felt the wind of isolation, the breath of physical closure, after his hospital time, and the pants were a moment of comic relief that warned that even when he could go out, his very body would be that of an altered and ailing man.

All this became clearer a few days later when Julia came to work uncharacteristically quiet and subdued. Father asked if something was wrong, and Julia said the evening before she had worked another, utterly depressing case. Her other patient was an elderly man, with sight impairment and a mobility problem, whose doctors had told him that morning that his motor vehicle license was being revoked. If he could not drive, the man had said, he did not want to live and had chosen as a first step towards his demise to discontinue Homemaker services. Julia told Norm that this was indeed a suicidal act, because the man could not get his food or go to the bathroom without help. She asked my father what she could do to help her client, to convince him that life even now was worth living. "Leave him alone," Norm said, "He knows what he's doing. If you can't do for yourself, there's no point in going on."

We looked at each other, Julia and I, knowing my father saw himself in her client, another old man for whom the automobile meant liberty and freedom. In driving was the power to shop and visit friends on a whim. Taxicabs, handicap vans, and the largess of willing family did not compensate for the loss of freedom disability brought but rather emphasized the proscription of one's world and the failing powers that led to its diminution. For those like my father who grew up with the automobile, who remembered the Packard and the Model T, the car was also a link to more youthful pasts. Today's commonplace was once a symbol of adventure, and the ideal of the car itself a part of the personal histories of these men. To be unable to drive was to have life proscribed, and without the capacity to drive, isolation would be as profound as in the loss of any limb. To be prohibited from driving for these old men was to lose what had been since adolescence a physical reflex that defined their world. Writing in her journal, Katherine Mansfield said of a point in her illness·that "the rest is rather like a beetle shut up in a book, so shackled that one can do nothing but lie down." That is what Julia's other client felt and what Norm understood as well.

My father saw his future in the other's distress, and I began to believe he had been serious when he said to me in the hospital that "I'm only living for you and for my other boys." It was not a responsibility I wanted, and each time he told me this, I said he had to live for life alone and for himself. Later that day, while Norm napped, Julia and I talked over coffee and tried to make sense of father's swings between determination and despair. Only later, reading Roland Blythe's *The View in Winter*, did I finally get a feel for the temper Norm carried in those days: "Now is the deprived time. They are aware of ceaseless deprivation and of everything being snatched from them or placed out of reach, and of being narrowed and lessened and ground out of their very personality. They are shaken by the extent of their impoverishment both spiritually and materially." This was the terror Norm knew, that Christmas, as Buffalo's snows began to fall. He saw clearly that returning health would be at best only a reprieve and that more than health had been taken in the hip's complication and hepatic ills. Even if he became strong enough to drive to work again, that mobility would be merely a temporary reprieve, an Indian summer in his own late fall. He had crossed time's bridge of fragility and would never again be able to take health or personal initiative for granted. He had become one of the spiritually disabled, shaken to his roots by the specter of helplessness and whatever dreams had troubled his sleep as his liver poisoned sclera, skin, and soul. Julia's client was Norm's soul mate, and as he talked to her he was speaking to me, letting us know where he wanted to draw the line and what, on a day of improvement and returning courage, he wanted me to remind him of in later days of fear.

Unable to accept that I was with him simply out of unarticulated love and by choice, Father insisted on giving me some money "for your time." He said he wanted "to be fair" to me, although I believe what sparked his offer was a need to declare himself, to regain control. And how else could Father assert himself except by a check written in his now shaky hand? I protested that I did not want to be paid and refused his demand that I "name a figure," an amount that would define the worth of my Buffalo time. "What is fair?" he pressed, and finally I took a scratch pad and wrote some figures before telling him that at Homemakers, Inc., rates, I'd worked the equivalent of $12,000 since August—not counting overtime and holidays. "That's impossible," Norm said, aghast. "I don't have that kind of money."

He decided to give me $1,000 for my time. That worked out to perhaps $10 for each 24-hour day I had spent with and for him in Buffalo. When the check was written, he said, "Well, I'm glad that's settled" as if it had been an issue of contention with me and not in fact an internal debate between his warring instincts as parent ("I want to be fair") and businessman ("That's too much"). He was pleased with himself, but I felt demeaned. My noble sacrifice had been diminished to the hourly rate of unskilled labor, transformed from a filial act to one below minimum wage. It was like the yearly discussions of my childhood, when he would sit with each son and talk "man-to-man" about what each should get as allowance. No labor contract was ever negotiated with more seriousness as we stated what was needed and he, in turn, what he was prepared to give, and when a figure between them was reached he would say each time, "Well, that's fair." I felt but did not understand how important the reprise of these old patterns was to Norm and the degree to which my resentment reflected frustrations with him buried in me since those long-gone adolescent years.

Soon money became the hub around which our frustrations ran, an issue each time another bill came due. The electric bill increased, the telephone bill doubled, heating went "through the roof," and he worried. "Never mind," I would say, "winter has arrived and the days are shorter; two people now live where before you were one, and that means double the dinners, double the electricity, and double the usage of everything." Still, with each bill he scrambled, trying to tally in his brain the cost of existence against the scrutiny of savings, and each debit brought forth his father's poorhouse fears and the reality of Norm's own seventy-four years. I asked what he was saving for if not the security to live as he chose, and he said for the future, of course. "If I spend it all there will be nothing left." What concerned him most, I think, was not the affordable cost of life but the eventual depletion of his worth, the dispersal of those ledger figures spelling not only independence but also legacy in his soul. The former was his pride and the latter a future to assure he would be remembered not as the dodderer who needed care and love but as a man of generosity and substance.

My brothers and I gave him a remote-controlled, color television that Christmas. We had wanted to replace Father's old black-and-white set for several years, but each time he had declined the offer, insisting remote control was an unnecessary extravagance and color a luxury he did not need. But now he was bedridden, and we decided it was a necessary convenience. Certainly I encouraged the idea because our nightly time before the television tube had become something of a trial to me. It was tiresome to stand and switch channels constantly at Norm's command, to continually get up and go to the set and modulate the sound whenever someone telephoned. Throughout the hepatic siege he had dozed continually, nodding off while his favorite shows were on, waking with a start to ask if an episode had started. Would I please turn the volume up and explain what was going on? Please, would I turn the volume down because he wanted to sleep? Remote control, I was convinced, would be my salvation, and for his part Father was thrilled when, on Christmas day, I set the television up in his bedroom. It took him a week to master the simple mechanics of remote control, but afterwards he delighted in its power. What most pleased him, I suspect, is that so exorbitant and expensive a gift would be given so gladly by his sons. It was the signal of worth, a testimony to his value despite incapacitating illness and age. For a man who could not talk of love without figuring its cost, this gift was transformed through his mental code into a munificence that said we believed he would survive and that perhaps survival remained a worthy goal.

Walt returned the day before Christmas for the unveiling and, he said, as much to give me respite as to visit with our father. The strain on me of recent months had become clear in our telephone conversations, he said. A certain harshness and anger had crept into our conversations; a brittleness was submerged in the undertones of my speech. His presence was to give me a bit of leisure, the chance to read a few hours a day and to catch up on household chores. Father was equally delighted, both to see Walter and to have the opportunity to cut down Julia's hours during the holiday season. "She deserves to be with her family," he said by way of explanation, adding, of course, that with us present she was not really needed and "I can save a few dollars, as well."

A friend from the hospital, another volunteer, insisted on bringing in a traditional Christmas dinner for us all. Mary-Ann and three of her daughters arrived late Christmas day and, while my father had hoped I would allow him to receive guests in the living room, accepted with good grace the necessity of a bedroom soiree. The Christmas dinner, like Thanksgiving's gift, was the traditional cooking he loved: turkey with gravy and dressing, two types of potato, home-baked rolls, three vegetable dishes, and two different pies for dessert. For me the excitement of guests unencumbered by years of acquaintance and of people full of chatter from the outside world was the greatest gift of all. Mary-Ann gossiped of the hospital and their mutual friends, who, she assured him, were waiting for his return. Her daughter and I talked of growing up in local schools, and for a brief time the sickroom became part of a house again and company lost its solicitous, funeral air.

During the visit he seemed his old self, full of charm and a deprecating wit. With "ladies present" he seemed for a while to recover a portion of his old confidence and self-respect, but it was a heroic effort and short-lived. After dinner he was exhausted and filled again with nagging fears, which exploded into a brief argument with Walter, who was smoking father's cigarettes while comfortably ensconced in an easy chair sipping wine. Father asked Walter if he'd prefer a scotch and Walter said yes, but he already had finished the bottle. "How could you?" Norm complained. "Someone might visit, and now there will be none for company." He asked how Walter could have so depleted the house's supply when he had been home so short a time. My brother ignored the question, and as he smoked, Father kept reminding him that it was their last pack and that in the morning he himself would want a smoke. Walter kept promising to leave a few for the morning and, the next day, to buy more for them both. It became a litany, question and response. After the fifth repetition, Walt rose from his chair, walked to Norm's bedside and slammed the half pack down on Father's night table. "Keep your damn cigarettes," he shouted angrily, and my father was clearly shocked. That was not the way his sons talked to him, he thought, or the way we who had pulled him through this illness had reacted to his sometimes peevish ways.

Walter then went upstairs for the evening, and I captured the chair he had vacated, waiting for the tears which Father had been holding back with a visible effort. Soon they came, and with them a request that I tell him he had been right in his frustration. Perhaps, I said, but once was enough. It is galling to be forced to promise, again and again, what one has already pledged to do. I suggested he had been wrong to worry about the depletion of the household scotch, which neither Father or I ever drank. "But scotch is so expensive," Norm said. It should be a "treat, not drunk like water," and, he explained, it was "bad manners" to finish a bottle in someone else's house. "This is still my house, isn't it?" he asked. He wanted to make the rules, to rule as before, but worried simultaneously that Walter would "be mad at me" and "now won't come back to visit again." I assured Father our family history was filled with petty angers and disagreements which had always passed overnight. My memory was of factions and reconciliations, tears, shouting, and hurt silences throughout the years of our growing up. Father remembered nothing but idyllic moments and saw this disagreement with his firstborn son as a catastrophic sign of his own waning power. If he could not control the liquor supply, what would next slip from his grasp? Finally, he went to sleep.

It was as if, for a brief time during dinner, reality conformed to memory, and despite the changes imposed by illness he was a younger host to outside folk and not the invalid who had, that morning, stared at him from the bathroom mirror. There had been sons, a friend from work, and children present, all keeping the volume of chatter at a reasonably high decibel. But in his memory the world was an idyl, and the dream had shattered with Walter's irritation. Norm was again the older self who could be challenged by a son in his forties, a geriatric to be put to bed by a youngest boy who was himself beginning to go bald. Upstairs, I tried to explain this to my brother who for his part was still angry with Father. "I spent $400 to be here with him and he's worried about a bottle of scotch," Walter fumed. The next morning, Walter vowed, he would buy two fifths and a carton of cigarettes for the house: "That will shame the tight bastard," he said. I agreed perhaps Father had been unreasonable and tried to explain, as best I could, the old man's fears of depletion. Walt insisted that age was no more an excuse for bad behavior than our parents had allowed youth to be in our childhood. I told him of Norm's fears that his son's love had been extinguished in the tiff and said that as once we worried that our transgressions might diminish parental love, so the fears were now reversed. Walter dismissed my explanations as "pop psychology" and "coddling." "He's not senile, for Christ's sake," my brother snapped, and there the discussion ended.

The next morning he bought a carton of cigarettes and a single fifth of scotch, which Father insisted on paying for. All was well, and Norm apologized to Walter, saying, "I am not the man I was. I have been ill." That was perhaps the hardest moment of all, the realization that he knew what had happened to him and understood he would never again be filled with confidence, that whatever the level of his final recovery, some barrier had been broken and, indeed, he was not the same man at all. The man we had known for a lifetime died in the autumn, in the hospital, and both Norm and I were left with a ghost, a specter who resembled him in some respects but differed in crucial ways. Walt left two days later, and after two weeks and several phone calls from Colorado, Father still worried he had lost his first son's affection with that one act of holiday petulance. I assured him he had not but knew by then that some other process was at work and nothing I could do would quiet these fears, which had grown and metastasized since autumn.

I asked Uncle Jules who could explain these issues to me, help me understand the complex process Father and I were engaged in. Much had been said about dealing with death, but I did not think Kubler-Ross or the writing of others concerned with terminal disease would offer me insight about living in a perpetual twilight. Maybe there was another literature, another arena of wisdom that would apply. Uncle Jules referred me to Sam Fletcher, a psychologist who offers classes for the children of elderly parents, and Fletcher said I was wrong. Kubler-Ross's books on death and dying offered the key to what I sought. I made an appointment to talk to him, but a lake storm settled in, an epic Buffalo snowstorm that shut the city down for a week and kept us housebound for days. So Fletcher and I talked by phone. He had a fat man's tenor, smooth, round, and comforting. He sounded like a storybook uncle into whose lap a child could climb, curling against the contours and abdominal rolls while adult stories are told.

Fletcher believed that the stages defined by Kubler-Ross—denial and isolation, anger, depression, acceptance, and perhaps, finally, hope—are not merely the levels we each pass through when faced with the timetables of terminal illness. Death is not so unique either for the individual whose demise is imminent or for the world that waits upon it and prepares to live on. We mourn throughout our life, the psychologist said, pass through these stages many times, and old age is merely another dress rehearsal, a practice run for the final dissolution. My father had lost the work that gave reason to his existence, the independence that gave it meaning, his wife who made living a joy; furthermore, he had lost his strength to old age. These were reasons enough to mourn, Fletcher suggested, reasons enough for denial, anger, and depression.

I told him of the battles over money and the incident with Walter and the cigarettes and Scotch. Fletcher said that was it, exactly. In years past my father could have gone himself to buy these things and seen their expense balanced against his salary. But now he knew his ability to earn was gone and with it went not only a sense of purpose but the underpinning of his independent world. Father's concerns were manifestations of depression about that fact; the scotch and cigarettes were symbols of his helplessness and immobility. It was not the money, Fletcher continued, but what the whole signified to Norm that my brothers and I had to understand. We talked of the visits with Ed Sterman and this psychologist seemed amused at my naivete. Locked in an internal battle to deny the reality of his condition, I had tried to force my father to confront in the presence of a stranger those very problems that he did not want to consider even by himself. Because it had been at my urging, the whole issue of counseling had become a battleground of wills. If Father had to accede to Sterman's presence, he could still fight a rear-guard action of noncompliance, something like a five-year-old child sent to bed who lies there whispering to himself, "I will not sleep I will not sleep I won't." Money, Sterman, the scotch and cigarettes all were symptoms, Fletcher said gently, and only my father could decide when and if he wished to accept the central fact of age and the physical frailties that had become, for him, its companion.

How was I bearing up, Fletcher asked gently. Had I denied the possibility of my father's death? Did I insist on my own ability to offer all care or refuse help offered by others to maintain the chimera of a simple visit home? I was locked into the same progression towards hope he had defined for my parent, Fletcher warned. It would take time for me to accept this new reality, to come to terms with my months of participation in Father's medical siege. I could not expect to walk away without undergoing the same process of traumatic reevaluation as Norm, he warned, because "after all, this is your history, too." Later I learned that much of his practice was in counseling the children of aging parents who, like me, were torn between their own adult lives, their parents' needs, and the distance between those poles. No, I insisted, there was no problem. Like Norm himself, I was sure I needed no outside help.

When the storm finally blew itself out, we had been through what local newsmen described with no small pride as the worst blizzard in decades. Almost four feet of snow had fallen in eight days, and for much of that time Father and I were housebound together, unable to shop, have aides come to work, or get away from each other.

During that time we argued and bickered almost constantly. I tried to convince him to complain about his medical care, to write letters to the hospital's review committees and thus to take charge of his own health. I blamed both Stryon and Pangless for the tape burns that were unnecessary and had taken so long to heal; I reminded him of the substitute doctor who had proscribed Lomotil for a postoperative patient everyone worried would contract hepatitis and argued that had we been told the dangers, we would have been better prepared when the problems began. Finally I said that with minimum home care instructions I was sure the cycle of hepatic recurrence could have been broken at its beginning.

But Father refused to consider a complaint and resented, he said, my "bossiness." Sitting in his chair and staring at the snow, he simply shook his head each time I raised the question and said to me, "You don't have to live with these guys. I do. They have my charts. So leave me alone on this." He was so passive, so accepting of his fate, that it made me want to hit him. I insisted he did not have to live with bad medicine and offered to find him better, more personal physicians. But he said he liked and trusted Pangless, whom he had known since they were children: "I don't want to rock the boat at this point in my life."

Partly this was an old argument, a matter of styles and inclination. My father had never been a protester, a man to write letters or to "fight city hall." I had chafed from youth against his passivity and when, for example, I was in trouble at school, he always would say sanctimoniously that "round pegs get pounded into square holes, and you, sonny boy, are a round one." But there was a new theme present as well. It did not matter to him that the attitude of his physicians had increased the cost and severity of his illnesses because, I discovered as we talked, he remembered only bits and spotty patches of the period of his convalescence. He did not remember insisting that Walter meet him at home in August, for example, or the fall that had bruised his back that first day. I would mention events occurring during a hospital visit and Father would shrug as if to say "how do you expect me to know about that?" Father did not want to dwell on what had happened, to be told he'd been close to death, or to consider his own fragility. He did not want to find new doctors because that would acknowledge a recent past he did remember and signal preparations towards an infirm future he feared and yet could not discuss. To change—physicians or personal patterns—would be to weaken the already shaky structure on which the remains of his life still stood. The long past, for Norm, had become sacrosanct and holy. The physicians or habits he carried with him into the illness were things to be clung to and cherished. The future had shrunk for him to a vision of the coming spring when all would be "back to normal," which meant being as it had been before.

I, of course, wanted him to take charge of his life, to protest and change and act in a way appropriate, perhaps, to a man in his thirties but a way that a man more than seventy years of age could not abide. Failing that, I wanted him to grant me the right to order these things in his name as I had ordered so much during the previous months. But Father wanted to hold his own, to reassemble what he had, and that meant putting me back into perspective as a son and not as a caretaker. And so each day we argued until he would refuse to discuss it and I would stomp out of his room. As the storm abated and the roads cleared, Father said one day that it was time for me to leave, that he could see I had run out of patience. I denied it, of course, but knew it was true. Julia was able to drive to the house again, and I booked a flight to Denver, where I would visit with Walter and from there go on to Vancouver. My other plans were long outdated. There was nowhere else for me to go but where I had already been.

I wrote Father a letter in Buffalo but never gave it to him. I wrote it during the Buffalo storm and have kept it ever since. I wrote this one but could not mail it. He would have read it and shrugged, insisting it was more of my bossiness. If he could have accepted its vision of us, the writing would not have been necessary.

It is bitterly cold, and I write upstairs while you rest in your bedroom below me. I start this now and will mail it when I leave, a hedge against both our futures. There are so many things to say, all buried in the injunctions and restrictions, the remonstrations and the issues of recent months. Now is my chance to say them.

I leave you with pride, a great deal of trepidation, and some resignation, Pops. The pride comes from your recovery to date which has been my principal accomplishment over these last months. Now you can use the walker and soon will be on the four-pronged cane again. By summer you will walk on nothing but your legs, and if only you show a sense of moderation, nothing more should impede you.

The trepidation is based on my certainty that moderation and accommodation are things you will not do. Just as you insisted on bending—and falling—after the operation, so now you'll choose to drive your car and work again as if nothing had changed at all. To the extent you do not accept the limits physical frailty requires, you endanger yourself and the progress which has been at such cost to us both across these recent months.

You remain among the walking wounded with an emotional—maybe a spiritual—frailty I neither understand nor can change. After Mother died you bemoaned your solitary status but have done nothing since that a widower should to ensure companionship and contentment. That's the type of intransigence which I worry about. I talk of inviting people into your house and life, working—as we all must—to create and strengthen and expand the bonds of human relations which tie us one to another. You talk about how it was when Mother was alive and live a half-life of volunteer work and solitary dinners.

Trepidation, I say, because you see your life as done, as finished and meaningless except to the extent it lives through me and through the lives of my brothers. This is more dangerous than your leukemia, for there is no magic pill to restore a sense of value. Our arguments about money have had nothing to do with bank accounts and financial resources. They have been about what makes life and what makes individuals valuable.

No one can set up conditions for living and no one should try. "If only I can drive," you say, "have a certain bank balance, do this work, and eat there—then will I live." It doesn't work that way, not for anyone. I have never understood those gamblers who take pride in the random roll of legal dice when the numbers come up smiling. Why moan when craps is the result or when a storm bends plans out of shape or when the flow of blood into the head of a femur is disrupted? Random chance works on us all. Nothing can be done but accept it.

You don't have to like it, but, Pops, there is nothing to fight on this field. Just as you fought last summer not to look in the mirror, what I'm urging now is that you look with care and accept what this Norm can and cannot do.

You think I am impatient with your illness, but I am not. I am tired from it, as you are. But what frustrates me is watching you make yourself unnecessarily miserable. It is like a parent teaching a child to bicycle, as once you taught me. The parent can see what is needed, remember in his bones how it should feel, but the child, wobbling and afraid, can find no point of balance.

That's how I feel towards you, wanting to grab the seat to balance your ride but aware that it is something you must feel yourself. I know the feeling of riding in this life and know you no longer have it. I know the joy which comes from a certitude and mastery of that daily balance and now know, too, the feeling of watching someone who has lost it.

Sometimes I think this is merely willful refusal on your part, an insistence on a vision of life which sustained you for so long. And who am I to dynamite a perch which has held so stable for decades? Maybe it is the rigidity of your years, a willfullness of vision and temperament, which must be accepted—like the calcium accumulations in your shoulder and hip.

But I am still either too young or too optimistic to accept that. I believe one can change at any age. Do not whip yourself with might-have-been's. All lives drown in past possibilities, if we let them. You have done what you could and lived as you thought proper. No person can say more, and many, I suspect, whisper to themselves that they have in fact done less. You have money enough to sustain you. Relax and enjoy it.

If you can't do it for yourself, maybe, just this once, do it for me who remains, in hope and fear but still with love.

Your son

I left at the end of January, and we both cried as the cab waited at the door. "God bless you," he said. "I had lots of things to say, but you know what they are." I hugged him fiercely and said simply, "I love you. The cab is waiting," and walked out the door.

I sat at the Buffalo airport in something of a stupor, ticket to Denver and Walt's house in hand. Colorado was a way point, a first destination. From there I planned to visit Vancouver and arrange my taxes, visit the bank, and bring my life up to date again. British Columbia was where my life had been based for years, but it had become merely a point on the map whose center was Buffalo and my father's house. The months had transformed my city into a datum, the line on a ticket that says "From" and "To." Vancouver was one side of a telephone conversation, the origin of the voices of unseen friends, and I was returning with all the thoughtful determination of a homing pigeon freed from captivity and his keeper's cage. Before I left, Uncle Jules had invited me to Maui, where he would be vacationing in a few weeks, and I thought maybe from there I would sail on to Kiribati and the story I had long promised myself a chance to do. A boat would be leaving from Hilo in about six weeks, and maybe this time I would be on it. But sitting in Buffalo's airport terminal, watching plows struggle to clear the runways of new-fallen snow, all I knew was that I was leaving the city and with it, my father who was now in Julia's care. For the moment, it was more than enough. They called the flight, and I shuffled to the gate, sleepwalking in the afternoon.

My seatmate was a woman who, as she sat beside me, tucked a

cardboard box beneath her legs. We nodded politely to each other as strangers who find themselves companions usually do. She was well dressed and had the air of a person who directs the lives of others. Nurses have the attitude, and so do longtime schoolteachers. It says they are in control of lives other than their own, and I admired this woman's self-assurance. The stewardess, checking to make sure all passenger luggage was safely stowed, tried to shove my companion's container beneath the seat in front of us, but, alas, it was too big. There was an occasional meowing from the cabin floor. "What is that?" the stewardess asked sternly. A paw came out from beneath the box's cover, waving slowly against my seatmate's leg as she reached down to push it back. "Regulations forbid the carrying of pets within the cabin," the stewardess began, but my companion, a woman in her early forties, cut the lecture short. Both ticket counter employees and security station guards had assured her that as long as the cat was secured and sedated, it could be carried onto a plane, she said. Hers had been given a sedative and was in a box, she continued, emphasizing the point with a gentle kick. "But, but, but—" the stewardess sputtered, and the woman smiled, as at that moment, the captain ordered cabin attendants to take their seats.

After takeoff my companion leaned over and asked if I minded a cat companion, and I said no, not at all. My sympathies were in fact with the stewardess. It was she who would have to contend with the situation if a cat hater were to complain. But it would have taken too much effort to say this. To have a position one needs a base, a posture from which to move, and mine had been for six months borrowed from an adolescence half-remembered. I felt like someone who had been in the hospital or in prison. There had been a break, a gap in my life, and it would take me months to develop a point of view again. It was easier to be agreeable than not, so I smiled and politely congratulated her victory. As we chatted, she said her name was Gina and that she was from Princeton, New Jersey, heading for Santa Fe, via Denver. By then the plane was fully airborne and the cat was displaying unusual vigor. Low muffled screams came from its box, and ever more frequent paw thrusts past its confine's ties showed how eager the cat was to be free. "I gave it a very nice dosage of Librium, but I'll bet it spit out one of the pills," Gina said with a smile. "It's just like my patients. Secretive, willful, and with a mind of its own." She grabbed the box and some pills from her handbag, excused herself, and strode towards the washroom. Minutes later she returned, her hands cut and bleeding. The cat had surely taken the tranquilizer this time, she said grimly, and should soon be docile and fast asleep.

I asked what she did for a living and learned she was a physician closing out a suburban practice in the East to work at a rural clinic in New Mexico. She was bored, Gina said, treating mundane cases of flu, high blood pressure, and minor ills. Now she was moving to full-time work in the villages where "interesting medicine can happen." As she talked I helped clean her hands, which were raw from the battle with her cat. "You're pretty good," she said. "Where did you learn first aid?" I told her I had been nursing a geriatric parent who needed medical care, and she listened sympathetically as I described the tape burns, therapies, and the nursing necessities that had filled my days since August. As we talked she looked at me strangely, as if we were members of a secret order who had forgotten the identifying handshake. Stories like mine, Gina said, were a part of every suburban doctor's practice. It is not simply that the elderly are fragile or that simple problems become critical procedures in geriatric care. The worst part, she continued, is the feeling of neglect and dislike on the part of many who work with the elderly, who themselves seem too often filled with futility and resignation. What I had done might have been mundane work, she said, but that I did it at all was surprising.

"In the Pueblos they have nutrition problems, tuberculosis, alcohol-related diseases, trauma, and a host of other difficulties. But at least they take care of their own." She asked if I was an only child, and I said no, there were three other brothers but they were too busy to help with more than the occasional visit. Even when they were present, I laughed, they were mostly useless, terrified of illness and the mess that sickness creates. Gina nodded and said that was exactly what she meant. In native villages it was not only that families stayed together and that two, three, or four generations lived in close proximity and offered mutual support but, more important, that age and life were believed to have value in and of themselves. Our natural squeamishness over the vagaries of senility, distaste at incontinence, and displeasure with the realities of geriatric infirmity had no parallel in the world she would enter.

"Do you know the one thing I saw a lot of in New Jersey that I never see at all in these rural areas? Child beating and elderly abuse. The Navajo may be violent at times, but never against the very old or young." I thought of something an aide, Margaret Ringer, had said one day to me. She was a sometime replacement for Julia Shea, a nurse who in the 1950s had given up her profession for full-time parenthood. One day while Norm napped, Margaret had talked to me of all the physical and mental abuse she had seen the elderly endure throughout her career: nurses who spanked men for lack of bowel control and aides who thought it was their right to take whatever they wanted from a patient's refrigerator or helped themselves without a second thought to small things from a client's home. Margaret had laughed when I asked if the patients' relatives had not objected. They were usually so happy to have someone else in charge, she said, to be able to abdicate care for their aged, that they never listened to the elderly's complaints or credited what he or she said. "As long as they could believe someone else was doing something, the families were quite content," commented Margaret.

As Gina talked I stared out at the dark. Our plane passed over towns whose names were lost in altitude, and existed only as clusters of light, earth beacons of luminescence against the night. I saw myself reflected in the airplane's windows, and in reflection I grew old and frail, skin curled against the forehead and lips pulled tight against rotting teeth. I saw myself as I would be in forty years and then again as I was at that moment, a simple thirty-six. In recent weeks I had searched my reflection in the mirror each day, looking for the signs of aging that Father so clearly displayed. Elsewhere, I inspected strangers passing anonymously on the street for liver spots upon the skin, for telltale watery eyes or a shrunken back. If no such traces were overt, often I would impose them, adding signs of geriatric decline to people barely out of adolescence.

Gina and I passed the rest of the flight in pleasant chatter about gerontology and cats, about countries and cities where we had both worked. When the plane landed, she put her hand on mine and wished me luck while warning that my father's illness was not ended. "This is only the overture, you know. Usually it gets worse from here." As we walked into the terminal at Stapleton Airport, my brother was waiting, pipe in hand, and saw Gina and me walking together. We separated with that delicate feeling of empathy that belongs to those who have shared time together only to become strangers again.

I promised to write and so did she, but neither of us ever did. "Who was that?" Walt asked, and I said a woman I had met on the plane. Yes, he had figured that out, he said, and where did I want to eat dinner?

Those five days in Denver passed in a blur, with only fleeting memories to sustain them. I remember waking each night in Walter's guest room when the forced air furnace would click on with a loud, hollow sound. Each time, I heard my father coughing, calling, whispering for me to come downstairs, insisting on my presence. Every morning as I shaved I'd examine my face in the mirror for new wrinkles, my hairline for the diminution that would spell more balding and signal the rapid onset of overt age. One day my brother and I went into the mountains to shoot his pistols, and as I pointed a long-barreled .44-caliber revolver across the river at a distant tree stump, squinting across one hundred yards, I saw in miniature my father's face buried in the snow. Firing, I shot high, but to this day I do not know if I missed on purpose or if, despite a concerted effort, I simply overshot. I would like to think the bullet went wild by plan, but suspect I was desperate to hit the stump and the face that seemed to have materialized upon it.

Walt and I talked of many things, but the conversation continually returned to Norm. Time and again we went over the incident of "the cigarettes and the scotch," with Walt insisting he had behaved properly and that my "pampering" and concern for Father only made his sense of being an invalid worse. In my brother's mind the episode showed that one could ignore the emotional frailty of the handicapped and force a "mature" response by "being tough." To me it showed how little Walt knew of Father's life in its geriatric present. We talked of the vision of money Father had and the extent to which we had or had not inherited it, and we talked of our mother, dead nine years, and what she might have said and done.

There was the sense that whatever we meant when we referred to "Father," we were each speaking of a different man. For Walter, Father was, although sick, fundamentally the same parent who twenty years before had laid down curfews, considered allowances, and signed our high-school report cards. Proust speaks of those for whom love "has been so nearly continuous that the image we retain of them is no more than a sort of vague average between an infinity of imperceptibly different images." The weight of those memories across Walter's life made Norm a constant whose condition might change but whose reality never would. The only alternative was to see a "vegetable," my brother said, a shell emptied of its past and history—an "Alzheimer's zombie," in his words. When I spoke of Norm it was of a frail man whose diminished power made him successor to but not participant in those shared memories of his sons' youth. Father had become, for me, a patient as well as the constant who spanned our communal past. My Buffalo months of total care had ruptured the inviolate creature of familial memory and patched into its place this pastiche—part remembered past and part uncertain future—who was parent and patient combined. Walt spoke of "our father," "Dad," and the "tough old kraut" but always with the sure sense of being anchored to the image of a man we both had known since birth. Increasingly I referred to him as "Norm," a new acquaintance in need of care, a being distinct from that other man who had dominated and informed our lives.

There were, I said, an infinity of shades between the "zombie" emptied of personality and the parent—"a moral presence" that Walt and Norm both insisted was still there. The man I now knew lived somewhere between those poles. Just as Norm had seen in his reflection the traces of his own past days, so he now became a mirror for the different visions of Walt's memories and my present world. Walter saw in his father the same healthy legion of selves that Norm still claimed: the parent, businessman, and concertgoer who, even if ill, remained in alert charge of life and life's goals. I saw the emaciated, anorexic Other who required help just to stand, the Dachau demon whose reflection had leapt accusingly at our father in the August episode.

For his part, my father faced a similar confusion of roles in relation to me. I was both Tom or Thomas, the man to whom he had given responsibility in August, and "Tommy," the youngest of four sons, the child who he remembered wearing a cowboy hat and red boots at age four. If his memory was filled with a legion of selves, each vying for attention, I was the mnemonic for our communal past, and in the hospital or sickbed it was as if I had been hauled out of time with him. He saw not simply my present but our history, a mental pastiche of old home movies in which I could be any age. It was sometimes quite confusing. When groggy from hepatitis, he would ask how my day at school had been and, later, warn me of the dangers of walking alone in the Buffalo night. In December he would blink with uncertainty each morning as if trying to choose which of the many Toms—each one from a different year—stood at that moment before him.

From Denver I flew to Vancouver and stayed, at first, with friends who gave me a spare room and then left me alone to sort things out. I told everyone I was just passing through, getting my affairs in order. Letters of inquiry were sent to Hawaii to discover if the sailing ship had left yet for Kiribati or if it was still in Hilo preparing for departure. I worked on my taxes, talked with editors and radio producers, and tried to function like a businessman. My dentist gave me an emergency appointment when I complained of an excruciating pain that had begun to throb in the back of my jaw. "Wisdom teeth," I muttered, biting down on the X ray plate as a hygienist readied her machine while clucking over the plaque and tobacco stains she had seen in my mouth. The dentist called me that afternoon to say, cheerfully, my teeth were fine. No wisdom tooth had begun to protrude and no cavities or abscesses were visible. When I asked what was causing the problem, she said it probably came from clenching my jaw and grinding my teeth. "Try relaxing a bit," she said cheerfully. "Take a vacation or you'll get gum disease." I laughed and said a holiday was on the agenda, but I knew as we spoke that it wasn't. It had slowly become clear to me that a vacation at that time was impossible. I wrote Uncle Jules, by that time already in Maui, and said I would not be able to join him. The first draft was cheerfully regretful, pleading the press of business and the necessity of ordering my affairs. The second said simply that I was exhausted, that moving anywhere for any reason was beyond my power and that even so delightful an idea as a Hawaiian idyl was, for the moment, more than I could bear.

I felt like a marathon runner who was stumbling and panting five hundred yards from the finish but knew he could run no more. The simplest decisions had become excruciating dilemmas, and real choice had become impossible. Each morning I would do some chores and end my midday at the beach, trying to take some action, to make a decision or plan. I would spend the afternoon staring across English Bay towards Howe Sound and the mountains that rise beyond. There were foreign freighters at anchor in the harbor, skiers on the hills above, and in the distance snow-capped peaks stared blindly back towards me. Each day I would walk on sand wet from tides and rain, trying to understand what had gone wrong. I seemed to have no energy or enthusiasm for the business that had been my joy before.

It became a matter of geographies, and just as my father saw his world's anchor in Buffalo—with each street and store a memory—so, too, this Vancouver that I had left the previous year became a site to which I needed to cling and which in its solidity sustained me. I would walk slowly through its neighborhoods, each day a different one, and marvel at the region's youth. Vancouver had aggressive hope and confidence, which after Buffalo was a refreshing change, and I would wonder why I felt so old, so like a ghetto district in my father's geography: burnt out, gutted, and alone. Discouraged and desperate, I would end the afternoon at a coffee bar with endless double espressos, trying to focus on the page of some book carried to give my leisure at least the appearance of purpose. Finally I decided to find a new apartment in Vancouver. Despite assurances from both Father and Julia that he was regaining a measure of health, I expected each day a telephone call announcing some new medical catastrophe. My life was frozen, locked in a present whose future seemed uncertain, and it seemed to me that a geographic base was the antidote my ennui demanded. Near the university I found a three-story building whose vacant, two-bedroom apartment was ideal. It was, like so many Vancouver apartment buildings, a stucco creation of the 1950s, and I liked the fact that it was near the university that first had brought me to the city and liked, too, the fact that the building was relatively new. Its contrast to Buffalo's old, brick structures and solid, nineteenth-century feel was refreshing. The building stood opposite a small convenience store whose neon sign blinked, "The Roseland Market" nightly into what would be my living room. The same movers who had stored my boxes of books and furniture the previous year returned them to this new home. One of them remembered me, asked how I had liked the Olympics, and said he had watched the television, searching for a glimpse of me.

Thus began the period of my convalescence, of long walks through my new neighborhood. It was everything North Buffalo was not, and the contrast between them, more than anything else, satisfied me with my new location. My father's street was purely residential and always quiet. Vancouver's 10th Avenue was a noisy and commercial location. In Buffalo everything was dispersed, but this block to which I had moved became a concentrated symbol of my world. Across the street a bicycle shop was delighted to advise me on cycling techniques, and nearby was the White Dwarf bookstore, filled with science fiction. Two blocks west, past the public library's branch, a small fish store stood near a bakery with the best bread in town. The Varsity Grill was also close, and there I lunched on oyster burgers and smiled smugly, thinking of Buffalo snows, as spring blossomed on the coast.

One day I realized that I knew more about my immediate vicinity than I did about my father's neighborhood. His environment had been simultaneously too old and too new. The people known a lifetime were seen again, but I had ignored the scores of new stores and new families that had invaded North Buffalo since I had left the region eighteen years before. It was as if during my Buffalo tenure I had taken on Father's long view and rooted insolence. If someone or something had not been present in my youth, they were not worth knowing. The stores my mother had patronized and her friends still visited were worthy of attention. Others, newcomers present for less than a generation, were to be dismissed. Now, in Vancouver, I began to rediscover a present geography and those who inhabited it with me.

I remained obsessed with the signs of age, just as Norm was determined to deny them. We talked by telephone several times a week, and each time he told me how much stronger he was and how impatient to return to work. He was intent on driving again and waited only for the doctor's permission. His Chevrolet stood in the garage, and twice a week, on Norm's instructions, Julia would go out and let it run so the "battery won't be ruined." As spring came, first to Vancouver and much later to Buffalo, Julia would drive the car to his door and wait with him while he sat immobile in the driver's seat, listening to the engine run. His rusting, mundane four-cylinder automobile became for Father a symbol of all that had been lost in the fall from health. Like an adolescent waiting for his sixteenth birthday, he saw that Chevrolet as liberation, and like any teenager pleading with a parent, cajoled Julia into allowing him to drive up and down the driveway, one day, just for the experience's pleasure. I told Father to act his age and urged him repeatedly to give up the idea of driving. In recent years he had become one of those elderly motorists who straddles the lane marker while coasting down the street at twenty miles per hour, often blissfully unaware of stop signs or signal lights, of younger, impatient folk trying to pass both to the left and to the right. As a frail, convalescent motorist he would be, I said, a danger both to others and to himself. "Well, we'll see," Father replied each time. That phrase was an incantation from my youth that meant his mind was made up and it would be useless for me to argue. It was the quote from Emmanuel Berl's *Sylvia*, come fully to practical life: "I can scarcely make myself out at all in the pictures my memory offers. What have I in common with this character arrived at Le Touquet in a blue pseudo Morand racing-car with a pseudo Van Dongen young lady? If all these puppets, all these mere imitations make up my memory, then my history is not me."

It was as if, as strength returned, the mirrored image Norm saw every morning became again that of potency, while his geriatric face, the stooped and quivering old man of August, faded into no more than an afterimage. That was the face I had carried from Buffalo and tried to present to Walter, but for Norm it was a truth rejected for the more flattering legion of older, stronger selves that waited, hidden inside his body for vanity's inspection. Age was an indignity that he was intent upon denying, a trespasser that had broken in upon his self-esteem and was continually being barred from his soul. To accept his history and its inevitable present was to put an end to memories in which the car and potency were what defined Norm's place in the world. Whatever the danger, I knew he would drive again because narcissism demanded it. To do otherwise would be to accept the mirror's vision of an old, weak, diminished man, and that he could not do.

My new Vancouver neighbor in Apartment 104, Mrs. McPhee, had the same capacity for self-delusion, but for her it had more immediately disastrous results. She was the building's oldest tenant, a proud and private ninety-one-year-old. Hers was the demeanor of a stern old aunt who has spent a lifetime brushing hair until it lay absolutely straight, who smiles with grim satisfaction only when each follicle has screamed at the bristles' abuse. Other tenants who knew her, Rachel in 205 and Hillary in Apartment 106, for example, worried about Mrs. McPhee in an absentminded way. She was, they said, somehow "failing," and her tenure in the building seemed to be somewhat insecure. I would meet the old lady as she hobbled down the stairs, balanced precariously on her cane, to our mailboxes. Sometimes we would chat while she waited impatiently in the vestibule for a member of her church group to take her on an "outing."

When it was damp—which was almost daily in those late winter months—walking was especially difficult for Mrs. McPhee, and I would fetch her mail while she waited for her ride. The old lady would exclaim bitterly over the number of bills she had been sent or the presence of advertising circulars. "You see, another thing from the church. Probably asking for money," she would say with malicious triumph. "Here is some advertising booklet—as if I could go running around looking for bargains or afford to have dinner at restaurants." When a trip had been arranged for her, Mrs. McPhee would be downstairs at least twenty minutes before the scheduled time and would wait with mounting irritation for the driver who, while on time, always seemed tardy to the old lady. Like my father, what apparently bothered her most was that she had to depend on others at all, and she seemed genteelly furious at a life so devoid of excitement that a trip to the beauty salon or grocery store was a major event.

One afternoon two women came to my door and introduced themselves as members of Mrs. McPhee's church. Had I seen her in the last hour or so, and did I know where the building managers were? I said both Rachel and Don, the building's comanagers, were at work, while my neighbor was presumably in her suite. "We were supposed to pick her up for the church group," one of the ladies explained. "But when we came she wasn't out front waiting, and, well, maybe you know her—she just is never, ever late." The driver, who was middle-aged, launched into a long explanation of why she had been a bit tardy that day. She apparently felt guilty about the quite reasonable five-minute delay and seemed to live in fear of disappointing her client. That was understandable. The old woman had the same effect on me. Both worried that Mrs. McPhee had grown impatient and decided to walk on her own. "She's done that before, you know. She just hates to wait for anyone," the driver said. The church women had cruised the eight blocks between their center and our building, looking up and down each street to see if they could find their charge, but both had searched in vain. "Maybe she has fallen in her apartment and injured herself. We knocked and telephoned, but there was no answer at all," one of them explained. "Do you have a master key, by chance, or know where we can get one?"

I called Don and he returned immediately, telling me as he arrived that Mrs. McPhee's disappearance was nothing to worry about because "this has all happened before. She gets forgetful." We entered an apartment filled to overflowing with late Victorian end tables, chairs, and cases, the remains of what obviously had been, years before, furnishings for a house. It looked like an obstacle course, and as we threaded our way through the apartment's rooms, I realized that the clutter assured that at no point was the tenant ever more than an arm's length away from a sturdy piece of furniture to grab should she stumble or begin to fall. Like Norm in his hospital room, swinging from commode to bureau to night table to bed, she could maneuver without a cane by handing herself across the furniture. It was a maze, but an intelligent one assuring her physical support. For those of us without mobility problems, however, it was a terror. With each step we were sure to knock something askew, and we knew that if anything broke, Mrs. McPhee would be slow to forgive our intrusion.

But she was absent, and the church ladies were extremely apologetic to Don and me. "I just don't know where she could have gone," said one.

"She'll turn up," Don sighed. "She always does, and if you'll excuse me, I have to get back to work."

That evening Rachel told me Mrs. McPhee's children had called to say their mother was in the hospital. She had been waiting for her ride, fifteen minutes early as usual, when she had collapsed in the building's vestibule. A passerby had called the ambulance, which came screaming and whisked her away to the hospital. "I was afraid of something like this," Rachel said. "What do you think we can do when she wants to come home?" The building's owner was worried, she said, that he might be liable if Mrs. McPhee returned and injured herself on the stairs. We talked for an hour, working out a method to help our neighbor return to the place she had lived in for years. I suggested that if Mrs. McPhee would agree not to walk up and down the stairs alone and if her apartment had a few safety features—like a portable telephone—she could and should be able to come back to us in safety. I promised to help with chores and knew that Hillary would do the same. She and I had chatted about the old lady, gossiping in the communal laundry room. Rachel liked the plan because she disliked the idea of the building without its dowager, and said she would talk to Mrs. McPhee's family.

But she never had a chance to push our plan to the building's owner. Rachel later told me that Mrs. McPhee's children had long argued to their mother that she was too frail to remain alone, but their protestations were denied by her and the obvious fact that she was indeed looking after herself. The fall was their justification, and while she was in the hospital, they made arrangements to send the old lady to a nursing home. Anonymous moving men came to remove Mrs. McPhee's belongings from our building, and within a month several college-aged women moved in. The old apartment soon sported ready-made, knock-down furniture instead of old and somber, Victorian chairs. The walls, which recently held oils of English hills and flowers painted slightly past their bloom, now sported posters proclaiming Peace on Earth and life-sized images of current rock stars brandishing garish guitars.

I had begun to write for a radio show on health and did a short item on "the dowager tenant," talking about how easy it would have been to rearrange the place for safety and how sad it was that she had been sent away. "If only the woman had been less rigid, less insistent in her stand against age," I said. "If only she had accepted its infirmities and allowed us, her neighbors, to help." Writing the words, I thought how easy it was for an outsider like me to see what the elderly find impossible to accept. Hearing the words when the story aired, I knew I'd written the epitaph not only of Mrs. McPhee's independence but of all those who, like my father, let pride stand as a bulwark against time and change.

Throughout this period I slept each night with a light on in my bedroom. It had begun in Buffalo where I would read myself into exhaustion, waking from a doze in the early morning to answer Father's calls. With a light on it seemed that all night sounds were more overt and if Father needed me, I would be able to rise more quickly. In Vancouver I discovered it had become a habit I could not break. Each night, I would turn out the lamp by my side and lie in the dark, heart pounding, alive to insignificant sounds. Eventually—sometimes after fifteen minutes and sometimes after an hour—I would roll over and admit defeat by turning on one or another light until the room was lit and I was free again to sleep. I knew this was a symptom of stress, a legacy of the Buffalo time, and only hoped that it would end and rest could become, as it had once been, as automatic as the moment when a current's flow is interrupted by a toggle switch.

4

Paradoxical Existences

In the old person that we must become, we refuse to recognize ourselves.

Simone de Beauvoir, *The Coming of Age*

Adolescents who last long enough are what life makes old men of.

Marcel Proust

My brother Brian called one day to say he was going to Buffalo for the weekend. He said it was "his turn," and while glad to hear of his plans—Father complained of loneliness and certainly wanted the company—I was irritated at his words. He could not equate a quick, convenient three-day visit, I said, with my months of the previous year. His "turn" would be mostly a holiday in which they would go out for dinner or visit the local art gallery, while mine had been a siege. But Brian had never been a man to balance things nicely, choosing instead to deal with life wholesale while leaving the fine points and small details for others to do. Like Norm, he was a furniture man, a salesman who bought and sold container lots to be resold later at the trade shows Father once had haunted for his store. "Even blind, he'd make a good living," Norm said of Brian to me with pride. "He is a hell of a salesman. As long as he can dial a telephone, Brian will do just fine." Vision was a legitimate concern, because Brian had been sightless in one eye since his earliest years and, more recently, a cataract had developed in the other. He denied it was a handicap and, since reading had always been a difficult visual task for him, took defensive pride in being in his words, a "doer" and not—like me—a "reader."

Brian had been one of those large, cumbersome children whose growth comes years too early, a giant in the primary grades when strength always takes precedence over subtlety. He grew and matured but never really changed. Life for him was to be attacked headlong, and physical barriers or handicaps were irritations to be knocked down or ignored. My brother dealt with his visual problems as Norm had the dislocated shoulder of youth and, later, his pinned and osteoporotic leg. Both viewed their disabilities as irritations to be denied when possible and bemoaned when not, but never, ever to be accommodated. Despite their similarities and closeness, or perhaps because of them, that visit of Brian's to Buffalo was less than ideal.

He called me on Saturday night to say that Father looked "old, he's become an old man" and to worry with me over Norm's future. For his part, Norm called me a few days later upset that during their visit Brian had smoked incessantly and that he was grossly overweight. If Walter had vanquished the house's liquor supply, Brian "drank a gallon of Coca Cola a day and didn't have even one glass of milk."

"You're trying to be a parent," I laughed, "to make your boys drink milk and go to bed early." Brian, then about forty years of age, was well past parental injunctions, I said, old enough to choose his own mistakes.

"He's still my boy," Norm insisted. "I don't like to see him damaging himself like that."

I reminded Father that food and tobacco had been his vices too, ones my mother had called the "occupational hazards" of a furniture man's life. Selling and decorating and stocking the store had been for him as it now was for Brian a seventy-hour-a-week job, with fattening restaurant lunches and overflowing ashtrays a constant of that world. Brian, having assumed the mantle of Norm's profession, had picked up its deficits as well. Father and son, each worried about the other and neither could discuss those fears except through me. This visit brought home to my brother, as telephone calls could not, the frailty that his surviving parent had become, and the naked fact of that fragility made him uncomfortable. Norm saw his past in my brother's vices, and perhaps wishing to have been different himself, wanted better for his second son. Father did approve, however, of Brian's business success. During that trip my brother was often on the phone handling office problems by long distance, and that was something Father had loved. After Brian left, Norm proudly told his friends and sister how kind it had been for "Brian to take time out from a busy schedule to visit his poor old dad."

There was criticism implied here of me. By telephone he would ask each week if I was working and when I would again be fully employed. What was I doing for money, and where would I go when my savings were spent? When, he would ask over the long distance wires, would I do more than free-lance work, and did I need a loan? His concern irritated me, especially since the questions were ones I asked myself. Long-term employment was a problem that also worried me. The crux of the problem was whether I should even look for full-time work or simply continue as a free-lancer while holding ready to return to Buffalo. How much would he need me in the future, and what exactly did I owe to Father in terms of my life and time? If I took a full-time job, would it prohibit me from returning to Buffalo should Norm again require help? These were issues I had to puzzle out, and while he insisted I was to lead my own life, claiming, "I don't want to be a burden," that was, after the Olympics, exactly what he had become.

After one of his calls I wrote a few pages in a burst of anger, a collection of images from my Buffalo time. I had nothing to say, really, merely fragments of memory that invaded my sleep and frus-trated my working hours. Instead of seeking new assignments, I would sit each morning before the typewriter and think about a hospital visit or an incident that had occurred in, perhaps, November. I would see again my father's wrinkled, withered flanks and the burn scars that ran along them. The act of writing soothed me, placing Father's aging within my context. It allowed me to set down on paper what we had lived but could not yet accept. I thought of sending it to him and to my brothers so they could see what my "business" had been in recent months.

A mass of notes began to build in a file on my desk, and I was uneasy with its size. Catharsis for a journalist is writing about him-self, but for a daily newsman, it is the hardest work he can do. We are trained from the beginning to be unreflective. Reporters are taught to write and think like a mirror, reflecting everything that comes before us but keeping it all at a distance. Reporters are like bank tellers who handle money eight hours a day but keep none of it for themselves. Maybe it is more accurate to say that a newsman must be like the lantern illuminating a shadow puppet show. Lighting the cutout figures on stage, the reporter is never anything but a background brightness, a presence before the proscenium. It was an idea I had always taken seriously, believing the reporter's role to be that of recorder, an observer but never a participant. Now I was center stage, a principal in the cast, and found as I wrote of Buffalo that memories of my early years intruded. There were incidents of family, fights, and friends, details that had been long forgotten but that became again as real to me as the Roseland Market whose neon sign illuminated my apartment each night. It was as if Norm's insistence on past abilities had set me searching for a common base. My childhood opened like a forgotten book, and memories of my brother's Christmas visit set me puzzling over holiday periods long past.

None of this had any focus until one day I visited friends in Victoria on Vancouver Island. The passenger ferry takes ninety minutes, a wonderful trip on a fast boat that shoots across the Georgia Strait and then twists between a score of islands before coming to rest, thirty minutes from downtown, at Schwartz Bay's ferry terminal. As we steamed towards Active Pass, fishing boats motored slowly by with down riggers ranged like open arms to welcome sailing boats beating towards the wind. In the distance, barely visible, were Thornby and Lasqueti islands. I had sailed these waters years before, and this proximity—even in a power vessel—restored to me a measure of calm.

In Victoria I stayed with a close friend, the psychologist Patrick Michaels. He is a big man with gross features. About Michaels's body and face there are no finely sculpted lines but instead a general impression of solidity and comfort. He looks like a half-finished cartoon, an impression dashed off in haste. Patrick had the demeanor of a summer camp director, the type whom children instinctively adore. Indeed, there was something almost childlike about him, an innocence that was the professional mask he wore with practiced ease. It is easy to mistake intelligence for stupidity, a trick professional jesters know. Patrick used innocence and a feigned ignorance to draw my stories out.

We talked at first about my time in Buffalo and then of my father's condition. I described the medical problems, the battles with doctors, and my father's preoccupation with money. The story had been repeated so many times it had become a polished piece. Patrick said how strange it must have been to live so long in the shadow of my own history and, agreeing, I described the pandora's box of childhood memories that my tenure in Buffalo had unlocked. "Maybe that's what your need for a night light means," he said as I laughed, remembering how Mark and I had fought over the presence or absence of one in the room we had shared in our early days. At different periods first he, then I, would insist on having the room lit at night, but it was something we could never agree on. I remembered how scared I had been, once, in a lightning storm and how Mark had said I was a baby when our mother had to come and comfort me. "These things can come back to haunt us," Patrick agreed.

Everyone carries into maturity a reservoir of fears and anger from their earliest childhood years. Usually they are buried in the issues of adulthood, never to be considered again, but being in Buffalo for so long had forced my past back onto me. My friend suggested that I was caught in a time warp, locked in a battle between my history and Father's present. Norm had his illness and I had our past, a pathogen as consuming in its way, Patrick said, as the hepatic retrovirus. It was especially serious for me because I was in a profession that prohibited self-reflection and had accepted the situation at face value, ruling out the use of reflective knowledge as forever inappropriate. Thus, he said, I had no mechanism, no habit of dealing with conscious memory. The irony was how similar Norm and I were in our approaches, how attached to a present fashioned and customized from a common base.

"Why did you stay in Buffalo?" Pat asked. "Your brothers came and left. You could have too, you know." To say that Father needed me or that to do anything less would have been abandonment really said nothing at all. Words like loyalty and love, gratitude and pity would have been better answers but they too spoke after the fact and not to the issue. The answer was that I had stayed out of memory, Norm's and mine. As his world crumbled, I had anchored our shared history and of all the things that had held me there, that journey through our respective visions had been what was most compelling. I chose to stay in Buffalo because I had been transfixed by a reflection. Perhaps it was myself in Father's action or him, for the first time, in mine. Maybe it was the fact that childhood and adulthood had, for that Buffalo period, stood side by side. Certainly love was a part of it. There was duty involved, a belief that children owe their parents more than an anonymous nursing-home bed. But the other part was the chance to sort through a communal past and the opportunity, perhaps, to write new emotional equations.

Months later I was to learn that Patrick had been so drained by his time with me that his wife suggested I not visit again until my problems were worked out. "I know he's our friend," she said to her husband, "but you can't kill yourself counseling on weekends and then spend your work week doing the same." As I had sat and talked to my father for hours, listening to his fears and troubles, so had my friend listened to me. Just as my excursion into Father's life and fears had exhausted me, so too had Patrick's journey into my confusion been tiring for him. But I was my father's son, and had taken Pat's help for granted just as Norm had presumed on me.

Patrick and I first had met long before at an Aikido martial arts seminar where we heaved each other back and forth across the mats, beginners in a master's art. In the years since that first meeting I had become an instructor and in Buffalo had sorely missed both the release of hard practice and the community that comes in small but close-knit schools where each person is known to his fellows. On this visit, my friend asked if I'd teach a class, because the local instructor had been called out of town. Sure, I said, and at his school was immediately captured by a new student, a woman who had not been on the practice floor before I went to the Olympics. That is how I met Becky—flying across styrofoam mats taped to a community center's gym floor. She was filled with energy and determination, tiny and blond, with laughing eyes that mocked the formality others showed amidst the dojo's ritual Japanese bows. She was a nurse, and after class Patrick introduced us by telling her of my recent travails and me of her plans to move to Japan. Then we chatted, and I told anecdotes from Buffalo while she laughed in sympathy at my stories of Norm's travails.

Rebecca asked if I would be free sometime to talk with her about Japan, the possibilities of work, and what it would be like for a foreigner interested in practicing martial arts there. It was, as Patrick had known, a subject I liked to talk about. I had worked in Asia several times and had practiced in Japan over the years. I asked if she were free that night, and she said perhaps for coffee. The afternoon passed in a blur, and I left for Rebecca's that evening, the first of several visits. She lived in a small cottage next to an old boat yard at the edge of a simple, almost forgotten inlet that squirrels its way up from the Gulf of Georgia into the edge of Vancouver Island and Victoria's outlying regions. It is an old cut, a final half-forgotten dividend of the last glacial age that so obligingly folded British Columbia into a maze of convoluted coastline and mountain range.

There had been no time in Buffalo for companionship, because Father's illness and desperate need for the company of a son had demanded my constant attention. Since returning to Vancouver I'd found old friends in new alliances and had not looked for new friends who would force me to responsibilities anchored in a present time. Becky did that for me. Our interests were in many ways quite parallel—from the martial arts to literature and the ethics of medical care. As a nurse, she had seen many like Norm, and with her I could return again and again to the issues of the previous six months and my fears for the coming year. She listened with patience and understanding as I came to understand how exhausting my time in Buffalo had been and how much it had shattered the world I had known before.

In our family one never talked about how he felt, but tried never to show vulnerability. It was not simply among Norm's sons that this held but also in our whole Buffalo family and world. One did not cry and did not complain, whatever the justification. Certainly our parents set the tone, and whatever travails Norm suffered in business or disagreements he and my mother shared, we were never privy to those problems. Even during the hepatitis attack, Father had refused to discuss his concerns, and from Buffalo to Los Angeles by telephone, he had spoken of the logistics but not the emotional essence of his then pending hip operation. What he had wanted to say, I think, was that he was afraid he would never walk again. "Remember Jack Risotto?" I had asked. Norm's reply that Jack's implants had been removed was as close as we had come to frankness—his fear encoded in bare datum. I had taken the message at that time and refused to apply a translation.

Becky forced me to understand this, to face the emotional weight of my childhood years translated through the months of Norm's care. She asked what I felt and how it seemed until, one night as we sat in her room while her son was visiting elsewhere, I surprised myself by admitting how the uncertainty of Norm's condition had made of my world a fragile base. Later I wrote about this in my notebooks, and include a piece of that confessional here. "The entire world that I had built and lived in has disintegrated and I feel like a sailor with a broken mast, trying to get from sea to land, waiting for the tide to pull. It was so easy before. I was a newspaper man and liked what I was. I went out and reported other people's problems, and sometimes it helped them and sometimes not. But now I'm taking care of an old man and have no control over it at all."

I talked about how scary it had been to have another human as my charge and how confusing it was to have that person be my father. For the first time I admitted to myself at times I had wanted to hit him, to spank him, and how that desire had scared me. "I don't even know him anymore," I said to her. "He's like Lewis Carroll's Cheshire Cat. Sometimes he was there, whole and complete, but sometimes the man I knew had faded to an afterimage one could barely see." I said that he and I seemed to be mirror images or, perhaps, parallel tracks, for I saw his habits and traits in me; if I could change him, perhaps I would change myself as well. For her part, Becky let me know that what I was experiencing was not unusual, that aging children of elderly parents often felt confusion and fearful frustration when present times were overlaid upon a familial past. The conflict engendered between children and parents who once had been strong and were now weak is something every nurse has seen. That, she said, echoing one of our aides in Buffalo, Julia Shea, was one reason people hired others to care for those they loved the most. "Patients can be wonderful, but often they're cranky, unpleasant, and angry at the world," Rebecca sighed. "And that means we who care for them know the absolute worth [or worst] of their souls." For the first time I had a hint of how bitter it must have been to be Norm, and for the first time I understood how his frustrations could become an expanding, concentric pool that engulfed those who stood the closest.

Becky asked, as had Pat, why I stayed in Buffalo, and, searching for an answer I did not have, I said it was because I had to believe we all are of value. "I want to show him that it isn't economics, it isn't what one contributes or some bank balance but life in itself that is valuable. He has always believed that those who are not able are diminished, and I've always insisted that isn't so. If I hadn't stayed in Buffalo he would have won the argument," I said at last. "If I had lived my life and just visited for a weekend in the fall, I'd always have heard him say in my dreams, 'You see, life is for the able.' Patrick asked me why I stayed, and maybe it was simply because my other brothers did not. But I think it was a need to know, to show them all and to show myself that we all have worth, no matter how miserable we feel."

I lay awake much of that night, watching Rebecca sleep, and came to understand during that time that my confessions had been incomplete. What I had not said was that a part of me had enjoyed my role in Buffalo, preened at the idea of the noble son sacrificing himself for the parent. What had been admitted to neither Patrick or Becky was that the situation had given me control over Norm and that I— like all children—once had dreamed of the day when all-powerful parents would have to listen to me. It had been a childhood fantasy, when I was sent upstairs at night, to order my father to bed. When dessert was withheld because I disliked my vegetables I once had fantasized about having the power to insist my father eat things he might dislike. This whole geriatric complex of role reversal had given outlet to desires buried and forgotten since my earliest years. If the price had been isolation and sexual inactivity, it had been a price I paid willingly.

With Rebecca came another understanding and a bit of pity for my father. I was his mirror and he was mine, and if the situation had been my fantasy come true, it must have been for him a fear confirmed. Like King Lear, he had reached the stage where children could control and, also like Lear, he stood naked on the hill with no one to administer to. Even the hospital, his last defense—"my salvation"—had become not a place to work but the domain of nurses and physical regimes that he was expected to obey. His fight against hepatitis and the restrictions of his hip was more than a battle against infirmity but, as critically, a way in which to regain control and the power of self-esteem. In the interim, he had only his history as a parent to affirm the personal power whose diminishment he felt so sorely. So of course he had kept me at his side, and of course he had berated Brian's diet and smoking habits. How else could he show he was entitled to respect—to regain time's order—when, on the evidence of his present, Father had jettisoned the core weight of work and power on which his sense of respect—for others and himself— was built?

My relationship with Becky marked a major change for me, and with her the world held promise of again becoming an ordered place. Much of what she taught me was temporarily set aside; it was too much to absorb all at once, and I buried some of these reflections for a time. But with Becky's support and visits between us, Victoria to Vancouver and back again, my life began to take shape. Small jobs began to come my way, like the radio story about Mrs. McPhee, and the images that had grown in my folder began to fit together like a jigsaw puzzle in which the borders but not the central image are defined. The whole of that first phase of this battle began to develop like a photographic print whose figures are revealed in the darkroom's chemical baths. From the negative projected upon treated paper first comes a general gray, and after that the deep blacks develop, slowly washing up to the whites and a fully integrated image. That is how I began to understand the process of living with age, from the depths of my indecision through the highlights of Becky's time until it began to become a story in which both Father and I were entwined.

Throughout this period Norm and I continued to talk by phone several times a week, and, while still fragile, he reported a steady improvement. Soon Father reported he was again on the four-pronged cane and that his walker had been stored in the bedroom closet—"just in case" Julia said—but he, more optimistic, vowed "never again." The weather cleared, and spring became first a promise and then a certainty across the Great Lakes. Although Lake Erie remained choked with ice, Buffalo began to bloom. Its trees came if not yet to leaf at least to bud, and flowers made their presence known after the long months of snow. People traded heavy parkas for lighter jackets, and snow boots were set aside for walking shoes. Father and Julia went outdoors one day for the first time since autumn of the previous year, and in one evening conversation, Norm reported to me with pride that he had dined with his sister in a restaurant. Small things still upset him, and he was less able to cope with even minor problems than before, but, Father told me, he was learning. On his own initiative, he began to prepare his own breakfast each day and then cut back on Julia's hours to celebrate the feat.

Anxious to return to work, he was still not driving—Dr. Pangless had apparently discouraged it—but Norm still waited in hope for the day when he could get into his Chevrolet and have the luxury of its freedom again. Work and driving were synonymous to him. Both were so bound up in his vision of self that the idea of using buses and cabs for transportation was something he could not accept. This led to a major battle between him and his oldest friends, the Bees. The autumn before, Mrs. Bee had been one of the most constant and concerned of my father's circle, and her husband, Roy, had been a close acquaintance of my parents' for years. So I was surprised when one day Norm called to say that he had been betrayed by these people. Eager to return to work but still unable to drive, Norm had asked his friend Roy to drive him to General Taylor in the morning and if possible pick him up at the end of the day. Since his friend's office was near the hospital, riding in Mr. Bee's car struck Father as the perfect solution. But his friend, who was several years Norm's senior, had declined, and that, Father said, was inexcusable.

I called them to find out what had happened, and Mr. Bee told me that my father was still shaky on his four-pronged cane and that he worried that if he agreed, Father would fall getting out of the car or slip on Buffalo's still icy streets. "I couldn't take the responsibility, and if he needed help, wouldn't know what to do," Roy said to me. My father took this as a breach of faith and a lack of confidence in him on the part of an old, old friend. Norm could not accept the judgment of a peer that he was anything but able, and for several months relations between them were strained. Finally, Norm did return to work for a few hours on a beautiful day in late March. He traveled by cab, and when he arrived, no words could have been more welcome or kind than those of a coworker who said, "We have your old chair waiting." Still weak, unable to work for more than a few hours at a time (and then only twice a week), Father was reassured he would be useful again.

"It's over," I said to Rebecca when she next came to visit me in Vancouver. Her plane ticket for Tokyo was confirmed, and this was the last time we would be together until I could join her there. It was important for her to go, we had decided, and important for me to work. I was not happy with this and wanted her to delay the trip, but Becky said she would not change her plans. We had a dinner party in Vancouver for friends—hers and mine—and, puttering about the kitchen, I thought how strange it was that the chores that had seemed oppressive to me in Buffalo were in this context such a delight. We said good-by and promised to write. Maybe I could come to Japan as early as June, but, I said, it would probably be September before I would be able to visit. "Just come," she said. "Whatever else happens, come to be with me in Kyoto."

I no longer needed a light when I went to sleep, and the fears which had disturbed my nights slowly slid into memories. It became an automatic reflex to turn off my reading lamp when I went to bed and to know again that sleep would follow in no more than fifteen minutes. Dreams that had been a part of my nighttime now were consigned to subconscious oblivion. They had been horrible things, and often in the previous months I had waked in a sweat and written them down in an attempt at exorcism. Sometimes they showed Father and scenes from my earliest youth. In one recurring dream he was changing my diapers in the early morning, and as I watched, he sighed and grew old until the final safety pin was inserted by shaking, arthritic hands. In the dreams his face sometimes would be transformed from one that was middle-aged and firm into a wrinkled, yellow mask that dissolved in turn into a naked skull around which a single, blue bottle fly would buzz. There also were cancer dreams in which my mother rapidly metamorphosed from health to pain-racked, terminal disease while my father stood by, crying helplessly. In others it was I who was dying while both parents sat reading the newspaper.

I dreamed again and again of one of my brothers and the day he contracted a dangerous illness. That was the trauma of our childhood and, I believed, the root of many future ills. He had been rushed from the house bundled in a doctor's car, but in the dream, the person who returned in the family station wagon was a stranger. That was how it had seemed to me in real life as well. Before his illness we had been impossibly close, individuals only in a nominal sense, because the first person personal "I" in fact meant "us" — him and me. But after his illness Mark was changed, and in my dreams I relived the day when, months after the illness had passed, he had put his hands around my throat and squeezed until, gagging, I turned blue. "Boys will be boys," my father had said when I cried to him, warning me not to be a tattletale. But in dream's memory, while reliving that moment I was as angry with Father as I was afraid of this stranger brother. In the dreams I was choked again, but then my hands went in turn around my father's throat until, gasping, he turned hepatic yellow. "Yes, Tom. I understand now," he would say, and then I could release him, although afterwards his strange coloration did not change.

That was the most vivid and recurring of my dream places but by no means the only one. Night after night old family battles were fought again, but in most of these dreams the ending would change so that my triumph was, if not certain, at least a possibility. Most times, however, I awoke too early to discover the outcome of an image and would simply lie in sheets soaked wet from sweat while waiting for the radio to soothe me, to quiet the pounding of my heart and let sleep come again. These nightly battles had been common before I knew Rebecca, but after she left, they were replaced by dreams of us in Japan or on a ketch-rigged boat from Molokai to Oahu.

This complex of past experiences, so buried in my unconscious, erupted in the silence of my new-found freedom as if, after years of careful storage, a box of old photographs had tumbled from the closet shelf to come alive. Proust speaks of our "successive selves," the varying masks we wear at different ages before the changing world and in conjunction with a "permanent self," the quintessential person who lies at the center of their orbit like a sun around which planets and asteroids revolve. Norm's trauma had awakened a succession of those earlier masks in me which, like puppets before the curtain's rise, sit ready for their master's strings.

What I did not know then and learned only much later was the degree to which my father's and brother's worlds stood in similar states of disrepair. My father's identity, his permanency, had rested for years on the roles of parent, husband, and businessman. Being a widower was the easiest fracture for his persona to voice and thus one he had lamented ad nauseam. By insisting on my presence in the fall, he had fought to hold onto his parental role even at the cost of abdicating the rule of his household's schedule. Now, at last he was a businessman again, back to work, but the hours had been so severely decreased by his continued weakness as to make even that reestablished posture as tenuous as his returning health. For my brothers, the strain was less overt, but they had to face the fact that all children eventually ascend the familial ladder and overtake their parent's dominance. Brian's discomfiture with Norm's age and Walt's battle over the Scotch were early tremors of their own internal battles. Identity is both a character we act before the world and a representation, a presentation we put before ourselves. We were all fighting valiantly to hold those internal, worldly postures in place, but the strain of maintaining an internal face was, for each of us, beginning to take its toll.

The week after Rebecca left for Japan I saw an old friend, forty-year-old Peter Waters, who had woken up one day the summer before, while I was in Los Angeles, to find his right side paralyzed. Nobody knew what had caused his symptoms, and from Buffalo I had called him perhaps once a week through the late fall and early winter. Maybe it was a stroke, the doctors first said, but later they talked about the possiblity of a brain tumor. For months Peter had endured an unceasing round of tests, increasing impairment, and tests again. Perhaps it was not a brain tumor or stroke at all, the doctors now thought, but a case of multiple sclerosis. Day to day his condition changed, one day improved and the next diminished. Finally, on a good day, he came to dinner. Talking with him was like talking to a drunk. He had the same slurred speech and vacuous stare, but here one knew there was intelligence and power locked away, held by some errant disease. Peter seemed to handle it well, and when accustomed to his speech impairment, one heard hope and strength instead of anger in his voice. Often he joked, but humor, he admitted to me, was his last bulwark and best defense. "You should introduce me to your father," he said that night at my house. "We probably have a lot to talk about. The doctors said my brain is half its normal size and that I look, inside, like an eighty-year-old man."

Peter, by profession a therapist, had spent his life with others' problems, and now, I said, he had to work on himself. "Nobody ever does as well with themselves as they do with other people," he sighed. "I'm trying to figure out how to get by with half a body. It isn't pleasant, you know. Indeed, it is very frustrating." I remembered something Sam Fletcher had said that day of the Buffalo blizzard: "One can be old at any age, you know. Or young whatever the circumstance." I repeated it to Peter and he laughed a crescendo of rising S's, spraying the dinner table because of his speech impairment. His wife, Monica, wiped the spittle from his chin with a table napkin. "It's a good line," he said. "If I ever get to the point where my clients can understand my speech again, perhaps I'll use it on them." He sounded like Norm, with his hopes for work and his fears about disability. But a difference was that Peter was determined to improve for his daughter, then three, to see her grow up and to live to a point where he could enjoy her adulthood.

Peter, like Norm, slowly improved through the late spring while waiting for the doctors to define his disease to a certainty and then issue a verdict on its potential for a cure. My Aunt Janice in Buffalo sent me a touching letter, informing me of my father's progress and praising my efforts with him. She was enjoying retirement at that time and, freed from worries about her brother's health, was traveling a great deal to see family and friends along the east coast. Being retired was hard work after so many years of labor as a social worker, she wrote. The structure and purpose were gone from her world, and it took time to find replacements. My father was frankly envious of her, telling me on the telephone how his sister seemed always to be traveling to visit her sons who lived in distant cities. "She sure seems to be enjoying herself," he said. Aunt Janice wrote that she was determined not to make her brother's mistakes. She would travel, exercise, and enjoy herself precisely in the way that he had not; where he had been rigid, she would bend. It seemed to me an irony that he who was parent and brother to us should have as his greatest gift a life exemplary in what not to do.

I also received a note from my Uncle Jules, who wrote how saddened he had been by my letter, written in January, informing him that I would not be visiting Maui. For him retirement was also a trial but not simply because he missed his work. There was, he wrote, more than enough at home and with hobbies to keep him busy. The problem was that in age, he said, chores that once had taken no time at all now sometimes required days for completion. Uncle Jules felt himself slowing down, and it was frustrating, he said, to find difficulties where once there had been relative ease. It was, he cautioned me, hard to understand for those who had not lived it before.

I wrote back to both of them and to my father weekly. For his part, Norm began to reply by letter, short ones at first, but then longer ones as his strength returned. In one he mentioned in an offhand way that he was driving his car again. It was said casually, for he knew that I would be angry, and I called on the telephone to ask that he reconsider. Partly it was because his body was so fragile that any accident would be a disaster and partly because his driving abilities had declined so markedly in recent years. I had come to hate riding with him because he no longer paid attention to the road and did not see its potential dangers. As he drove on streets traveled for forty years, it sometimes seemed to me as if he saw not the road at that instant but a pastiche of trips made over all his decades of residence in that city. It was not that he didn't see, but pehaps that he saw too much, maneuvered his car across time and not simply through the immediately crucial present. Each turn and bump held past memories that made concentration on any specific trip quite minimal. He was an automobile accident waiting to happen, but when I asked him not to drive, he said on the phone that driving was his life. Without mobility he would die.

The week before Easter he almost did. While crawling up Hertel Avenue on his way to a fast-food store, a young man in a fast car pulled out of a driveway and broadsided my father in his Chevrolet. It happened at dinner time about a mile from the house, and pushed his old car into a tree while hurtling Norm into the steering wheel. Father, of course, was not wearing a seat belt because he didn't believe in them. "I've been driving almost sixty years and never needed the things yet," he would say whenever, in the past, I had insisted he buckle up. And each time over the years I would reply that "you'll only need it once." Without it, this time, his ribs and shoulder were thrown forward, and he was shaken up, terrified, in pain, and confused. The police called a tow truck to take his car away, and although they wanted Father to go to the hospital, he insisted they take him home.

Father told his sister, and she telephoned a family friend—a lawyer, Brook Samuelson—who rushed from his dinner to handle the paperwork and help Father if he could. With Aunt Janice, Brook tried to get my father to the hospital, but despite their entreaties, he adamantly refused. Eventually, he did call Dr. Pangless, who told my father that if he felt fine an examination would serve no purpose. "Nothing is wrong," Father shouted at us by telephone as family and friends called in, one by one. "I'm okay but my car is ruined. See what you can do about that." Brook checked the police report, and finding the other driver was clearly responsible, called my father's insurers. In tears Norm called Brian to talk about the accident and about his anger over being without transportation when the ability to drive was again so new, so recent. My brother, wanting to help, said he could get a deal and would buy a new car in Atlanta and drive it to Buffalo for Father. Then Brian called Walter to tell him what had happened, and Walter said the idea of a new car was outrageous. Maybe the old car should be fixed, he suggested, arguing that to drive 1,800 miles and save, at best, $1,000 made little sense. Walter in turn called me, and I then dialed Father, who said he had not wanted me to know about the accident because I had been so insistent he give up his automobile.

For days after the accident Father was sore and in pain. He could use his cane only with difficulty because his shoulder had been so badly bruised. On the telephone he told me he was taking Librium for his nerves, and maybe, I thought, that was why he sounded somewhat disoriented and confused. Father did not know what he wanted to do about the car and complained to me that "Brian is pushing for me to buy a new car but really, I don't want one." I again talked to both brothers by phone, and although neither was free to travel, both said they were worried about Father and the idea of his being alone. "Someone has to go," Walter agreed, "and it looks like you're the best."

Two days later I returned to Buffalo and Norm's house again. When I called to say I was on my way, Father agreed that Julia would work throughout my visit, but when I arrived in Buffalo, it was to find he had canceled all Homemaker services. "There's a holiday and that means paying double time," he explained. When I angrily reminded him of what he had promised, Father shrugged his good shoulder. "Well, I forgot. So sue me, and anyway, with you here I don't need anybody else." I spent several weeks in Buffalo getting the car repaired and again caring for Norm.

In my first week he needed constant help, and twice I caught him as he fell. "Just lost my balance," he said both times, immediately dismissing and then, within hours, entirely forgetting the incident. This latest travail was an "act of God," he insisted, something he was at pains to explain to me because Father was sure I would act like a parent whose son has stayed out past curfew. "Even the police say it wasn't my fault," he said again and again. That he was driving despite my warnings was to Norm of no import ("look, I have a license; you're not the State of New York"), and his refusal to see a doctor immediately after the accident was irrelevant because, after all, he had telephoned.

Norm forgot things every day and became even worse about money. When I called my mother's sister in New York City, Father twice asked me to get off the phone because the charges would be too high and he "was not made of money." Angrily I told him to shut up and purposely dragged the conversation out, berating him for cheapness when the call was finally done. Both Aunt Janice and I urged Brook Samuelson to submit a bill for his time spent on Norm's behalf, and when a bill came for $250, Father was outraged. "I asked him to send it," I told Norm. "He deserves to be paid for emergency work, and that's what lawyers get these days for a house call." But my father could not accept it, insisting instead that Brook was simply a "shyster" making money on my father's bad luck and that Janice, his sister, had been the impetus behind the lawyer's bill.

He was still sore a week after the accident, and his skin again had a yellowish tint. He lacked strength enough to go outside, and as he walked within the house, lurched and tottered with precarious steps. Finally I insisted he be examined by Dr. Pangless, and Norm agreed, he said, to put my mind at ease. X rays showed Norm had a fractured clavicle, which explained why he had trouble using the cane, and there was a deep black-and-blue welt over Father's liver where he had slammed into the steering wheel. Pangless ran some blood tests and said that Father seemed to have sustained no further permanent damage than that. Norm's balance problems and tiredness were simply symptoms of emotional distress, he suggested, and would pass in time.

Throughout the trip we had one good day together in which Norm spent hours talking to me about his father and their depression years. That afternoon I happened to drive him past a lovely house that my paternal grandfather, "Junie," had considered buying in the 1920s when the family furniture business was doing well. Finally Junie decided to stay with apartment living "in case a depression happened." It did, of course, and that cautious pessimism made a permanent impression on his son. Junie had been a gentle, kind man, a traveling salesman with no head for figures, Norm said, retelling old family tales. My mother and everyone who had known him said my paternal grandfather was the "nicest, sweetest man you'd ever want to know." My grandmother, however, had been a powerful woman who had ambitions enough for them all. In the early 1920s the family had lived in elegant style, but during the depression, when the business collapsed, my father had worked to help support the family—his parents and sister—because his parents refused to acknowledge their relative poverty and lived beyond their reduced means.

When I asked if that had made him angry, Father shook his head no, that was the way it had to be. When my aunt had married, their mother had ordered an expensive wedding that Father ended up paying for. "Why didn't they just have a small service?" I asked, and Father smiled at my ignorance. You never knew my mother, he said. Economy was not her style. I thought of the times he had spoken disparagingly of his sister and decided that while he had never blamed his parents for their extravagance, he had never forgiven his sister for accepting the largess of her marriage day. My aunt's eventual divorce more than twenty years later had somehow confirmed for my father the waste that her wedding had been to him, the diminution of his own capital given freely at the time but later held in memory as a grudge.

Every day I cooked for Father, made his breakfast, made his bed, and helped him with leg-strengthening exercises. He was almost childishly grateful because, he said in a moment of honesty, what he had really needed was a son around. I offered, as I had done in the past, to move back to Buffalo and care for him, but he refused the offer because "you have your own life to live and I don't want to be a burden." Father than said how fortunate it was for him that, unlike his other sons, I was out of work and had chosen this time for a visit. I tried to explain that I free-lanced precisely so I would be free to come to his aid when needed, but he shook his head and told me that "it just worked out that you decided to visit me now."

I hated being in Buffalo during that trip and resented the impositions his cheapness placed upon my time until, at my insistence, Julia finally was allowed to return to work. She told me one day while Father napped how difficult her supervisors found him. Sometimes Norm would call the agency to cancel her hours on days she was scheduled to work, and often aides brought in to relieve her on days off would refuse to work again for Norm after that first "tour of duty." I asked why, and Julia shrugged. She had no problems, she said, but others found him insulting and abrasive. He resented anyone he did not know.

Both Walter and Brian wanted to know how Father was progressing, so each night after Norm was in bed, I would call them and bring each brother up to date in turn. Both insisted that Father's context was to be handled "communally" and that, while the responsibility for details was clearly mine—"After all, you're in Buffalo," Brian said—any major decisions would be made by us together. They were free with suggestions of how I could spend my time in Buffalo working on our father's house, handling the damaged automobile, and working in Norm's garden. I said caring for him was a full-time job, and after Walter said, "Come on, how hard can it be?" I grew angry and short-tempered with them both. Finally I flew back to Vancouver, vowing as I climbed into the plane to leave the next trauma for my brothers to handle. They were so lavish with advice and care at a safe distance, but how, I asked myself, would they function if either had actually to cope himself?

Since both brothers had asked individually for a "progress report," I sent them letters written after my return to Vancouver. A copy went to Mark, too, explaining that our father was weak, fragile, and plagued by a number of chronic complaints. I said that while the accident had apparently not been too serious, our parent needed a wealth of emotional support, which could only come from his sons. I asked Walt and Brian to visit at least three or four times a year and suggested that Mark should write or call at least that often. Walter was the first to respond, informing me he would do what he could but refusing to be held to a schedule. It was his position that unless Father's condition was grave—and the presence of an oldest son absolutely required—he was free to continue his life. "Thank you," he said, "but I can handle relations with my own father without your help." Brian said that my letter was "dictatorial" and he hadn't liked the tone. Mark did not respond at all, although from Walter I learned that he, too, had thought my letter an imposition. It had always been a tenet of our parents' faith that "all our boys are equal," and Norm had repeated it to me when, irritated at my brothers' distance, I had suggested to him that it no longer held true. "I'm here and they are not," I complained, but Father would stand for no criticism of my brothers from me, and by telephone my brothers had been at pains to remind me that "we're all in this together." But age had changed the equation, and equality had disappeared. They were concerned at a distance, while I was present at close range, and I promised myself that the next time they could take over Norm's necessities and run his geriatric circus themselves. That there would be a next time nobody, I think, ever doubted.

In the meantime, however, I had assignments to complete and plans to make for a late summer's trip to Becky and Japan. In mid-June I would attend a martial arts camp, and all these new things crowded much of my exasperation with them all to the back corners of my mind. But a small, mean, childish part of me smirked in hope and anticipation. It could see Norm in extremes and hear his—and my brothers'—pleas for me to come back, come back to Buffalo, while I sat smugly in, say, Kyoto.

5

Ceaseless Deprivation

Modern geriatric psychiatry speaks of the aged as being wounded in their narcissism—a poignant term and one which eloquently compresses the whole business of what we once were and what we must inevitably become.

Ronald Blythe, *The View in Winter*

As we age, there are two changes in our immune functions, both of them disadvantageous. . . . At the same time that we become less able to defend ourselves against our [body's] enemies, we also become more likely to mistake friends—our own body cells—for foes.

David P. Barash, *Aging: An Exploration*

For seven days our of every year my world is reduced to a martial arts camp and six hours a day of Aikido practice. It was and is an exhausting exercise, with more than 60 adults taking over a children's summer camp on Gabriola Island, everyone sleeping in sixteen-bunk cabins and eating from a central kitchen. Gabriola sits off the coast of Vancouver Island, a five-hour sail from the mainland, and the camp is so placed that from it one can see nothing but British Columbia's mountainous coast, a lumber mill on the horizon, and the boats that occasionally sail by.

My father had always admired this side of me, the insistence on fighting and physical defense. "Uncle Frank was a boxer, you know, and one of my favorite people," he had said when, as a teenager, I began to study judo. He never watched me practice, but showed his support for my study by chauffeuring me to practice in the days before I could drive. For himself, however, Norm abhorred physical violence of any kind and throughout our youth frequently lectured his sons on the need to avoid confrontation. His father, Junie, had been a physically powerful man and in the immigrant, German-Jewish community of Buffalo, a peacemaker when disputes arose. "They'd call Junie, and he was so strong," Norm had told me that May day when we talked for hours, "so physically strong that no-body dared start anything when he was present." Junie's brute strength and physical prowess thus enforced his negotiator's role. Norm adopted his father's perspective (discussion and compromise are better than confrontation) and tried to pass it on to us, but without Junie's certainty and strength, the whole became something passive and, to me, unreal.

Those who knew Norm best had suggested, over the years, that this posture was as much a result of Norm's high school injury as it was of his father's example. "I think he changed after that," my mother once said to me. "That dislocation was his turning point." When trying to explain her husband to a son, she would tell us of a time before their marriage when, on a date, Father's shoulder had dislocated spontaneously as he reached for the salt and pepper at a restaurant. He had not told her of his injury, and when he fell writh-ing to the floor in pain, she had been scared. "I thought he was an epileptic," she afterwards said. Incidents like that—there were several over the years—humiliated the former high school football hero and made him cautious and careful beyond his years. Like Norm's sister, his wife knew that Norm might have better accommodated to his disability, but as wife and not sister, she knew as well that with the injury some essential part of Norm was set and had become a part of the whole she knew. It had made him quiet and unathletic while still admiring and longing for the grace and assurance amateurs gain who spend their hours in any active, physical endeavor.

To Norm I was the inheritor of his athletic interest, his father's strength, and Uncle Frank's combativeness. That I was free to pursue it in my adult years meant to him a son freed of personal limits he acknowledged in himself but never truly accepted. It fascinated him, I think, that a university-educated son would find such archaic arts both valuable and compelling. So, when told by telephone that I would be at my annual retreat, he promised I would not be interrupted by his context. "I want to hear about problems, though," I said, and he agreed to have Julia take the camp's number and put it in a conspicuous place. He was humoring me, laughing at the fact that I was a "worry wart. You always were, you know." Julia, for her part, said that if problems arose during my week's retreat she would call Walter or Brian. As a precaution, however, I called my oldest brother to give him the camp's telephone number as well. "Just in case," I said to Walter, and he replied that if something came up "I can handle it as well as you." Like our father, he saw me as overly concerned and in need of knowing that Norm's world could get along for at least a week without his youngest son.

But on the camp's second day, my oldest brother did call, apologetically, to say he didn't know what to do. Father, it seems, had fallen the previous night, passed out and finally come to, hours later, lying on the kitchen's cold, linoleum floor. He had just "blacked out," Norm confided to his sister, who initiated a chain of phone calls from Julia to Walt to me. My brother asked me what we should do. All Father knew was that he had gone for a glass of milk before the 11 o'clock news and woke up early in the morning stretched in the space between the refrigerator and the sink. No one knew why he fell or what it signaled, but all agreed it was a miracle that he had not seriously injured himself. Julia said Norm's skin color was yellowing like old parchment, regaining the hepatic tinge, and that day by day energy seeped from him like a balloon collapsing in upon itself. What, Walt asked, did I suggest? How should we handle this situation, and what ideas did I have while sitting on that small island off the Pacific, Canadian coast? "Let me make some calls," I said. "Let me ask some questions." I immediately called Aunt Janice, who said she was convinced that Norm's hepatitis was returning if leukemia were not the culprit. At her suggestion, I called Julia, too. Over the months of daily association she had grown to like my father and took pride in her skills as his guardian. She lamented that "he was doing so well until the auto accident, until that day in May."

I called Father, who was angry that I had been told about what he dismissed as a very minor incident. A brief lapse, he said; nothing at all was wrong. He refused to tell Dr. Pangless about his fall and got angry when I insisted. "I don't need any mothering," he said.

"I can look after myself." Each day or so I received new progress reports from Aunt Janice or Julia or secondhand reports from them through Walter, and none of it was encouraging. Finally Father agreed to go to his doctor—to "put your mind at rest." Dr. Pangless ordered a series of tests and told me, when they were complete, that Father could add "hemolytic anemia" (brought on, perhaps, by chronic leukemia as well as the hepatitis) to his list of physical problems. It meant, he said, that Father would be constantly tired and that bacterial infections were a danger as well. The hepatic scores, while somewhat increased, were at present nothing to worry about, Pangless continued. But none of this explained Father's blackout, and for that the doctors had no immediate rationale. "Should I come to Buffalo?" I asked. The doctor said that he could not tell me what to do but, while the situation was in hand, "I know your father always likes to see you."

From Gabriola Island I called Father again and tried to convince him to stay home, to rest. He agreed he would "take it easy. After all, resting is what I do best." However, he insisted on continuing to work at the hospital. "After all," he pleaded, "I don't want to get fired. Work is what I need, you know. It's the best medicine of all." I argued with him, and in his turn, he became angry with me: "Stop badgering and pushing. These days that seems to be all our conversations are. You bugging me and telling me what to do. I sleep most of the day, just lying in my room like a corpse. I like my life—at least it's my own—so please, just get off my back." I thought I could hear bravado and fear in his voice, knew the terror he must feel at increasing and constant exhaustion. The blood scores read to me over the telephone by Dr. Pangless meant each step and every action of Norm's would require an exhausting effort because his red blood cell count was so dangerously low. I knew and, perhaps, so did he that only will power and sheer determination got Father out of bed and away from the house each day. Norm was caught again between what he had—an illness debilitating in the extreme—and his persona of astute patriarch and active businessman. Between the two there was no reconciliation and my "badgering," well meaning perhaps, emphasized the growing distance between his diminishing physical ability and his eroding, emotional self.

Walter suggested that "one of us" should go to Buffalo if the situation did not rapidly improve, but because he was working on a major contract, would not himself be able to get away for anything less than a life-or-death emergency. Maybe Brian could visit for a weekend, he suggested. For his part, Brian was equally busy and said, with some reason, that since Julia was watching over Norm there seemed nothing more for anyone to do. What was needed, both agreed, was for the situation to be "watched." Walt had asked our Father if he wanted company, and Norm had replied, "Only if you feel like a dull vacation." That, in my oldest brother's mind, absolved him of any responsibility for an immediate trip to our ancestral home. He apologized again for interrupting my camp but admitted he no longer knew Buffalo or its information network. Who to call and when was my metier, he implied. Buffalo in its complexity was my expertise, and Walter asked would I, please, when back in Vancouver, continue to monitor things.

The camp was over in mid-June and then, from Vancouver, I called Buffalo every day to talk to Father, his sister, or Julia. If I did not call, someone called me. Day to day Norm either berated me for "babying" and "badgering" him or complained of the constant physical tiredness he felt and the burden his life had become. I telephoned Uncle Jules to ask for his advice, but he had just been released from the hospital and was himself too weak to do more than give me encouragement by phone. I called Norm's next-door neighbor, Sam Elaine, who said every morning he watched from his window as Norm lurched along the driveway towards the old Chevrolet with uncertain, halting steps. Each evening it was both a surprise and relief, Sam continued, to see that the car had returned to the driveway and thus to know Norm had made the trip without incident once again. "It's been downhill ever since that damn auto accident," Sam lamented. "He looks terrible, he really does."

One night Father again talked to me of suicide's attraction, complaining as he had the previous year of the burden life had become. "I should have had a heart attack, something like that, while working at the store," he insisted. "This isn't how it's supposed to end." The ideal of suicide became a way to rectify what seemed to Norm to be God's oversight. He was sure that nature's plan did not include a final, shameful half-life of corrosive and embarrassing age. It was as if longevity itself had become a betrayal, as if to have lived so long and then be forced to accommodate, to change, at this stage of life was in violation of life's moral and natural design. Of course he refused to take any responsibility for his own situation, bemoaning instead his lot as if, like Job, Norm was an innocent party subjected to a series of unfair trials visited by malignant fate. That is what angered me the most, and one night I wrote him a letter insisting that he, too, was responsible. It said in part:

I asked, begged you not to drive this year and for years have insisted you wear a seat belt. But you chose to ignore it all, and this is what I feared. You have talked of suicide for a decade, whenever life seemed lonely or difficult, and now you are doing it again. Your first problems came when you fell at the house, ignoring Paula's advice. You, Pops, are in charge of your life. The things you make sound like an act of God are as much an outcome of your own decisions as the stock portfolio you've been building for years.

The letter was filled with good advice and mailed with a sense of high purpose, but I was in Buffalo before it arrived. On June 25, Norm was again admitted to the hospital, active chronic hepatitis and hemolytic anemia the diagnoses entered onto his clinical chart. All my brothers were busy, so at their urging, I flew again to Buffalo the day after Dr. Pangless admitted to me that even he was concerned about Norm.

At the hospital and in a semiprivate room, Father lay violently jaundiced and immobile, buried by a single sheet pulled over his head like a shroud. I ran to the nursing station, where a duty nurse said no, my father was not dead, merely asleep. A nurse's aide preceded me as I returned, relieved, to Norm's room, and I stepped back, out of Norm's line of vision, to see how he behaved with her. Setting a basin and wash towel by the bed, she woke him and said it was time for his bath. "I can do it myself," he said, and as she protested his hands made ineffectual, dry swipes across his body to show her he was able. "I can do it. Really," he insisted. "Anyway, they gave me one this morning." Then he saw me at the door and told the aide to look. "Tommy boy," he called to me as I came into the room. "What brings you to Buffalo?" Turning to the aide, Norm asked her to leave "because, you see, this is my son."

She left us with a shrug as Father began to ask, as if mine was a social visit, about my Vancouver life and work. I asked in turn about his condition and about how he felt. He was tired, he shrugged, tired all the time. Yet he seemed happy to be in the hospital again, to have his body the subject of such concern, interest, and professional expertise. "They take a gallon of blood each day," Father said with pride. "It's a wonder I have any left! They gave me these pills for water retention and now, wow! When I have to go it's Niagara Falls." He wasn't sure what had made that treatment necessary but told me his bladder just wasn't strong anymore and admitted that sometimes, on his way to the bathroom, it was "well, touch and go." I asked if he wanted to go for a walk or sit for a while in his hospital room chair, and Father said that would be nice if I could just bring him his cane. I started to help him stand, but when we pushed back the sheets I saw his legs, which looked as if they had been painted a splotchy yellow-brown. Bending to examine them more closely I found the indelible, fetid smell of stale urine, something like the odor that seeps from an uncleaned bus station's bathroom stall. "Haven't they washed you this week?" I asked, and Father replied with dignity that "I'm not so old I can't wash and clean myself." When I pointed to his legs, Father stared with interest—as if they were someone else's—and said, well, when he had rushed to the bathroom earlier that day perhaps his limping gait had been a little slow.

If I had not seen him with the aide, I would have been angry, but it was hard to blame others when the decision to be dirty was so clearly one he himself had made. I left him in bed and walked to the nursing station, where the woman in charge was talking on the telephone while searching through a stack of papers on her desk. She had about her the harried and distracted air of a schoolteacher at the end of term. She was surrounded by charts, lists of medication, and scribbled physicians' notes for patients on that floor. Each page had to be appropriately filed in the correct folder, and it did not help that there were two patients named Koch—each unrelated to the other—among her charges. It simply added to the confusion. When she was free, I told her what I had seen. She shrugged sympathetically and explained that my father was what nurses call a "hider," a patient who masks problems and sometimes symptoms to keep intrusions to a minimum. If the patient refuses help, she said, there is little the staff can do. I asked if I could wash him, and she took me to the supply room where piles of fresh towels, soap, wash basins, and sheets were stacked waiting on endless shelves. "Have fun," she smiled, and returned to work.

I brought warm water, a stack of washcloths, and towels back to where Father still lay. When he asked what I was doing, I said he was going to get a bath from me. No, he said, it wasn't my job, and anyway the nurses had washed him that morning.

"Look at yourself," I said, gesturing to his legs. "You tell them you've done it, and now you tell me they've done it for you." I explained that he had no choice and that, in his words when I was young, the "conversation was closed."

Father protested that "I'm not a baby, you know. I have my rights."

But I ignored him, saying as I began to wash his legs and feet, that he had abdicated them through arrogance, pride, and stupidity. "I'm taking over now," I continued while soaping his legs, torso, and back. He insisted he would clean his own bum and groin, and there I happily acquiesced. Then I helped him to a chair so that I could change his bed sheets while he complained continually that I "was being silly. It was done in the last day or so." Finally I trimmed his toenails, which were overly long and curling. Then I helped him back to bed, where he lay crying, pristine but defeated.

"I hate you waiting on me like this," he sobbed. For Norm it was preferable to be dirty, wet, and uncomfortable than to admit to nurse or son he was unable to care for himself. It was better, his actions said, to sleep a night in weakness on the kitchen floor or lie uncomplaining in a dirty bed than to acknowledge his body's treason and the necessity of help. It was not simply the indignity of incapacity that upset him, although that was a part of it, I'm sure. Juvenal once said that "a perpetual train of losses, incessant mourning and old age dressed in black, surrounded by everlasting sadness—that is the price of a long life." Norm was living the cost and hated the premium existence extracted in dependence for even a foreshortened future. The worst of it, for him, was the injury done to his self-esteem, and the best thing about the hospital room to my father, I think, was its lack of a visible mirror. One hung in the bathroom but at such an angle that patients could use the facilities and never have to see themselves. I remembered Roland Blythe's words, read the previous spring, and wondered how far my father would go in the name of vanity, self-sufficiency, and self-esteem: "Modern geriatric psychiatry speaks of the aged as being wounded in their narcissism—a poignant term and one which eloquently compresses the whole business of what we once were and what we must inevitably become."

None of this did I say to him. The activity and excitement of that visit wore him out, and soon Father was sleeping again. As I went towards the door, his roommate that day, a man in his fifties, called me over to say that watching my father walk to the bathroom and back had been the high point of the man's hospital stay. "He totters, leans, and then almost stumbles again. I'm always afraid he'll fall near me and that we'll both have to wait for some nurse." That man was to be discharged the next day, but before he left, wanted somebody to know what he had observed with trepidation and, apparently, with interest. Father tried to time his walks for the hours when he was alone, of course, when no nurse or visitor could see how frail he was and order him back to bed. I thanked the man for his concern and said I surely would discuss it all the next time I saw Norm's doctor.

From there I went to Aunt Janice's for dinner and afterwards, in Father's house, telephoned my brothers. All wanted to know what their father's prognosis was and what the doctor had said; each asked how their father was feeling or described to me a recent telephone conversation with him. I had little to report except that Father had been bathed by me, and to that Walter reacted as strongly as had Norm. "That's not your job," he said, and when I replied that it had been necessary, he insisted it would not have been had he been the one in Buffalo. "Don't they have nurses on his floor?" he asked. I tried to explain that it wasn't simple. It certainly was, Walter insisted, and accused me of "just playing doctor and nurse again." From Denver he explained that I should have ordered nurses and nursing aides to do their jobs because "we weren't raised to rinse out bedpans."

This was not simple class snobbishness, although perhaps that played its part. Walter's reaction, while similar to Norm's, was based on parallel but not identical fears. If his father had reached the point where even the simplest physical acts required the help of others, then Norm's presence as parent and power, an image both had nurtured and polished for more than forty years, was nothing but memory, and Walter's world would be bereft. He could accept that his father was in the hospital and under "professional care," but that I, another son, was so involved robbed the situation of polite fictions and impressed upon us all Father's helplessness. I embraced the fact to justify my presence again in Buffalo just as Norm had insisted after the automobile accident on the fiction that my presence was a fortuitous, social visit. If our father was wounded in his self-esteem, Walter's sense of time's balance was simultaneously injured now. A patriarch and historic resource needs to be seen as self-sufficient, and that memory was what I began to destroy in my brothers' worlds that night.

The next morning, before hospital visiting hours, I walked through my father's house, whose disarray was a compliment to Norm's physical condition the previous day. There were piles of bills and banking slips, old checks, form letters and past-due notices piled on the floor beside or behind the bed. It was the accumulation of weeks in which he had been too tired and sick to handle his own affairs and too proud to ask for help. Papers had been simply dropped in fatigue or hidden so neither Julia or Janice would see them until Father felt better. "I'll get to it tomorrow, or the day after," he certainly had muttered to himself. "This will pass, I'm still working at the hospital. I can still do it. I know I can." If his caretakers had seen the residue of bills unpaid for several months, he had guessed, they would have insisted that I or another take over his affairs. Father had gambled for time and lost. That morning I sorted through the untouched and unanswered mail, paying the most urgent accounts myself.

Julia said she had done her best, but Father had insisted his things not be touched. She had tried to clean and dust but his night table and bedroom bureaus had been, on Norm's orders, inviolate. So on his bureau, where family pictures stood framed in rows, there lay a coating of dust punctuated by fingerprints where he had edged along with his free hand, seeking support from the furniture while the other hand held his cane. The fingerprints were unevenly spaced, as if made at various times and with a lurching gait, or perhaps when nobody else was looking, he had grabbed for support with a guilty thrust. If Mrs. McPhee had been less fastidious perhaps each table and chair in her apartment would have carried similar marks. But it was only on the bureau before those photographs that the traces of fingertips were clear, and it all seemed vaguely familiar, although at first I could not recall the image they evoked.

Then I remembered seeing similar marks long ago in Guatemalan churches where penitents, afraid to touch the image of a saint, prayed before some shrine and left their fingers' prints on an altar or at a saintly statue's feet. I decided that was probably close to what happened on the bureau beneath Norm's family photographs as well. Walking, he had paused to rest in front of those images of our communal past, slipped into a moment of memory as each awoke old visions, while his hands rested on the dusty surface beneath the picture frames. Maybe his hand, shaking slightly, had touched in evocation the image of my mother smiling at the world from a sunny day on the coast of Spain when they had been on vacation twenty years before. The instant photograph that recorded that moment is faded now, as is a Polaroid that he had pointed out with fondness to me in May. It recorded a day more than thirty-three years before when we boys had gathered in uncomfortable ties and itchy suits for a familial photograph. Mark sat on Walt's lap, and I rested on Brian's. I thought of Peter Waters, whose brain had shrunk, and wondered what he swept under his life's rug and whether he stood before the toys his young daughter used and remembered, like Norm before those photographs, how it had been in his own long ago.

For several weeks Father's condition followed the course it had taken the previous autumn. The hepatitis became this time, like before, daily more violent and then, slowly, retraced its advances and promised eventual remission. Each day I visited Norm at the hospital, whose nurses had gladly abdicated to me the ritual of his daily bath. Most of my time was spent waiting, watching his almost constant doze. He slept at least sixteen hours a day, but when awake, liked to know that he was not alone. Incontinence was a recurring problem, as it is for so many elderly whose muscles give up their strength to age and illness, so a urinal was placed by his bed "for emergencies." To him it was a signal of shame, like wet sheets to a child newly toilet trained. Norm would have preferred to race from bed to bathroom with his lurching gait, he said, but the nurses had insisted it was too dangerous and ordered him to stay in bed.

Brian called one night to say he needed someone to talk to. In childhood I'd been his confidant, but as we chatted, I came to realize that, inhabiting Norm's house and caring for him, I was assuming other roles of his as well. Thus that night "Bri" came to me for personal advice, which otherwise he would not have done. He told me that he was unhappy at work, impatient with life, and curt with his family, that in sum, "things just don't seem to be working out." I suggested this was a kind of "midlife crisis" brought on in him by Norm's dissolution. When he was young, Brian had wanted to be "just like Dad," as we all did, I guess, at some point in our individual childhoods. But only he had adopted the outside forms and gone into furniture sales. It was as if my brother had borrowed a family destiny and now, as Norm waned, Brian suspected that his eventual conclusion would follow a similar course. His own end might not be the storybook picture of grateful, grown children attending the benign elder, which my brother had presumed he would become. Brian saw his own future in Norm's condition, took as a personal sentence some future time in which care became something professionals would give on an hourly or per diem basis. The sequel to *On Golden Pond* had become, to this brother, a semiprivate room where nurses worked in shifts, and that vision had robbed his life of its balance.

The problem, I said to him, was that he had tried to live by Norm's reflection, and that mirror had changed from one of pleasant esteem— businessman, parent, and home owner—to a refracted image in which these public postures inevitably would cease. Like Norm's sons, Brian's daughters would grow up and move away. He, like Father, would retire to find years slipping away while time dragged at the scale of the individual day. A parent to grown children and deprived of work, he, like Norm, someday would be adrift upon a sea of uncertainties and regret. If Walter's concern was for memory's frame, Brian's was for the future. No work, the equation ran, no life. But as Norm's "Bri" now knew, sometimes existence continues anyway. Later I came across a quote by Robertson Davies that explained this nicely, a prognosis at one remove from Norm's frustration throughout the whole long slide. "The danger of a busy professional life is that it will eat you up. One of the serious troubles with our modern world is that far too many people have become so identified with their public life and their public role that they have lost sight of the private person that they must also be. The public figure is a giant: the private person is a dwarf."

Men like my brothers and father, who define themselves through work, sacrifice without thinking their private, personal, nonfamilial lives at the altar of professional respectability. When that public purpose ends, however, their persona diminishes as well, just as Norm's body had shrunk when the pitted, osteoporotic spine compressed beneath his body's own weight. Our father's decline had affected us all differently, but the central fact was that the public person had slipped away and none of us—Norm included—knew how to deal with what remained. "Man is in love and love is what vanishes," T. S. Eliot wrote. "What more is there to say?" Only this, I told Brian: illusion narrows to solitude, and we all become at best a presence in the memories of others and of ourselves. Norm's illness had shattered all illusions of a pastoral future and broken a set of perceptions ingrained since our collective childhood. With that trauma came a realignment of memories, a reordering of personal histories, that shook us one by one. Norm was the first to feel the seismic shocks, and now Brian, at his remove, was learning them as well.

I borrowed a bicycle from a childhood friend and began cycling each day to the hospital. The physical release was invaluable, and day by day I pushed myself to ride faster and faster, to burn my anger and frustration away in the pedals' revolution. Sometimes after leaving the hospital I would simply ride to exhaustion through Buffalo's streets and remember how, in early adolescence, my old, red Schwinn had defined for me the city's range. What I had not remembered was that cycling in Buffalo was like walking on the moon. Hard winters and a lack of maintenance guaranteed that huge, deep potholes—almost craters—littered every road and path. Bicycling in Buffalo was a dangerous affair because at any moment one could drop a wheel into a five-inch-deep hole, somersaulting in a pinwheel over the still spinning front wheel. I grew to know each hazard on the route, however, and safely arrived at the hospital each morning out of breath and drenched in sweat.

Before entering, I would stand on the street for a moment, cooling down, and consider the complex that is General Taylor Hospital. Unlike facilities in newer cities or suburban regions, this was an old structure sitting squat and permanent, as much a part of its ghetto neighborhood as the local Salvation Army's mission. Despite its almost constant building program and modern facilities, the hospital had about it an antiquated and military feel. Originally opened during the Civil War, the hospital is encircled by a high, linked fence ringed at the top with barbed wire. It is, in the end, like an army station squatting near combat lines, and I half expected to discover some morning that land mines had been laid beneath local streets to keep the indigenous population at bay.

To gain entrance to the hospital, everyone has to show a pass before the omnipresent guards will allow one past locked security doors. Staff, even volunteers like Norm, wear identification badges that include on them the individual's picture, name, and position in the hospital's hierarchy. I have seen the same overt order at hospitals in cities like Boston and New York. In others—those in cities like Denver or Vancouver, for example—the signs of status and privilege are usually more covert. The hospitals of those cities are not in combat zones, and they do not need the fences and guards that are so much a fact of General Taylor's life. Identification tags may be used in those places, but there they don't necessarily carry rank and station, only the bearer's name. But in those cities the general population is younger and less formal than in Buffalo.

At General doctors, of course, are at the top of the pecking order and tend to keep their badges obscured beneath sport or suit coats and ties. They don't need them, really, being more easily identified by a formal, officious look than by rarely glimpsed badges that carry the accolade "M.D." Residents and interns usually display theirs more prominently, the latter keeping the new stethoscopes dangling around the IDs like frames. Less sure of their futures and their skills, many wear their identification like small diplomas that they can pin to their clothes. Nurses' badges, on the other hand, often are pinned at the waist to uniform pockets or belts. Having gone as far up the ladder as the hierarchy allows, nurses have no need of show. Like them, orderlies and aides take no special care except to make sure their IDs are displayed where the security guard can see them. Visitors, however, are issued large passes like the oversized keys primary-school children get when they leave the class for restroom privileges. At security checkpoints these are to be returned as one leaves the building. One day when I thoughtlessly walked out with my foot-long pass, a security guard came after me, hand on gun, to take it away and question me. I told Norm about the incident, and he said I was just "making trouble" and if I were arrested he would be all alone.

On July 20 the telephone rang at 8:19 in the morning.

"Would you please come to the hospital immediately," an anonymous voice asked me politely. "There has been a change in the patient's condition, and your presence is requested." The woman's set piece had the stilted formality of an invitation to dinner with a minister of state, the ominous ring of an official announcement that an IRS audit had been commenced.

"What's wrong?" I asked. "What's happened?"

She said she was just a secretary and didn't know any more than what she had been told to say except that if I would inform security it was an emergency, they would let me go without delay to the patient's room. I no longer had to wait for visiting hours.

"Yes, of course," I said, "right away."

But before I could hang up the woman said wait, there was something else she needed to say. She had called my aunt with a similar message, but there had been some hearing problem and she didn't know if the message had been understood.

I hung up the receiver and headed for the door when the telephone rang again. It was Aunt Janice telling me to listen, not talk, because her hearing aid was broken and without it conversation was impossible. The hospital had called and would I please meet her at my father's room? "Yes," I shouted into the phone, and Aunt Janice said that while things would be difficult, we'd "make it through somehow."

At the hospital I rushed to Father's ninth-floor room, where a full complement of residents stood waiting with my aunt for me. "Where is Dr. Pangless?" I asked. The residents told me he was off that day, and because my father's situation was critical, Norm had been put on "hospital service," which meant that they were in charge of his care. Pangless had been consulted, of course, but the problem was such that, for the moment at least, Father's fate was in their hands. He had begun a massive internal bleed that night, losing a tremendous amount of blood. It began when, alone in the bathroom, he passed enormous volumes of a black, diarrhetic, tarlike stool. He had been found on the tile floor, ineffectually trying to clean the mess up, ashamed, he said, of his "mess." Maybe the bleeding was caused by his liver, the physicians said, and maybe it was something else. But whatever the cause, if it wasn't stopped he would die from a lack of blood. The flow seemed to have lessened for the moment, and with Father's permission, the doctors had started to transfuse him while debating what else to do. I told them he had a history of ulcers and the residents—two men and a woman—nodded to themselves. If the bleeding came from that type of problem, one said, perhaps there was a chance. They could try emergency abdominal surgery—which most doubted he had the strength to survive—or give endoscopy a shot. What did we the family want them to do?

Aunt Janice looked at me. I asked what the patient wanted, and the residents said he hadn't made any decision except to say he wanted to talk to me. I asked if my father was conscious, and they said yes, but extremely weak. "Give my aunt and me a minute alone, and then I'll go and see him." The residents tried to impress upon me the need for speed, and I told them I knew the situation's urgency but first had to speak with her. We walked down the corridor, and because she was so deaf, then stood like lovers cheek to cheek as I spoke loudly into her ear. "Can you hear me?" I asked, and my aunt said yes, faintly, but would I please speak up. She told me that I would have to decide for Norm, that this was not a decision for her to make. But she also said that if this was to be his end it would be something of a relief, that she hated seeing her once strong brother lying so weak and so frail. I said that if Father could decide for himself it would be his choice, but that if it were up to me, I'd let him die quietly. From here on things could only get worse. Aunt Janice told me to do what I thought best.

Arm in arm, we returned to the doctors, who stood like horse-players waiting to see the replay of a hotly contested race. I told them I would authorize no procedures and that, if it was left up to me, Father should die. "He's been miserable since this hepatitis began, and has constantly complained about the minimal quality of life that is all he has left," I explained. "Sometimes one just has to let go, and this may be one of those times."

The doctors looked one to another and tried to tell me that surgery had a chance and that the endoscopy offered at least some hope.

"I'll explain his options to him. Now please," I said, "I'd like to see my father."

That was when I lost their support, then and forever more. It is treasonable to tell doctors to leave a patient alone, heresy to suggest that the potential for survival is sometimes not worth the risk. Armed with an arsenal of protocols and drugs, they have been trained to use them at all costs. For these young physicians nebulous phrases like "patient approval" and "quality of life" are courtroom games for lawyers and psychiatrists, not real boundaries to a patient's care. Like auto repairmen faced with a wreck, they are conditioned to fight for continuance whatever the cost or problem. Just as my father chose in May to have his ruined Chevrolet repaired even though the cost was greater than its worth, so these doctors demanded a chance to work on him. Now my father faced these young, eager body mechanics for human beings, and they wanted to get on with their job. They read upon his body a specific illness and sorted through protocols for its potential cure. But I saw my father's crisis as malignant age and knew it could not be halted or reversed. I believed that he would choose to die because life could no longer be lived on his own terms, and continuance would be by definition in a diminished form. Were he to survive surgery or other procedures, the residents could not guarantee that his faculties would be unimpaired or that other and related complications would not follow the resolution to this crisis. But for them these were irrelevancies—the only issue was an internal bleed, and their only concern, its treatment. But I could no longer separate Norm's body from his condition and just wanted his unhappiness and our trials to end.

Janice stayed with the young doctors, smiling and nodding as they explained to her deaf ears the need for haste, while I went alone into Norm's room. The sheets were still stained by his blood, and the floor near his bed needed cleaning. Father smelled of sulphur and shit. His hands were cold and clammy. Overnight his jaundiced, yellowed skin had taken on an almost unearthly, paste-white coloration. I had a suspicion that he had done this to himself, taken an overdose of Tylenol to end his life on purpose. He had threatened suicide often enough, and knew that nothing is surer than thirty tablets that go directly to the liver, turning it into a sieve. I had intended to ask him if that was what had occurred, but he told me immediately that he had just gotten up in the night to go to the bathroom where "it felt like I dropped a load and left my life behind." This wasn't a man who had planned his own death, but one terrified at the physical dissolution that had begun six hours before at three o'clock in the morning. "What is going on?" he asked, and calmly, gently, I told him.

"You're bleeding internally," I said. "Nobody is sure why. Maybe it is your liver. Maybe it is from an ulcer or something else." He said that in June he had complained of stomach pains, but Pangless had said they were probably not important and told him to ignore them. "Whatever the cause, you have to make some choices, and if you can't, they'll be left to me. If nothing is done, you'll die later today. If you refuse all surgery or help, it will end. Do you understand that?" I asked. He said yes, he wasn't afraid of dying and had told the doctors he did not want either intrusive surgery or intensive care. I asked again if he understood that without treatment he would die, and he again said, yes, he did. Then I said he could have an endoscopy, which meant that a tube carrying a camera and other tools would be inserted into his abdomen through the throat. With it the doctors could try and find the trouble and, perhaps, then fix it. The chances were not great, I finished, but they were all he had.

Father said he always had hated the idea of a tube stuck down his throat but that, "well, perhaps I should give it a try." Here was the chance he supposedly had longed for—a guaranteed quick and virtually painless death. Here, too, was a procedure that symbolized the intrusions he detested. And yet here was Norman Koch, considering it as if it was a stock investment and he had all the time in the world.

"Look, Pop," I said. "If you want to die, just tell me you don't want any more blood transfusions, and that will be the end."

He thought a minute and said he didn't want the endoscopy but, since he was in the hospital anyway, figured he might as well have the blood. Then I said that without an endoscopy the blood would just pass through his system and the transfusions would do no good. This was a package deal, and the choice between certain death or a little more life was his.

No more, no more, my mind screamed silently at his. In retrospect I see that my mistake was in believing he did not want to live, in still not understanding that what he really wanted was merely the clock turned back to an age where health could be taken for granted. He sought not release from life but a return to the world of health once reflected each day in his bathroom mirror, the old one of strength, choice, purpose, and hope. Failing that and given even one small potential for any future, he wanted to go on, and I was probably a fool to think he would do anything but accept the risk. What he finally said was that since he was already in the hospital, he figured he might as well give the endoscopy a shot. That was his decision. "Tell them," he ordered, "and then let me rest. I'm really very tired."

The physicians smiled with relief when I carried Norm's decision to them. It would be a while before he was stable enough to begin, they said, and in the interim, we could visit with him. I excused myself and went back to his room to tell Norm they would continue with the transfusions and do the endoscopy later that day. Father asked for Aunt Janice, and I brought her in so he could tell us both that he was not afraid to die. The only thing he would regret was leaving his boys behind, Father insisted tearfully. He also wanted us to know that he had a clear conscience, having lived life as he saw fit.

Aunt Janice was crying and at a loss for words. She held his hand for a moment and then, for want of other words, said, "Norm, I just want you to know what a wonderful boy your Tommy is."

Dad looked at her and shook his head. "You don't like my other sons, but, you see, you just don't know them as well as Tom." Then he asked for a cigarette because if he was going to die, he said, "I might as well go out smoking." I told him nicotine could cause the bleeding to start again, but caught up as he was in the bravado of the moment, Father said he didn't care. He was facing death with a smile, with courage, and ever since the movies of his adolescent years, those moments had called for a smoke.

For all of us there was, I think, an unreality to that day, a surreal sense of mediocre theater, of set pieces badly written and incompetently acted many times before. For Janice and me it was a moment dreaded yet expected, discussed and anticipated since the previous year, but Norm's bravado—"I might as well go out smoking"—came as something of a surprise to me. Maybe it was a denial of his own mortality, or, perhaps, simply a failure of imagination. Proust's lines came to mind: "No doubt the discovery that they have grown old causes less sadness to many people than it did to me. But in the first place old age, in this respect, is like death. Some men confront them both with indifference, not because they have more courage than others but because they have less imagination."

I went to the lounge with Aunt Janice while nurses bustled through Norm's hospital room. A friend in the volunteers' office sent up coffee and a deck of cards for our use. My aunt and I passed the day playing gin rummy and sitting in silence while holding hands. Several times I tried to get her to go home, and each time she refused. There was nothing either of us could do at that point, but Aunt Janice said she wouldn't leave me alone and, for my part, I couldn't leave her brother. I told her exactly what Father had said, and she shook her head in despair. "After all that talk of suicide since your mother died, all his stuff about loneliness, he throws away his chance like this," she laughed. "He finally gets his heart's desire, and then decides against it. Typical Norm, he's always been like this. Ever since he was a boy."

She spoke sometimes of their distant youth, hers and Norm's. It was as if her deafness had made our conversation her soliloquy, and despite my presence and Norm's proximity, she spoke exclusively about their mutual past, sorting through memories as she shuffled and reshuffled that old, tattered deck of cards. I think she was choosing which pieces of their history to keep. Norm, she said, had been their mother's pet, while she had been the family's bane. He was the first born heir, good in school and athletics, while she had been a tomboy in the days when Shirley Temple reigned. Their mother had wanted her in ladylike attire, but my aunt had loved sports and sporting clothes. Their parents and friends had lauded Norm's athletics, while her talents were derided or ignored. "Do you know why I took up golf?" she asked, and when I said no, Aunt Janice explained that no one—including her brother—would play tennis with her in the 1920s when a fast service and good return were not "ladylike" things. "Oh, I worshiped him," she said. "But whenever I asked him to play with me or go somewhere—even to a movie— do you know what he would say? All he ever said was 'Well, Janice, we'll see. Well, Janice, we'll see.' But we never did see, and unless my mother insisted, he never took me with him." Although she spoke across fifty years and two generations, the memories were as raw as yesterday, and his thoughtless arrogance at the age of eighteen something she had never been able to forgive.

I laughed and said "We'll see" had been Father's stock answer in our childhood as well. It stood in the gray area between acceptance and refusal, a convenient way to promise potential but commit himself to nothing. His other stock phrase, I remembered, was "You're coming along." If I built a model, worked at basketball, practiced my penmanship or showed off a school painting, I was, in Norm's words, "coming along." Where I sought praise, he offered the same conditional approval promised to customers worried about the warranty on a sofa at his store. "Well, it will stand up to hard use,"

Norm would say, "but remember it's a sofa and not a football field."
It occurred to me then that he had done it again that morning. He
had said "perhaps" when faced with his death and "We'll see" to the
blood and endoscopy. That was what Aunt Janice had meant when
she said his decision had been "typical Norm."

Finally it was time for the endoscopy, and I helped load Father
onto a transport cart and wheel him to the operating room. There
had been further bleeding in the morning, and it was afternoon before
both he and the hospital staff were ready. We snaked through narrow
corridors into the oldest part of the hospital to an ancient room in
which nothing but curtains separated one patient's gurney table from
another's. There they anesthetized his throat and inserted the tube
into his stomach, and as they worked, Father gestured for me, and
I was brought to stand beside a doctor so I could grasp Norm's cold,
cold hand. "We'll see," I whispered to him. "We'll see." It didn't
take long to find the bleeder. A doctor passed the viewer's eyepiece
to me, and I could see the duodenal ulcer, a V shape in the organ's
wall, and behind it, a small vein whose exterior had been corroded
by the gastric juices spilled out in frustration over months by Father's
body. "Just one?" I asked, and the resident said no, there was another,
smaller point nearby. As he worked, isolating the problems, he used
a cauterizing tool to staunch the bleeding points and, he hoped, seal
the hole through which the night before my father's life had poured.
The physician worked swiftly and with practiced ease, an artist freed
of the planning stages and deep within his craft.

Soon Father was back in his room with orders not to eat anything
for a while and not to smoke at all. One of the many effects of
tobacco is the raising of blood pressure. This could, for Father, put
more pressure on the wound, which sat like a bicycle tire freshly
patched, unable to hold back the volume of air an impatient cyclist
immediately wants to pump in. The physicians said that if the tech-
nique held for a day or two, Father's body would begin to mend.
"We'll have them call you if anything changes. There's nothing more
to do." A floor nurse gently insisted I go home. Throughout the
day she had been attentive to both Aunt Janice and me; she was the
one, as existed on every floor, whose perceptions and feeling go past
the patient to those who sit and wait for news. I thanked her and
told Father I was leaving for the day but would return the next
morning. "Cigarette," he ordered through his bruised, sore throat.

"I'm not afraid to die." "The hell you're not," I said and took his pack away.

Then I drove to Aunt Janice's. She had left the hospital an hour earlier to buy some food because "we still have to eat, you know." Neither of us felt like it, I'm sure, until we sat at her table, but then I discovered I was ravenous. It was a strange affair. Sitting at the kitchen table, Aunt Janice spoke in her monotonous, deaf voice as I shouted at the top of my lungs, intent on giving such volume that even she would be able to hear. Occasionally she asked me to speak up. Both of us expected the hospital to call at any moment and say that Father had died. As we talked about what to do, Aunt Janice suggested I call Paula Debillio, Norm's nurse the previous year, and ask if she would help. When she had retired that spring, Paula had told Father that should the need arise, she would return to work for him. I called her and explained the problem, and she promised to be at the hospital the next morning. Then she rang off to arrange for an overnight, private nurse to make my father comfortable.

I went home and called my brothers and brought each of them up to date. If the endoscopy held, Father had a chance, I explained to them one by one. If it failed, they could try again but the chances of a second procedure working would be significantly less. Walter, whom I talked to first, was furious when I related how Norm had decided to have the procedure and my impatience with that choice. He was angry not with Norm but with me and my statement that if the choice had been mine to make, I'd have allowed Father to die quietly. "You don't make that choice for him," Walter ordered. "Or for us. Our father must be given every chance." He insisted that major decisions regarding Norm's life were "communal"—something to be discussed and debated among his four sons. When I protested that there had not been time enough to reach and brief all three brothers, Walter cut me off. "You make time," he shouted. "You don't choose alone for our father. Period." But there had not been time, and they had been long absent. Mark had not seen his father in years, and neither Brian nor Walt had visited in months. They had not seen the evidence of his decline, the dusty icons of Norm's bureau shrine, and to me their distance meant they had abdicated the right to help decide his fate. But I did not debate the issue with Walter that night, and when I talked to Brian and Mark, told them only that Father's condition was critical and he might not last the week. Both asked if they should fly back to Buffalo, and I said simply that it was up to them where they chose to wait. There was nothing more anyone could do. Brian had planned to take his children on holiday that week and asked if he should cancel his plans. "Hang on," I replied. "Wait a day or two and see if he makes it through." Privately, I hoped they would stay away. I did not want to make decisions about Father's care "communally" with brothers who had been so long from the reality of our father's life and my own life.

The next day it all began again. I was at the hospital by 8:30 in the morning to find Paula already in full swing. While cleaning Norm and the blood-spattered room, she told me that a few hours before he had begun to bleed again. He dozed throughout and seemed too weak to hear. My aunt arrived soon after me, and periodically Paula would stop everything to shout a word of comfort or encouragement into Janice's ear. I watched in admiration as Paula worked. It seemed as if at any one moment she was engaged simultaneously in fifteen separate tasks. Three intravenous lines were slung and set flowing into Father's arms while she chatted with me, bathed my father, and tried to clean his room. When he would wake from his doze, she would hold his hand, and as he slept she conferred with the physicians, who popped in and then left on a regular basis. A resident tried to tell Paula what to do, and she lifted one eye from her patient to ask how long the lady had been a medical student. "I'm a doctor," the woman said angrily, puffing up to display the ID badge pinned to her breast pocket. "Oh, you've made it to resident, have you?" Paula asked sweetly. "That's great. Now please, Doctor, get out of my way." Other, older staff members knew better. They stood to the side as she worked, waiting for the bleeding to stop long enough for another attempt at the procedure.

The doctors again asked what I wanted to do, and after they left the room, Paula woke Father and listened as I explained to him that he had the same choices as the day before. I wanted a witness should he decide to die and Walter demand proof that it was not my choice for Norm. I told him that it was even chancier now and if he did nothing, that painless death—"what you've always wanted"—would come within twelve hours. While I was in the room he passed more blood. His hands were weak and frigid. Again he decided to have the tube inserted because, in his words, "I'm here anyway." Paula nodded to me, letting me know that the decision was his and that I should tell the doctors. But before I could leave he lifted his hand to call me closer and asked if I remembered, the day before, when Janice had waited for him to say something kind. Yes, I said, I remembered. A grotesque smile appeared on his face. "I couldn't resist giving her a little jab," he said, "a nasty to remember me by."

That day he was too weak to be moved, so orderlies wheeled the equipment into his room. Just before the procedure began, at the moment when doctors ordered me away, Father called me over and said, "Please, tell Mark I love him." Then Aunt Janice and I again played cards in the ninth-floor lounge, saying little to each other. By early afternoon it was finished, and Father was again in officially critical but stable condition. Paula arranged for around-the-clock private nursing. Everyone believed he would die that night and that the endoscopy, having already failed once, would not hold this time. A resident came to ask Norm what he wanted for dinner and Father said coffee, ice cream, cookies, and jello would be nice. Before the young doctor could leave I said that the day before Father had fasted for hours after his endoscopy. "Isn't a meal dangerous now?" I asked. The resident said his orders were simply to make the patient comfortable while we waited for Norm to die. "After all this?" I asked, and told him Norm was to be given nothing but a bit of broth. The resident looked as if he was about to object but then shrugged and said it was up to me. When Paula's relief came on I told her what had happened, and she said she understood.

That night I went straight home. Both Aunt Janice and I were exhausted beyond care, and each of us needed to spend time alone. In a daze I brought each of my brothers up to date. Walt said our Father wouldn't die, that "the old kraut has sturdy peasant blood and is stronger than anybody knows." To him the idea of Norm's demise at that point was simply inconceivable. Brian, who was Norm's executor, began to make funeral plans. He told me to keep receipts for all my expenses and that he was planning to rent a large car for Norm's funeral. Visitors would be coming to town to "sit Shiva," he predicted and the car was so they could be greeted at the airport in style. Shiva is a traditional, Jewish mourning practice which neither of my parents had ever followed and I wondered why anyone who had known them would think such a ritual necessary. I told Brian that Norm didn't have many friends left who would fly into

Buffalo except, perhaps, our aunt and uncle from New York; that Norm had always insisted there was to be no memorial service; and, most importantly, that father wasn't dead yet, not yet. As we talked, the idea of turning over control of father's life or death to Brian—or anyone else—made me violently ill. Hanging up quickly, I smelled the blood and bowel of that day and convulsed in dry heaves, but not solely because of the memory. I retched because I could see my brothers—after all had been cleansed—coming to preside over a religious funeral for this most agnostic of men. It was a strong, overpowering image, and after it passed I paused weakly at my father's bureau, fingers pressed to the dust where so recently his had rested. I stood, as he had, before a photograph in which my mother still smiled as she had on the day it was taken eighteen years before. Beside her but in a separate frame stood Mark and I dressed in cowboy hats and shorts. It was as if she were smiling through time's frames—photograph to photograph to now—knowing as a private joke what all our futures would hold.

The moment passed, and I called Mark. That day he had done nothing but debate returning to Buffalo, he told me, considering his father's life and death while at a continent's remove. When I gave him Father's message, the "I love you" entrusted to me like a deathbed promise, Mark began to cry. Like Brian, Mark again asked if he should return, and I told him it was not my choice to make. If he arrived the next morning, Norm might still be alive, I said, or he could already be dead. He talked about his memories of Father. Mark finally put off any decision for a day, needing time to search his heart, while hoping Father would pull through. Maybe this is always the way. Those who are most at distance, whose lives have left too much unresolved, will always take geriatric declines and death the hardest. While there is life there is at least the potential for resolution, but death—of sentience, mobility, or life itself—tells a claimant that time has passed, that the chance for changes has been lost forever.

My last call that night was to our Aunt Agatha in New York City. She was my mother's sister and, I thought, a friend of my father's as well. But on the telephone she said it would be hard for her to mourn Norm's passing. For twenty minutes she recounted a litany stretching back almost forty years of mean and petty things he supposedly had done to her. In coming days other old friends would recite to me their old grievances and petty stories nurtured across a lifetime's mutual association. None of these tales recounted major transgressions. Rather, Agatha, like Janice and the others, talked of minor, thoughtless acts such as we all commit: small favors he had denied but could have granted, kindnesses done for him that he never acknowledged, and sins of omission when one day something had slipped his mind. All of these joined Aunt Janice's memories and became an indictment, a stream of abuse that while damning, I decided later, was a distancing mechanism as well.

Faced with the prospect of another's imminent demise, people seek to remember the worst things possible, to convince themselves that this piece of their life and time was not so valuable after all. Remembering the worst ensures that these are memories that can be done without and that at the moment of grief a barrier of anger and resentment will rise up as a buffer for the pain. I came to realize that the litany of petty grievances leveled at my father was based in part on each accuser's fear that his illness underscored the potential for their own individual deaths. While he was an invalid, he could be ignored, his status as more than memory something most people had put on hold. Aunt Agatha, for example, had not visited him the previous fall but had called periodically to say hello. Norm's Buffalo circle—so present the previous autumn—had become more distant by the spring; Walter, who had visited the August and December following Norm's operation, now waited for my calls. At the beginning, his social world had presumed he would return quickly and naturally to their lives. But in those months of long convalescence, his status had edged towards that of memory, and now, when an end seemed imminent, his world pulled away as if afraid of a contagion that might affect it as well.

Temporary illness everyone understood. Norm as invalid, signifier of infirm age, was isolated from the daily routine of Buffalo lives but not recast in the communal history of those with whom he had spent his life. Now, hovering on the edge of mortality, he was signal to the dissolution we all sometime would face, and that was an insupportable insult to those like my aunts, who chose the worst memories to assuage not incipient grief but immediate and personal fears. For his friends, his contemporaries, he was the overture of their impending personal doom, a signal of the frailty of their own failing constitutions. His travails—the illness, loneliness, fear, and anger—all were rhythm to the slow dirge that others knew played in the elderly bodies each of them inhabited.

Walt denied as an article of faith the possibility that his father would not survive. Bri framed his fears for his father's life in the regime of rites that accompany death. Mark was caught between his memories and his love, unable to choose, but he, like his brothers, found it hard to take the parent of memory and translate him into this geriatric shell. Those who had known my father for decades as an equal had to take a different tack. By cataloguing my father's sins, they made of his illness a retribution. It was thus not age and happenstance, but a religious judgment that caused the failure of Norm's flesh, and that judgment was a barrier between his condition and their own perhaps fragile physical states. He was isolated from them, these golden oldsters, by the very elements of mutual history that once had entwined their lives. Had he suffered from syphilis, a common disease of their shared youths, each could have insisted that "he deserved it for sleeping with whores." Were he dying of lung cancer, all could have said "that's what comes from fifty years of cigarettes." But his disease had no clear, moral factor, so each had to find in shared history an explanation and distancing cause.

That night I slept next to the telephone, and on Sunday morning rushed to father's room to be greeted by Paula and Aunt Janice. Norm was alive, Paula said with a smile. Still bleeding some and terribly weak, but "the old kraut," as Walter called him, had made it through the night. Paula was pleased with the hospital physicians who had taken on the case and delighted that Pangless, whom she did not admire, had been so little present. All that could be done, she said, was to nurse him carefully and wait to see if the endoscopy's cauterizing patch placed the day before would hold. I held Father's hand while he muttered incoherently, apparently unaware of my presence. Paula said he probably knew I was there but was simply too weak to think or respond. "His body is buying time, but that may be all it is," she warned. "They won't go in again, and after all, he's had over twelve units of blood."

That, Paula said, was a potentially fatal problem in itself. Not only because of the risk of increased infection that it signaled but because at any moment his body might reject the newly transfused blood. Most people, she explained, think that blood is something like engine oil, that if it leaks there is no problem with replacing liters of the fluid again and again. The mistake, she continued, is in thinking of it as anything but a moving, vibrant, circulating organ as unique and imperative to the body as a person's heart or liver. Because it travels so far and does so much, blood is the easiest thing to transplant. Blood is the common denominator of the body's world and is welcome from brain to big toe. Its ubiquity requires a universality whose practical result is that it is far less likely to be rejected than an individual organ would be. But its flexibility, alas, is not infinite. Human blood is a chemistry textbook, a maze of cells, enzymes, and proteins set in conflicting profiles, all of which the recipient's body must recognize and accept. When faced with major transfusions, a donor's blood must be more and more carefully matched, masked ever more accurately to take on the character of that which the body cannot produce on its own. Eventually, the body rejects all substitutes, having learned to recognize that which is not its indelible own, and at that point further transfusions are useless. In his first five days of ulcer crisis, Father received over nineteen units of blood and more of plasma and glucose.

Paula explained all this to Janice and me as the three of us watched Norm sleep. It was as if he were our newborn child and we, the proud parents and their friend, were content to bask in his presence while admiring his ability to breathe. As we waited, Paula also told us that private-duty nurses were needed to assure Father's comfort and prompt attention should the bleeding begin again. The nurses' presence would guarantee that Norm, confused, did not try to get out of bed unaided or wake up in need and alone. Under nurses' care he would not mistake a bleeding episode for a bowel movement or feel it necessary to try and clean up himself. Private nurses would not only assure Father's comfort, but closely supervise the doctors as well and in that role were a precaution against inappropriate medical decisions. If a new doctor reviewed his case, something that happened every day or two, his nurses could assure that improper medications were not given. This, in fact, proved critical when weeks later a doctor decided that Father had Parkinson's disease and prescribed L-dopa for him. Paula immediately called other physicians to get the order rescinded because, she said, the drug would have caused uncontrollable convulsions in her patient.

As we talked I wrote a series of checks to two nurses, Sara Donatello and Bruce Foster, who had joined Paula on the case. Sara, Paula said, covered afternoons, and Bruce was overnight relief. It sounded, I said, like a strange sports team that I had bought and she managed. Some sport, Aunt Janice laughed, with Norm the ball and hoop. If he were awake, she added, the game would be over, because knowing his round-the-clock care was costing three hundred dollars a day surely would kill her brother. No, I said, not at all. The checks were from my personal account against hopes of eventual repayment. "That reminds me," Paula said to my aunt. "Do you know what Norm said to me when I came in yesterday?" Janice replied, "I'll bet he said he couldn't pay," and the nurse nodded, smiling. "You know your brother," she admitted. "He took my hand and said 'Paula, how good to see you. I wish I could afford to pay you because it would sure be nice to have you around.'"

Janice shook her head in exasperation while smoothing Norm's thin, fine hair in an unconscious gesture of affection. She would have stopped immediately had she known how maternal and loving it looked. "When I used to eat at Sue and Norm's on a Friday night he would make a point of telling me that while it might seem like there was a lot of food, any leftovers would be for Saturday's meals." Janice paused to see if we understood, and when Paula gave her a questioning look, my aunt sighed into her punch line: "That was so I wouldn't eat too much." Paula chuckled and told us that when she first cared for Father after his prostate operation in 1978, any food left over, no matter how little—a bit of salad, a few uneaten string beans—was to be saved in the refrigerator for use the next day. Then she, too, smoothed Norm's brow and talked to him as if he were a young and tired child. "That's what you did, sweetie, isn't it? Kind of stingy with the leftovers, I guess." At that I excused myself and went home. In the evening I talked to Brian who, with his children, had driven to Disneyland. He believed it was important to "carry on" as if nothing had happened and yet to be ready, should Father die, to rapidly return to Buffalo. When asked, he told me our father had never been cheap or tight but a generous, warmhearted man. Mark and I talked after that, and in the coming days I was to call each brother frequently to let him know if Father endured or if his death had finally come.

For several days Father remained in serious condition, bleeding daily but less each day as, incredibly, the endoscopy that no one had believed in worked a modern miracle. Too weak to move, he slept around the clock under the constant watch of his nurses, who kept a urinal first beside the bed and then almost permanently positioned between his legs because Father had lost all bladder control. In those moments when he was conscious, this incontinence seemed to embarrass him. It was hard to tell, because even when awake, he was virtually unable to speak, and when he tried, spoke in attenuated, broken sentences as if a knowledge of grammar and sentence structure had flowed away with his blood. He could not lift his head or stand, even with a nurse's assistance. If he had been saved for this, I thought, it was no salvation after all.

A new group of doctors headed by Dr. Fine came on the case at this time. Pangless was the physician of record, but it was the new team that now took charge of my father's life. The head of gastroenterology, Fine called in a squad of specialists to oversee Father's rehabilitation, worry about his incontinence, and generally fuss over his health. Fine genuinely liked Norm, I think, and visited us with frequency. The gastric bleed bothered him because he did not know its cause. I told him about Father's auto accident, and Fine said yes, perhaps that had contributed to Norm's condition, but how much, he asked, had the patient drunk, was he, ahem, a heavy consumer of alcohol?

The answer was complex. Since the hepatitis of the previous autumn, Norm had been on the wagon, but before that had enjoyed a few martinis a day for decades, and in his youth, much more. My parents had told us all of the prohibition days when drinking illegal gin was a virtuous, political act in which both of them excelled. "We almost drowned your oldest brother once," my mother loved to say, "when Hirsh came to visit us and we tried to give Walt a bath." During all our years of growing up, my father's return home from work would signal the "cocktail hour." Both parents always said they would have only one, but on most days both drank more. "I never really liked martinis before I met your mother," Norm would periodically explain to us.

"But her father was a martini man, and I drank them to be sociable." After a varicose vein operation she had when we were small, my mother was told by her doctor to have a drink a day as "an aid to circulation." From then on my father's nightly martinis were, he would say, "so Sue won't have to drink alone." These were polite but useful fictions that nobody really believed, not even Norm himself. My mother put it succinctly when she said he needed a drink after work. "And so would you," she said one day to my righteous adolescence, "if you spent six days a week in retail." But for a puritan like my father, the fiction was crucial. He could not admit to the enjoyment of it all, and less, of course, to the necessity of a tranquilizing moment.

Thus he was a "social drinker," rarely over the line ("I never drink during the day, of course") but rarely without a drink for more than twenty-four hours. Like others who use alcohol to relax, it was also his secret defense in times of distress, and then he would drink in excess.

I gave Dr. Fine the general picture but spared him the family details. He did not care why one drank, he simply wanted to know the quantities. Norm's alcohol history may have contributed to the recent bleed, he said. Even my father's "social drinking" could have caused some long-term, permanent liver damage that had made the hepatitis worse and this bleed inevitable. I didn't believe it then and suspect the explanation now. Not because my father did not drink too much, but because it shifted the blame for this illness entirely to his past. Alcohol did not invite the hepatitis, a bad transfusion did. Lack of home-care instructions had kept Norm exercising valiantly throughout the fall, thus assuring he would require hospital admission again as his therapy contributed to the disease's strength. I blamed bad luck and bad care, while even the most understanding of his physicians found a way to blame the patient himself.

Fine said he deeply regretted having been away when Father's internal bleeding started. If we had given surgery a chance, he continued, Norm's chances would have been better, and he deserved every chance he could get because "your father has a lot of good miles left on him." He isn't some damn car, I replied wearily, although that was precisely how he was treated. Like any mechanic faced with a machine that just won't run, doctors looked for some specific ill that could be repaired—bore out the carburetor, replace the clutch—so he could be returned to the road again. But with automobiles one doesn't worry about will, while its absence, the lack of any emotional conviction, was becoming a pressing problem in Norm's care. That intransigent core that in the past had pulled Norm through seemed now to desert him as he sank into unresponsive lassitude. Nobody knew if this was a result of medication, an aftereffect of his gastric bleed, or something more fundamental. Paula and I would try to force Father to at least attempt some exercise, but he refused us every time. When we placed him in a chair, his head would droop like a newborn child's, and like a baby, he would cry in frustration at that weakness. Once he had spoken with care and ease, but now Norm repeated his *b*'s and *d*'s, imitating a child's hard stutter. There was no medical reason—outside of general weakness—for his incontinence, but it continued nevertheless. Several times Paula and I tried to dress him properly, but each time he grabbed at his hospital gown and said "No. Leave me alone." Paula shaved and cleaned him, and in this—as in most things—he acquiesced. At the least excitement, his hands would shake and he would begin to cry, turning away from company to sob into his pillow.

Severely astigmatic, Father had worn glasses for sixty-four years but now refused to put his on. His eyes were usually watery and sometimes unfocused, as if he were crying within himself. Perhaps that wasn't far from the truth, and maybe the glasses did obstruct his view. He lived during those days in halls of memories neglected for years, and each past event mourned with him the indignities of his present. He needed neither bathroom mirror nor photograph as mnemonic, but simply took off his glasses and saw beyond the world's resulting blur those earlier days he now so preferred. Those visions of our past were better company than I, who lived to haul him back to the present's hard realities.

Only the specter of penury could lift him from this passivity. In the weeks after the endoscopy, some strength slowly appeared, and he saved it to tell me that I was squandering his money in many thoughtless ways. His condition became, to Norm, the money I was spending on nurses, the cost of everything from blood to food—anything that could show up on a bill. One day Father told me to bring his checkbook because he wanted to take over his own affairs, which, he informed me, I was bungling again. "You didn't do well last fall and now you're hiring all these nurses who do nothing but sit around." I gave him a check, and when he couldn't even sign his name, tore it up in front of his face and called him a mean-spirited, obnoxious man.

That was when I began to detest him and, simultaneously, to hate myself for being in Buffalo. On the phone that night I told Walter the story and said that if that was how Father felt, perhaps I would bill him myself. If money was the coin in which he counted out his love, that would be the medium through which he could acknowledge my sacrifices. Father's suggestion that I was "bungling again" had hurt, and the excuse of his illness did little to ease the pain. He had become the center of my world, and although I had done my best, Norm had judged it insufficient. I keenly felt the strain of these weeks and began to worry resentfully over my own uncertain future. Rebecca was in Japan waiting for me and I was in Buffalo with Scrooge. Even if he recovered, I asked, what would I have when this period ended but the ungrateful debris of this depleted, miserable man and my own life on permanent hold?

Walter criticized my "mercenary attitude" and, he said, was "astonished" that I would consider such a calculated, callous act. "You're not there for money but for your father," he lectured. "How can you think of such a thing?" Then he called Brian, who almost immediately called me to say that he was equally distressed. It would be a terrible thing for a son to take money for a parent's care, my second oldest brother agreed. When I mentioned in justification the thousands of dollars I had spent for Norm's maintenance while he was too sick to write a check, Brian replied, "Don't worry. You'll eventually get it back." That night I went to bed sick with rage and lay awake for hours. My anger became a fury directed not at Father alone but more clearly at my distant brothers and their claims of parental concern. I thought of him, then, as "my" father and not "ours," because I was the one who cared for his needs while they stayed safely away. I was the one who had given up a year to be with our father in Buffalo, and I was the one who had held his hand while the endoscope was shoved down his throat. Nor were they the ones who over the past month, while enduring his complaints of poverty, had been out of work themselves.

The next day I called Brook Samuelson, the lawyer who had helped after Norm's auto accident, and asked him what I should do. He explained that I needed a power of attorney to give me authority over Father's affairs and, yes, he would be glad to draw one up. No charge. I told him of my brothers' criticism and of the frustration I felt. "You've seen things like this before. Am I doing right?" I asked. Brook said ours was not an uncommon tale, and he'd seen such family battles many times—especially when there was any money involved. I asked him if I was right to want to take charge, if it was wrong to resent my brothers' advice from afar. "You're the one who is here, so you're the one to take charge," he said. "Do what you have to and don't worry about them." Mr. Samuelson, who had known Norm for fifty years, then joined the chorus of family and friends with stories of Father's past petty behavior. Now I welcomed these tales as evidence that Norm was no paragon, but a person deserving of rough treatment.

That afternoon I told Father he was going to give me the power of attorney so I would be able to sign his checks and handle the securities he had nurtured for years. His stocks would be taken from a safe deposit box and put into a brokerage account where dividends could be automatically collected. This, I said, would ensure that his affairs would not "be bungled" but instead managed by competent professionals. I told him I was tired of running to the bank for him, of spending my own money on Buffalo's bills while he was too ill to sign a check. Brook Samuelson would draw up the papers, I declared, as well as a codicil to Father's will naming me executor. It was time, I insisted, to acknowledge the limits of his condition and the facts of long-term illness. Father said he liked the way things were and wanted no changes at all. "It's time we made some changes for my convenience," I replied. He said he liked looking after his own affairs and insisted that things would be better soon. "Look at yourself, old man," I shouted. "You can't eat without help or pee without two nurses and a pail stuck between your legs." I told him his days of independence were over, and disease had taken its irreducible toll.

It took several days before he acceded to my demands. During these days of argument, Father would listen for perhaps fifteen minutes before becoming so upset that he would dissolve into tears and stuttering denial. I wasn't a businessman, he said. He didn't want anyone else knowing his affairs. I said that after months of handling his deposits and withdrawals I already knew enough. Father said he liked going to the bank and I told him that unless a miracle occurred, those days were gone forever. He asked Paula and my aunt for their support, but they told him I was right. Paula said she once had a patient who, angry with her family and their treatment of her, decided to spend her entire savings on personal comfort. The women's assets, all told, were about $100,000, and it had taken three years of home care and nursing before she had spent it all. "Of course, it would have lasted longer if she hadn't taken us to dinner so much. Give Tom what he wants."

Finally Father gave in. "I'll do whatever you say," he sighed. I called Brook and made an appointment for him to visit the hospital when the papers were ready for Norm's signature. That evening I told my brothers what had happened and what I was going to do. Walter told me he didn't want to know, that the events of the past week had so upset him he was backing off from it all. "You're upset?" I asked in wonder. "You've been in Denver." He said the phone calls and the potential of our father's death had been very hard on him. "Jesus," I muttered and said no more. He was still debating a trip to Buffalo caught between the present and his past. The next day Paula said that I should try to get away and that she was planning a long weekend herself. "I've had about as much of him as I can take," she said bluntly, "and I think you're over your limit. Go to Toronto or fly to Raleigh, but get away for four or five days. You need it, and when you get back, we'll have our work cut out for us." Father's condition was stable by then, and death had slipped from an omnipresent threat to one that stood at a distance. Now it was time for the hard, brutal job of trying to rebuild both his will and his strength, to see if he had been saved for anything but enfeebled vegetation.

"Go away and rest," she said to me. "When you return the hard work begins."

That night I wrote Becky and tried to explain my continued presence in Buffalo. In nine, single-spaced pages I poured out my heart and told her of all that had happened. When it was finished, I understood that the physicians' arena of life and death is far simpler than the one in which most nurses work. Once death has been beaten back, a doctor's primary job is ended. It becomes, then, a nursing task to nurture and revive both the human will and the individual spirit that illness often erodes. I tried in the letter to make sense of my brothers and me, of my place in all that had happened. Putting it on paper, dead carbon on wood fiber gave the situation a distance and perspective that living time had not allowed.

This has become a cancer eating away at me. Not only at memories of and affections for my father, but through my whole emotional structure as well. It is metastasizing to alter ties, historical and immediate, to my brothers and my friends. I have taken actions necessary to both the current situation and its future, but in all I have resolved, from here on, to act absolutely alone. It is in many ways a decision of desperation, one made in such cold fury and unrelieved anger that I am not sure I trust myself to decide anything at all. A number of things have led to it and uncovered not only the ugliness of my father but also an ugliness within myself. I would love to leave here forever—today—but self-esteem will not allow me to abandon him to the impersonal discipline of nurses and hospital necessities.

Then I tried to explain what most confused me—my brothers' relations with Norm and with me. How could they be so distant and so certain of what was right? Why should they worry and cry when death was close for an old man they saw only rarely and whose current condition they did not know except at second hand?

Their father is a memory visited once a year, an annual Christmas actor—like Santa Claus—feted for a week a year. Their father is a voice on the phone, and for my three siblings that is all it takes to keep old images alive. All are caught up in a world long gone, a past world of memories when Father was healthy, active, and strong. None wish to live in the present, in this half-life divided between an empty house now long outgrown and a hospital room filled with vials of blood and the smell of sulphured shit. None want to run his errands, but all want to think of themselves as sons and not strangers known long ago. Yet they criticize me and my angers as if I should be grateful for my responsibilities here.

I should charge them for my time, because it has been my presence in Buffalo which has given the other three their liberty. They can continue lives, family, and business while I'm caught between the cracks with a cranky old man whose chief concern is not spending the money he's saved. In a real way their father is no longer mine. Their father is a composite of past memories dressed up for the yearly, personal visit, and mine is a hospital charge, a patient who cannot sign his name or do anything but lament. There is the difference, in a nutshell.

What this says about us, and me, I have not begun to consider, let alone understand.

As I read the letter over, it occurred to me that lost in all this was my father himself. He was the reagent around which we changed, the gravity that held our histories together. During this period Norm seemed a thing of time steeped in its own history, a patient whose emotional needs were seen not as human entitlements but merely as an inconvenience. Only later did it become clear that Norm still led us in this dance and that as he sank into memories and fear, we followed the pace that he set. Sons and sister, lawyer and friends: all dredged up from their communal past shards of shared experience. Like Norm, we scoured our histories in an attempt to put this human puzzle—parent/brother/father/businessman/friend—into a perspective that would make sense not simply of his life but of our own as well. Unable by reason of infirmity to take over the acts that in his mind gave order to the world, he was engaged in a parallel hunt through a private past we could neither participate in or understand. His care became our search for his essential self and, on Norm's part, a scrambling attempt to find a mask to fit his shifting, ailing soul.

"Identity has a paradoxical existence," Norman N. Holland once wrote in an essay called "Not So Little Hans." "It is an agency, as it were, acting from the self out into the world. It is a consequence, the culminating return from these actions. But it is also a representation, my representation of someone's identity, even my own." So it was with us and with Norm. He was part of our identity, and so as he changed, we who knew him were transformed as well. Each of us felt the pressure as an isobar throughout the complex of historical associations and interpersonal histories that had bound us together in time. Father, for his part, had lost sight of his own identity and searched in his past through a gallery of Norms, none of whom were applicable to his new present. Nothing had prepared him for this, and without his glasses, he viewed an empty mirror and stood speechless before the world.

None of this was clear at that time; understanding came slowly to me over the months and years. My letter to Rebecca was mailed ("when are you coming?" her last letter had asked), and I packed a travel bag. The next night I was in Raleigh, North Carolina, visiting with friends. As the plane left Buffalo, I ordered a drink and felt my body relax. When I returned, however, it tensed up again as the plane made its final approach. My jaw clamped upon the back molars and both shoulders began to rise. Anger and tension had become a natural reaction, as much a part of my local geography as the Great Lakes and the December storms.

After a week away I returned to the house and called Father's room immediately. Paula was on a two-day break, and a male nurse, Tim Barber, answered instead. When I asked for my father he responded, like a butler, "Mr. Koch is indisposed. Who shall I say is calling?" This is his son, I replied, asking how busy could a man be who can't walk five feet alone. "He's having a bowel movement," the nurse said, and I laughed, promising to call back in five minutes. "How's my father doing?" I asked, and Tim replied that things were rather busy and he didn't have time to chat. A half hour later I telephoned again, and Father was given the phone. He was as pleased with himself as a three-year-old who has successfully used the potty. "Boy, it was big," he enthused, explaining his earlier absence. "I couldn't have taken a call from God when that was coming through." His voice sounded alcoholic, and his former sense of propriety had been metamorphosed into something like childish, unselfconscious pride. I asked if he liked Sara, the swing-shift nurse, and he said she was "a frizzle-frazzle." I had no idea what that meant.

Then I called Dr. Pangless, who said no new procedures were planned because they wanted to "build Norm up," which meant he did not know why Father was not stronger and had no idea what to do. Pangless said he had sent a referral to General's social services department, the first step in the process that would result in my father's eventual discharge. He suggested I give them a call, and, not wanting Father on my hands, I telephoned them immediately. A caseworker said someone would get back to me after interviewing the patient but warned that because of a departmental backlog, it would not happen for at least several days. "Take your time," I said. "I'm in no hurry to have him back."

That afternoon I talked with Dr. Fine, who now believed Father's ulcer might have been bleeding sporadically for a year. That, he said, would certainly explain the blackout in June and perhaps in part the hepatic recurrences of the fall, which drained Norm's strength and resistance when he needed them most. Father's stomach pains in June were merely the final warning signal, which, unattended to, had exploded in midsummer. Fine believed the endoscopy had solved that problem, that Norm's continued lack of strength and will were now the crucial issue. "The most important thing is to get moving, to use your muscles." he told Father each day. "You have to work on standing, getting some weight on those bones." The muscles would atrophy without exercise, and if that happened, Norm would never walk again. I told Dr. Fine about the financial battle, and he urged me to take charge of it all. "Maybe he'll get mad enough to want to get better himself," he shrugged.

The knowledge that Social Services had been called added an element of urgency that could not be denied. Although both Pangless and Fine promised that Father "wouldn't be put out on the street," hospital policy was to discharge patients as rapidly as safely possible, and despite the physicians' promise of a full recovery, Father was fit for nothing at this time but intensive care at a nursing home. He could not eat without assistance and lacked not only mobility but bladder control. His speech still degenerated rapidly into an incoherent stutter when he could be roused to talk at all. Could he be brought to the point where home care became a possibility, or, failing that, would he become strong enough for a halfway house whose rehabilitation unit could finish the hospital's job?

Doctors had told the nursing staff to make Father stand during each shift, but usually he refused, so each day they bodily lifted him from bed to chair, berating his weakness while they worked. "Keep your head up," Paula would shout as Father sat drooping and exhausted in the chair he had ordered as a volunteer purchasing agent five years before. He hated the dependence even while courting it. "You don't know how humiliating it is to be picked up like a sack of potatoes," he cried the day I got back. I told him if that was true, he should try walking on his own. "I'm doing my best," he whined. "You don't know what I go through." But when asked what, in fact, he was going through—what it was that seemed so insurmountable to mind and soul—Norm simply shook his head and turned away to stare inward and away from the world.

Dinners had become a daily battle in which Father would refuse to eat anything but cookies, ice cream, and jello. Paula or Sara, the afternoon nurse, fought to force him to eat an entrée, but each day he would balk because "it doesn't look good." Usually he was too palsied to hold a fork and too weak to use a knife, so when forced to eat chicken or ham, Father would simply grab the food in his hands and cram it into his mouth. One day I brought fresh grapes for his lunch, but Paula took them and his cookies away because Father had refused the grilled cheese sandwich sent up on a hospital tray. "No dinner," she said firmly, "no dessert." He pushed his tray away from his bed, crossed his arms, and cried. He had regressed in time and was enjoying childhood games. When Sara came that afternoon, Paula relented and told my Father he could eat the grapes I'd brought. "The treat wouldn't be fun now," he sulked, and she laughed while smoothing his hair in a loving, maternal gesture. "Grow up, Norm," she said sweetly. "Keep this up and you'll land in a nursing home and not back in your house."

What I needed to know was more about my father, not only the source of his fears but the hallmarks of his strength. Uncle Jules invited me to dinner that night, and as we ate, he talked about their teenage years, when my father had been a hero. "My father?" I asked in surprise. "Your father, " said Uncle Jules. Norm had been one of the first Jews to attend Putnam, a prestigious private school in Buffalo, and the first who surmounted its anti-Semitism to become truly popular and accepted. He had dominated the football field and excelled at tennis while compiling an enviable academic record, which took him to the University of Pennsylvania's business school. Uncle Jules said that he and other, younger Buffalo Jews who followed my father through Putnam had looked up to Norm, whose success set a standard that made their own high-school years much easier. "No one ever told me this," I said. "It was a long time ago," Uncle Jules replied. "People tend to forget."

Those who, like my uncle, had known Norm in those days said he had become quieter and more withdrawn after the senior year's football injury. "He could have learned to use his good, left side," his sister Janice had said more than once to me, but that was only half the truth. He could have, but he didn't set the equation in full. With that injury began the pattern I was seeing now, Uncle Jules suggested. It had been the first of a long line of incidents in which a physical crisis would turn Father inward, away from learning new methods and towards some quiet, safer part of his soul. He did not choose to learn to swing a tennis racket with his clumsy, unnatural left side. Better, instead, to give up tennis altogether. Nor did he learn to bowl, become a place kicker, or try a thousand other things. Instead he chose to back away from disability and live life as if a part of his world had not only ended but had never been. That was what he was doing now, and I wanted to find a way to blast him from this expurgated shell. Early patterns become tenacious in maturity, Uncle Jules explained. It gets harder and harder to find new ways. "That's what we mean by age."

The next day Brook Samuelson came to the hospital, and Father put on a show. His voice was no louder than a whisper and his speech so slurred as to be unintelligible. Brook explained the power of attorney, Father asked if it dealt with his wife's estate, and Brook said no, it was something else. "Stop it, Norm," Paula commanded. "You have worried over this long enough and know it's for the best. Now do it and don't play games!" At that Father shrugged and said that he would sign. On each page of the power of attorney he had to initial a clause denying my right to control military payments should Father decide to join the army. "I might want to, though," he protested. "If you could see my bills, you'd understand why I want some of the money the government's handing out." "If you could sign up," Samuelson replied, "Tom wouldn't need this done." Then we worked through the codicil to his will that made me Norm's executor. As we left the room, Brook, who had not seen Norm in almost a year, stopped to wipe his brow, shaking his head at the changes illness and infirmity had wrought. "You think this is bad," I said. "He's 100 percent improved."

I walked him to the hospital elevator and then returned to my father's room, where he lay, glasses off, with the sheet pulled over his head. Paula left on a coffee break, and when we were alone, I pulled the sheet away to find Norm staring at me with wet eyes in which the iris almost had disappeared, leaving pupils expanded to fill the void.

"You've got all my money now," he said distinctly and with bitterness. "So spend it and enjoy it." He closed his eyes then, as if to make me disappear, but I grabbed Father by his hospital gown and shook him so violently that his slack jaw rattled, lower molars against an upper bridge inserted years before.

"One more time, old man," I hissed. "I don't want your money. I'd like to be free of you, but I'm not. There's nothing in this for me." I felt him shaking and saw his head bounce against the pillow again and again. Then I let him go as if he were a hot stove I'd leaned on by mistake. "If you're so certain I'm robbing you, then show some balls and get better on your own." Every few words I would interrupt myself to ask "Are you listening?" and to order him to "look, look at me." When he tried to turn away, I'd push his head back into the pillow, pinning him so our eyes could meet. My hand pushed roughly against his jaw and my thumb caressed his throat.

Finally angry, he said in a clear voice that he could hear me perfectly. "I'm not deaf like my sister, you know." Then he asked why I had allowed the endoscopy, why I had forced him to live. I told him I'd gladly have refused the doctors and seen an end to both our trials but that he, he, he, he, not I, had made the choice. No, Father insisted, it wasn't true. This was something done to him and not carried out at his command. "You decided to live, old man. It was you who wanted it all, and now you're going to live, so make up your mind on that." He had no memory of it all, the crisis had slipped through him with the bloody stool and left my father barren of the dignity active choice should bring. Then I rushed from the room and saw Sara coming towards us in the hall. "Paula said you were with your father, and I didn't want to intrude." I told her that we were arguing and that at least he was awake, and she said that anything besides apathy was, in Norm's case, good.

I went to the cafeteria for a cup of coffee, and while it slowly cooled, my anger steeped and transformed itself into revulsion. If Aldous Huxley is right and "experience is not what happens to a man: it is what a man does with what happens to him," then neither Norm or I had lived this time at all. He had denied his own choices, lost life's affirmation along with the blood, and now blamed me for a hobbled, fragile continuance. His passive resistance in the face of disability had changed our triumph into a mistaken act, and it was that transformation that tripped me over the edge of rage. So I had taken the whole and danced it to the lip of a fury so real it almost blotted out our past, while pulling me into my own, personal abyss where violence stood as appropriate response to the changes of the world. Then I returned to my father's room, where he lay as I had left him—turned away and staring with sightless eyes at the wall.

As I entered, Sara left us alone again but said she'd "just be down the hall." Although a part of me knew she could not have seen my fingers locked on her patient's throat, her words were a cold, damp caution. I sat next to the bed and took Norm's hand and asked what he was so afraid of. Why wouldn't he help us bring him back towards health? "Don't you trust me, Pops?" I asked, and he said "I trust you, I really do." Then I asked again what he was afraid of, why he would not even try to walk. "They'll drop me," he replied, and I asked who. He said, "The women, of course." When asked what women, he responded as if it were obvious and said simply, "Them." When asked if Paula was one of "them" he said no, she at least was his friend. "You don't know," he continued, "how demeaning it is to be lifted up and down like a sack of potatoes." I told him that if he ate more and practiced walking and sitting by himself no one would have to carry him again. "I want it to be like before," Norm continued, "when I could do myself." That was his polestar, the one fixed hope in a universe that had spiraled so out of control and into chaos that childhood terrors and immediate memory stood simultaneously before the present. Then I promised—"Scout's honor, Norm"—that nobody would let him fall. It can be like before, I lied, everything can be better again. But first, I said, he had to help me by doing what he was told. Father said he would, he would, that he was sorry he had made me angry and now promised to be a "good boy" again. Then he fell asleep as I stroked his hair, a calming gesture his father perhaps had used in Norm's childhood two lifetimes ago.

Sara was standing at the door as I quietly stood away from the bed. I told her Norm was afraid of falling and that was why he refused to walk. Maybe he had been dropped as a child, or perhaps it had been some game adults played years before—tossing him in the air and threatening not to catch him—when the joking threat had been trauma enough for the Norm child to hold forever. It was as if his history were a mirror that had been shattered, and on the floor each memory lay out of order and against another, like a jigsaw puzzle for God to put together. "Are you all right?" Sara asked of me, and I said sure, just tired. But I wasn't. I was still scared at the violence I'd felt the hour before when, while holding Norm's head against the pillow, I'd desperately wanted to bash it against the wall.

Two days later the papers were filed, and in the eyes of the court, I was Father's "attorney of fact." I called his stockbroker to give him the news and arranged to set up a house account. Then I walked four blocks to the neighborhood bank branch that my father had used for years, deposited the power of attorney there, and was let into the vault. I filled four sheets of legal paper with company names before returning to the hospital that day. The next day I was back again to do the second box. Norm was not financially poor, but secretly rich. There were in all twenty-nine bonds worth about $5,000 each: school, sewer, and utility bonds he had gathered through the years. There were stock certificates as well, each representing shares in one of more than thirty different companies, almost all purchased in dribbles of five, twelve, or twenty shares. For each corporation there were up to fifteen certificates totalling two or three hundred shares per company and sometimes another for an equal amount representing a stock dividend or split. The financial value of it all was over $600,000, but I was less awed by the full amount than I was puzzled by the method. How strange, I thought. Why had he purchased so much in small, odd lots that, he had always told me, were more expensive than 100-share blocks?

I took the list home and studied it that evening until I broke its code. What he had done made little sense if the dates of his, say, Amoco (800 shares) purchases were looked at as a history separate from Norm's own. But it made perfect sense if one looked instead at the dates of all Norm's purchases over a period of two decades. Stocks had been bought, year after year, around specific family dates, and each cluster of purchases across a twenty-year period coincided with some auspicious familial event. Heavily invested months included June, September, and October (all months when his wife and sons had been born). When I understood this I saw that there were larger blocks bought in specific years of special familial importance. When his firstborn graduated from college, for example; in the month and year of Brian's marriage; and after the birth of the first grandchild—at all these times Father had invested heavily.

As some men buy themselves ties, a fine dinner, or a new sport jacket, as some women celebrate with jewelry or clothes, so Father would buy a few shares of Northern States Power or some Energy Fund to say to himself, "I feel good." These were not mere instruments of saving, but testimonies to exuberance and joy. No wonder Norm was loathe to have another see these stock certificates or handle these investments in his stead. His portfolio was not simply evidence supporting Father's posture of hardheaded business acumen, but more important, a personal, private notebook that catalogued a journey into his deepest self. Listing these assets was like reading a diary recording not merely moments of joy, but also details of despair. Nothing was purchased for almost a year after my mother died. If money was the measure of the man, how could Father, in those days when his world was in ill repair, have seen himself as having a surplus to invest?

For him, money had never divorced itself from the world in which it was made. Transformed into savings, it had held an emotional significance that none of us had known or guessed. He hid it expertly behind the mask of conservative Republican and businessman. By taking on the power of attorney that gave me the right to handle his stocks and invade this principal, I simultaneously had gained sovereignty over his life's principle and his past. Father had always insisted he wanted to leave his sons a legacy, to ensure that when he was gone there would be monies to remember him by. But that, in the end, was only half the tale. These were never mere investments in his mind, but a family commemorative. By willing them to his sons after his death, Norm would be giving back to us, the emotional source of those memories, the mnemonic he had sheltered and conserved to recapitulate our communal history. I wondered if, when a dividend check arrived, before depositing it he would remember some date or anniversary that had occasioned the purchase of that individual stock. To sell any of it now—no matter what the need—would be for him to divest a memory, and I knew for the first time my father.

Phillippe Ariès says that a "phenomena is characterized not so much by its origins as by the chain of other phenomena that it has directly determined." For Norm that phenomena—his attitude towards monies—had been misinterpreted by us all. Money was not a symbol of miserly selfishness as Janice and I had believed but stood instead as testimony to mute but powerful love. It was saved, however, in his private code, against a future in which we were to share unknowingly a remembrance of better days. "In the people whom we love," Proust says, "there is, immanent, a certain dream which we cannot always discern but which we pursue." Norm's dream was one of family and future, which he had tallied on a stock ledger's page. Throughout our youth his saving supposedly had been "for retirement" or a "rainy day." But when these events came, what he had defined and created as a legacy—as the future to be passed on—became endangered by the present.

Curious, I later talked with bankers and brokers, who all had stories of other Norms, of other men who had spent lifetimes buttressing against the chance of an old age that none could accept when it finally came. Some had more money than my father and others had less. All had bought equities—some in lots of a very few shares and some in blocks of a thousand or more—to celebrate family and success. What they shared, these old men, was a sense of time, of incremental saving for a future now measured by money (stocks, bonds, banking pass books and checking accounts) each man expected would live on after his demise. Against all expectations these old men had survived, but in frail longevity each man had become to himself an afterthought. In this transformation the money became to each man more potent, more real than his own life. Now some lived alone in single rooms, while others had been dispersed to nursing homes by relations unable to accept that solvency and feebleness could exist side by side. Retired and without work, each had lost, like Norm, an historical sense of purpose and all were left with nothing but the money to remind them of what had been. For most of their families, the esteem the old men had assumed would accrue like interest was frozen in memory as well. Their monies were not present objects of pride but future support for wives and relations who, like the old men themselves, saw the senile, stroke-impaired, and deaf old men as encumbrances and not continuations of the strength each once had known. Others more alone than Norm lived for the few times a year when some relative or pitying friend would stop by the nursing home to remind them of what had been. The irony was and is that many of these old men take pride in that benign neglect. "Walt's too busy to visit," Norm would say. "Isn't it nice Brian could come, even for a weekend?" He had taught us all too well.

I thought of these things while paying Buffalo bills with Father's checks, signing my name for the first time to Norm's account followed by the phrase: "Under Powers of Attorney." It felt odd, like stepping into his shoes when I was a child and feeling the strangeness of my size 7 feet in his 12 AAA loafers. The next day I talked to his accountant, Leo Stein, who suggested I use Norm's money to fund a custodial account on which he and I could both write checks. That way, when I was absent and while Norm was still unable, Leo could ensure that Father's bills would still be paid. It seemed so practical and sensible a plan that I asked why nobody had suggested it before. People were leery of being too involved, of pushing, in family situations like ours where the potential for misunderstanding and strife was so clear, he said. "If only I had known when this began what we're learning now," I sighed. "How easy it would have been when all this started to have a power of attorney in reserve and a custodial account in the wings." It's always easy to know after the fact, Leo replied, and hard for a person to know when to let go, or for someone else to know when to take charge.

6

Incessant Mourning

I can scarcely make myself out at all in the pictures my memory offers. What have I in common with this character arrived at Le Touquet in a blue pseudo Morand racing-car with a pseudo Van Dongen young lady? If all these puppets, all these mere imitations make up my memory, then my history is not me.

Emmanuel Berl, *Sylvia*

A peasant makes his old father eat out of a small wooden trough, apart from the rest of the family. One day he finds his son fitting little boards together. "It's for when you are old," says the child.

Jacob L. Grimm and William C. Grimm, *Grimms' Fairy Tales*

Buffalo lost its summer that year. At least so it seemed to me. On the day of Father's gastric bleed our world collapsed into a perpetual autumn even though leaves neither turned nor fell. It was as if July, August, and September had somehow disappeared. Summer had always been, for us, trips to the beach and hours spent sitting along the Niagara River's rapids while listening to the water's rush a mile upstream from the falls. It was afternoons in Delaware Park watching local baseball teams—each sponsored by a local bar, restaurant, or company—fumble balls and easy plays while laughing all the while. August was when we would sit on the house's front porch enjoying the cocktail hour or listening at night to thunderstorms when masses of hot, summer air were cooled precipitously above Lakes Erie and

Ontario. The Albright-Knox Art Gallery still had its summer, out-door jazz concert series each Sunday, but Norm and I were absent that year, and the photos run in each Monday's newspaper seemed to me dated and artificial. Summer had been, in the past, the hollow sound of an air conditioner humming in my parents' room, inhabited now only by the silence of empty beds and photographs on a dusty bureau. We made no trips together for hot dogs grilled at Ted's ("The best in the world," Norm would say as we ate together on an outdoor bench) or to Longo's for frozen chocolate custard, where each time he would remind me, "Your mother loved their lemon ice best."

These were our traditional rites of summer, and they disappeared into the hospital's world of starched white nurses and dull, linoleum floors. Sometimes while bicycling Buffalo's streets, I would be star-tled to see that the leaves were still a deep, deep green and to feel the temperature nearing ninety degrees. It was still August and on the coldest nights there was a hint, a premonition of chill to the air but one still so light it had to be sensed above the cicadas' murmur. A deep summer's silence still saturated the normal world. For us, however, July had segued into a November, and desolation crept along the road not as frost but as if time itself had speeded our year towards its inevitable end. Locked into the hospital world and room, Father had no feel for the seasons and lived outside them except for an occasional glance when half awake from his low bed to the high window beside it. From that angle only sky was visible, and robbed of its ground, that was unchanging, eternal.

I was wondering where the seasons had gone and trying to un-derstand why leaves had not yet begun to fall when I entered my father's room one day that August as a social worker interviewed him to see if he was ready to be sent home. His behavior was strange enough and his weakness so pronounced, however, that she rec-ommended instead he be sent to a nursing home. It was not his refusal to talk, inability to walk, incontinence, or feebleness in ex-ercise. These were, in fact, much improved. He was again wearing glasses and seemed more alert, and the battles over food were at least temporarily ended. But now his new-found waking hours were filled with delusions and hallucinations that the apathy had masked. Father had rejoined the world, but we found that his universe and ours were vastly different places. That day, for example, he opened his eyes and told me with satisfaction that "The Spiro Air people were here last night and found my keys." What keys and what people? I asked. "The people who bring air freshener and then tidy up the room," he said impatiently. "They were here last night and found my house keys on the roof. I'm just telling you what they said. They had the green key on the roof."

His house keys and wallet were at the house, we said, in the drawer where I had placed them. "You're not making any sense, Norm," Paula laughed. She tried to explain that, while real to him, his dream was bizarre to us. Therapists recently had brought up a Spiroscope used in respiratory therapy. His breathing was so shallow and body so weak that he had to be taught to inhale again. Each day it was set at a higher level, and when he inhaled properly, a circuit was tripped and the machine's clown face lit up. Norm had taken "Spiro" from that name, combined it with his worry about the absence of keys and wallet—symbols of independence—and created this business of a "green key on the roof." A few days later he called Walter and asked him to bring "the Rolls Royce globes." Nobody knew what he was talking about, and sometimes, perhaps, it was just as well.

He disliked Sara Donatello, he confided to me one day, because she had thrown a party for thirty of her friends in his room and it had been too noisy for him to sleep. "She's so inconsiderate," he complained. Early in the morning on another day he insisted so adamantly on talking to me that I was called at seven o'clock in the morning. Believing it was another emergency, I rushed to the hospital to find my father in hysterical tears because, he sobbed, I'd not invited him to my wedding. "All the nurses are talking about it. Even Dr. Pangless knows," Father cried. Even though he didn't like her, Father said, I should have told him that Sara Donatello and I were engaged. Despite my attempts to dismiss it as a dream, he remained unshaken in his conviction. "Well, should we invite her husband to the wedding as well?" I asked.

Sex became a topic of great interest to Father when, like a precocious six-year-old, he discovered the attention its mention would bring. One day I asked "What are you afraid of?" and his immediate answer was "Sex!" Paula laughed and said that since he had four sons the fear had obviously been sporadic. "What happened after the four, Norm?" she asked, and "More sex" was his answer. "Sex, sex,

sex, sex," he chanted. A placement officer from the old Sisters of Mercy Hospital—now a geriatric nursing facility—came to interview us and see if he would be a suitable client for their facility. He opened the interview by stating with a wink that he would move to Sisters only if Paula came with him. "I can see you two have a good, ah, working relationship," the woman said, amused. Then he calmly told her he wanted to go where there was good rehabilitation, and she replied approvingly that her aim was "to help you get stronger and, for that, you have to want to help us." When she left he looked smugly at Paula, who was amazed at how civil and rational he'd been. "I guess that means I don't need to go to therapy today and can have an extra dessert?" he queried. I asked if he knew what the Sisters was, and he said, "Yes, it's the f-f-f-funny f-f-f-farm."

I was uncertain how much of this was real craziness and how much was calculated to get attention, how much was real confusion and to what degree it was the "look at me" syndrome of a child bent on provocation as ballast against the inattention of an active and controlling world. Certainly he seemed to slip in and out of confusion, and his personality became a slippery, transient thing. The delusions were real—ever after he remembered the Spiro Air people and the friendly elephants which, Father said, visited his room at night. Certainly personality changes were occurring, and some were destined to be permanent. Clearly his short-term memory was failing. But some of these delusions were studied, I suspected, an actor's bid for attention in a world where activity had been denied. Rebecca wrote that I should not think of geriatric patients in terms of Kubler-Ross: "In many ways they more clearly resemble Piaget's studies of child development." In truth both models were active, although in different ways and at different times. What was clear was that Father would charm hospital nurses and therapists but reserved his nastiest face for Aunt Janice, private-duty nurses, and me.

It galled his sister to see him turn from charming patient to vicious relative with such apparent ease. To her he was cold, while to Paula he was warmly compliant. To me he could be accusing but to Bruce Foster, the night nurse, he was a pal. Father uniformly addressed the hospital's female personnel as "darlin" and "honey chil" but Sara he called a "snip" or a "bitch." The whole thing was very confusing. What Aunt Janice did not understand, I think, was that this changeling ability had been a part of his professional kit bag honed over forty years of retail sales and in visits to a thousand client homes. Years before he would regale us at dinner with tales of the "suckers" and "schnooks" who came and bought "schlock" at his store, but of course at his store he was the soul of courtesy. I first was taken there when very young and, he told me years later, asked in a loud voice which were the suckers and which the schnooks. I was, of course, taken home immediately by my mother and later given lectures by both parents on the difference between private and public postures. It was that distinction that had, for father, now become confused.

All his sporadic charm made little difference at the physiotherapy sessions that physicians had ordered he attend. The therapists did not care about Norm's craziness or manners, they cared about the individual muscles he needed to rebuild. At Paula's suggestion, I accompanied Father and Sara for the first of what were to become weeks of daily exercise sessions. We wheeled him through the hospital's oldest section, past rooms he had stayed in the year before and beyond the endoscope's operating theater to an area that seemed surreally familiar. It was in many ways like a trainer's room, the area off of any gym that every fighter has sometime known. It held the same smell of imbedded sweat and the obligatory whirlpool equipment set in an appropriate corner. Exercise tables lined one wall, like the rubdown tables found in most gyms, but here there also were sets of low, wooden steps on which stroke victims could practice walking again. Between the doors a rack had been hung that held a line of battered old canes, each ready for a new patient's use. They looked like testimonials at a religious shrine saying: "See Lord, I've been healed. I can walk again. I leave this aid as witness to your power."

As we entered, a young, very beautiful blond woman with short hair and swimmer's shoulders rotated, again and again, the left forearm of a very elderly, gaunt woman who sat smiling in her wheelchair. It was passive therapy, the type used after a stroke to help return to errant muscles a whisper of power and the ability of control. As we watched, the patient told the therapist how important she was and the blond woman then hugged her charge, thanking her for the compliment. "You make me feel wonderful," the old lady said, and the therapist replied, "Well, Elsie, you make me feel strong, too." Elsewhere in the room another ancient crone with a lovely, toothless grin sat gripping her cane like a barbell, raising it over her head in sets of ten. In the middle of the cane was a single weight, and this ability to lift perhaps five pounds was something that made her obviously proud. For a half hour it was her sole task and one she performed with such consistent joy that no one did anything but praise her: "Good, good Gladys. That's just wonderful improvement." While we waited for my father's turn he, too, watched from his wheelchair. "All these crippled old people," he said, turning to me. "What am I doing here?"

Finally it was his turn and they tested his quadricep, hamstring, and calf muscles for residual power and flexibility. They worked his arms and grips to test for strength and were encouraged by what they found. Because they were busy I helped supervise his exercises, simple leg raises with two-pound weights. Like a basketball coach I kept urging him on, ordering him to pay attention whenever he stopped to watch others in the room. "Stop heckling me," Father would say as he paused to look around. "Check out the women later," I ordered, "and get on with your job." Sara laughed and motioned me away, bending towards my father. "Come on, Norm. He has as much patience as you do. Let me help with this."

Therapy became a focus of his day and something Father would look forward to. It was something he could do, quantifiable tasks that offered the promise of measured progress. The therapists made no judgments about his behavior and were free of the expectations Aunt Janice and I based on prior association. For them he was a series of muscles to be exercised, and so long as he complied, they gave him full approval. He came to admire the therapists, who dubbed him the "Silver Fox" because of his long, white hair, and no matter how bizarre his behavior elsewhere, each day he anticipated his trip into their domain, where he was virtuous and compliant. He could see and feel progress, which, after months of passivity in the care of others, must have been a treat. In that first visit he had been shocked by the presence of others older than himself, and perhaps for the first time, he understood how he appeared to the world. Other patients were his mirror, his reflection with a proud and determined face instead of one cringing in fear. He wanted that posture for his own, and first in therapy but eventually elsewhere, used the example of that room to try to rebuild his world. None of this happened quickly. The changes occurred incrementally over weeks. At first he was silent and withdrawn with the therapists, sometimes refusing to walk at all or to do any exercises with them. Certainly his weakness was real. In the beginning any task seemed an impossible chore, but slowly he grew if not to full mobility at least towards the memory of power.

One day I went to Sisters of Mercy, a nursing home, to discuss his possible transfer there. General Taylor would sooner or later discharge him, and Father needed more help than I could give him at home. The Sisters' Marci Lapine showed me its facilities. An old, inner-city hospital which had been transformed into a geriatric facility, it was primarily a long-term home but had a few short-term client beds. There was a small physiotherapy department, a communal room where patients could gather, and a list of daily activities posted on the bulletin board for those residents both sufficiently mobile and interested. But its halls were so dark and silent that it seemed even sound and light had been invalided and sent elsewhere for care. The corridors were lined with wheelchaired, elderly people staring mutely, passively, into vacant space. One man slowly raised his leg and let it fall, raised it and let it fall, with metronomic regularity. Another woman with no teeth grabbed Marci Lapine's hand and said something in an unintelligible drawl gummed past spitting lips. Marci held the women's hand in turn and said yes, yes, as we hurried on. This was the most active, healthy wing, Marci explained to me. Upstairs the chronic cases lived, and did I want to see them? No, I said, not really.

Much more could be done for the clients, Lapine said defensively, if it were not for the chronic lack of money. It was, she knew, a dark, depressing, and frightening place for first-time visitors like me. Based on the caseworker's evaluation, she gently suggested another facility might better suit my father's needs. If he could afford the price, somewhere else might "be more agreeable to him." My father, she said, was too set in his ways for a facility that lacked the staff or setting to cajole him into either health or the acceptance of ongoing infirmity. After discovering that her father and my grandfather had been close friends, we talked at some length about geriatric care. What she said was nothing new, but in the context of Father's future, took on new meaning and immediacy. The issues being raised today in gerontology are the same ones that have dominated the debate over public prisons and mental hospitals for more than fifty years.

Are these clients with rights and dignity, or society's rejects to be warehoused and maintained? Does one mix clients of different levels of capacity, or segregate long-term and rehabilitative residents one from the other? Who pays and how much? Should the money go to helping the returnable few or towards long-term maintenance for the many? Lapine answered all these issues with liberal, enlightened views but admitted that ever-increasing demands and barely adequate financial support made the discussion academic. They did what they could.

The most frustrating thing, she said, was the knowledge that the government and insurers spend thousands of dollars each day to haul a patient back from death's door, but once that person's life is again secured, show little interest in continued support. It is as if we say through our policies that life—bare existence—is owed to everyone, but once the heart is beating again, the individual is on his or her own. "It's an argument for tobacco and alcohol abuse," I said as she walked me to the door. "With a tumor, a coronary, or a cirrhotic liver one can be assured of decent care. But watch one's health grow old and frail, and knock, knock—nobody's home." She laughed and promised to do what she could for my father if I was desperate for a bed, but we both knew that this facility was not what I wanted for Norm or what he would accept.

A few days later I visited another place Marci had recommended. Located in Buffalo's suburbs, it was brighter and more cheerful than the Sisters' and seemed, at least on the surface, quite suitable. The rehabilitation area was beautifully equipped, and the whole had a pleasant and airy feel. It was a church-affiliated, private institution catering to the suburban crowd, while Marci's facility was in the ghetto and housed a primarily black, inner-city clientele. Marci's staff had the appearance of grim competence one finds in busy, urban police, the real-life cops who deal daily with an angry humanity in despair. The staff had seemed efficient but harried, concerned but so overworked that a good day was one in which nothing horrible happened and the basic job got done. Here, in the suburbs, the staff had a small-town feel, like police in a region where speeding drivers and country-club party-goers make up the daily clientele. Staffers were more relaxed and had time to chat to patients for nothing but the joy of company. But there was a waiting list in the suburbs, and there were no old family friends to ease the procedures for entry. I knew that if Father went anywhere, this was where I wanted him to be, and applied for his admission on a short-term basis to the rehabilitation wing. But the entrance committee rejected Norm after reviewing his records because, they said, what he really needed was long-term care.

One day I tried to discuss Norm's options with him. In his room and on Sara's shift I asked what he wanted to do. He replied that what he most desired was to "end it" there and then. That morning he in fact had asked Dr. Pangless for cyanide pills and was angry that Pangless had refused him. "Still, I can do it to myself, even here," he boasted with a wink. I told him he was a fool. "You can't kill yourself without being able to walk. You can't get to the kitchen for a knife or into your bedroom's bureau drawer where those bottles of old pills are stashed." Then he again insisted I had chosen the endoscopy for him and created his predicament. None of this was his fault. Sara asked Norm what he would like to do if suicide wasn't an option. "I guess I can follow the hospital routine for a bit," he answered. "Just get along while staying here." "You can't," I explained, exasperated. "They're going to throw you out. So either work like hell with therapy or resign yourself to an old-age home where one sits for hours staring at bare walls." He said that didn't sound inviting and that I should leave him alone. "I can't, Pops. You know that, too," I replied, and he said yes, he did.

What he wanted was for me to decide, and I realized that my months of intimacy and service had been a very mixed blessing. He had learned to rely on me, to have me make his decisions, and had come to depend on our bickering, fighting relationship. Time had confirmed his suspicion that illness was the way to bind a son close to him. What he wanted was my presence, and if infirmity was the method by which that could be obtained, he was willing to pay the price. Also, I think, he enjoyed this freedom, retirement in the most fundamental sense. Illness had become his full-time job and brought the opportunity to say and do whatever he pleased. It was the freedom of a child to be bad and still be loved. He called me soon after I left that day, just when I had started to make dinner, and asked why I wasn't with him. "Because it's seven o'clock and I'm cooking dinner," I said. "Jesus, Norm. I only left you two hours ago." He started to cry, saying I had promised to eat with him, and I replied, rather curtly, that no such promise had been made and that he was being unreasonable. "Let me speak to Sara, please," I said, and when he handed over the phone I asked her what was going on. "He's pretty much off the wall," she sighed. "It's going to be fun and games tonight."

And so periods of bizarre behavior at night were balanced with teary sessions by day. Through it all ran the question of what we would do when the hospital decided he had been in their care long enough. The day I had submitted forms applying for the suburban home care was the day my father chatted happily about a pink elephant that had visited his room the previous night. The afternoon I spent at the Sisters was one in which he called Brian in Atlanta and suggested his two grandchildren each be given a horse. "But Dad," Brian complained, "I live in the suburbs. You know there aren't any stables around. Why should I give the children a horse?" "Because," Father replied as if it was the most obvious thing, "you know, horses eat apples." One day I asked him where he lived and he answered promptly that he was in New Jersey. "Why do you think you're in New Jersey?" I asked, and Father replied it was where the "n-n-n-n-nursing place is. The one with G-G-G-General T-T-T-Taylor." Norm called Walter one evening and again demanded his son bring the Rolls Royce globes, which Father insisted he once had loaned my brother. "But I don't expect him to drop everything and come here," Father said to me the next day. "He can send them by Federal Express." The overnight nurse, Bruce, reported one morning that he had found Father leaning precariously out of his bed, rummaging through a garbage bag taped to the supporting rails. "You're all robbing the government of thousands of dollars, throwing away old bottles," Father had explained when Bruce Foster rushed to his side. "I'm looking for them, you know." During the day he propositioned nurses, refused to eat anything but desserts, and did what he was told only in therapy. Once Father informed everyone that he was throwing a party but that I was not to make the arrangements because "the last time Mother was unhappy" with my planning.

Norm began to ask how things were "at our wonderful home," like a Florida retiree anxious for news of old friends, and I answered that things were fine. I did not have the heart to tell him how much I had come to hate the place and living alone within it. Constant in space, the shifts in time had made it unfamiliar to me, and I felt uncomfortable there at night. After the Olympics it had been a piece of geography filled with immediacy. It had been a piece of my history, and the memories evoked when I walked through its front door the year before were ones that had been cherished. In those first days of bandages, burns, and medical problems, each picture and piece of home furniture had held meaning. Now all of those associations were gone, worn beneath a new familiarity like the faint memories of childhood's innocence whose significance is lost forever to us all after puberty. Now in my father's house I was left only with solitude. But what I told Norm was that his house endured "the same as ever, waiting for your return." If it could have spoken, however, his home would have talked of other old, neighborhood houses now tenanted by new families with young children running through their yards. Houses need life to sustain them, it would plead. His was populated by histories and ghosts I dimly perceived.

Sara said to me one day that if I wanted, she would work for Norm in his house on a full-time basis when he was released. She needed full-time work because she was putting her husband through school and supporting their son. In addition, she had become interested in my father as both a professional challenge and as a human being. Something in her responded to his fears. Despite his bluster and craziness, he was weak and in need, and perhaps it was this that drew her to him. Paula was delighted at Sara's offer and, I think, relieved. She knew my father needed more than I could provide, care from someone familiar with drug protocols and physical therapy. My father needed nursing and more care than one person could give, and I immediately accepted Sara's offer. For her part, Sara looked forward to the work. She believed, as do others, that nursing's real challenge is in the transition from the hospital context to home convalescence. That year both she and Paula had lost clients nursed successfully to discharge who later died from preventable complications during home recuperation. "In ten years you'll see doctors making house calls again," Paula predicted. "Things are swinging back to home care." Sara argued along the same lines that nurses would become tomorrow's home practitioners as early-release hospital programs more and more rapidly sent the recently critical from their hospital beds back into their own homes. The ideal solution was to have a nurse coordinating home care, and that was what Sara proposed to do for Norm.

Walt called to say he would spend a long weekend in Buffalo with

Father, and I planned a trip to Vancouver to coincide with his visit. During my brother's four days of Buffalo time, Father's craziness diminished and a more normal sentience returned. He's doing wonderfully, Walter said by telephone. He's walking a bit, and we've had some good talks, he reported to me. I had exaggerated the seriousness of Norm's state of affairs, my brother lectured smugly by telephone. Sara and Paula told him that he had arrived just as Norm's crisis passed but to me Walter said the problem had been that I "coddled" Norm when I should have been "stern" with his nonsense. Two days after I left and one before Walter arrived, however, Father told me by telephone—Buffalo to Vancouver—that "I know you're busy but it would be nice, Tom, if you could visit me sometime."

While away from Buffalo my workbooks filled with notes on Norm's condition and his sons' relations to it. I would wake in the early morning amid dreams that my father was calling to me or that he had died. The issues of his age and illness, separate and entwined, compelled me, and distance from Buffalo brought no release from the obsession. While in Vancouver I sought something that would make sense of this time, and in letters and workbook came up with this much of an answer:

I think there is such a thing as local knowledge. It is called old age and dying. My father's world has shrunk to a bed, a room, to the immediacy of micro-geography. Climatology is what he sees through the window or an errant breeze which enters from it, chilling him at night. Time for my father has shortened to a long prehistory whose traces are sons and a few hours past ("What was for dinner last night, Dad?" "Who knows? It was so long ago!") and perhaps a few weeks of future. Summer reruns on television are fine because he cannot remember having seen the shows before and, indeed, at the end of the hour cannot remember its beginning. The real questions are who will be his nurse in an hour, can he walk five steps to the bathroom, and what can be done about the line of a crinkled sheet on mattress which is causing discomfort—now.

Like a child, he needs constant attention but has neither cuteness, grace, or potential. He will not come to the strength of adolescence and will never go to college again. And so, you ask, why am I here? There are several answers. Partly it is the simple belief that no one should die alone. Those who have spent their lives in the patterns of parenthood, with its necessary vision of hope and future, deserve better than an anonymous bed when their usefulness is ended. I do this as much for myself as for him, as much to test my beliefs of humanity as to minister from a past love to the present wreck of an often unpleasant man.

Simply the fact that he can no longer serve, help, aid, guide, or amuse me is no reason to abandon him. The universally accepted excuses that I have work, responsibilities, career—a life to live—will not serve. If we are more than a means of production, more than economic tools to be discarded when utility fails, then no part of life should be abandoned. If there is meaning for me in human relations it is in a vision of reciprocity, one person to another, which crosses any boundaries of convenience or utility such as my father would offer. We are joined not simply by individual histories but by a bond of humanity that says I owe life a debt, payable through him. It has, I have decided, nothing to do with his being pleasant or disagreeable, rich or poor. It has to do with accepting his age and seeing my future in it.

In short, my time is homage not to the husk that my father has become but to the man he somehow remains. He is a human being in need of help and my responsibility by default. To deny that would be to deny my better instincts and vision of the world. That would be to accept his definition of economic man, of utility as a measure of human worth. He lives now because of me, because I've always believed he was wrong. I remain in part to see how far I'll go in defense of these beliefs and in part because I'm in so deep that it would be impossible to leave until the job is done.

My brothers live by Norm's vision, which sees the commercially productive life as all-important. They live at a remove, worry about him from their homes, and insist he get the best of care as long as it does not inconvenience or impoverish them. This economic vision of life denies youth as anything but potential, denies children the right to individuality, and withholds power until they can earn a wage. Then it denies the elderly because, like children, they are no longer economically useful.

It is not the least of ironies that my father would utterly reject all this as sentimental foolishness. For years he argued that Down's syndrome children should be killed at birth because they could not offer society a full day's work. He fumed when the city began to make its buildings wheelchair adaptable, angered at the money spent on "cripples." And now he is as useless, mere dust that cannot function in the only way his world acknowledges as "useful," and he is broken by that fact.

Father's improvement was marked but by no means completed when I returned to Buffalo. During my absence we kept in touch by phone, and throughout that time he complained about the "bossy nurses," singling out Sara as the object of his ire. She was lazy and dictatorial, he said, demanding I fire her immediately. It was jealousy,

I think, an inability to share loyalty and love with anyone. His nurse had become my friend and, more to the point, met with Aunt Janice's unstinting approval. She was a woman I had hired and that, too, he resented. But mostly it was her relative youth that made of Sara an intolerable symbol of the dominion of these caretakers. Even Paula, whom he had always referred to as "my friend Paula," became contemptible to Norm. One day he complained to me that she had wanted him to walk with his legs straight, refusing to understand, he explained, that for him the task was impossible. "But it is possible," I laughed. "I've seen you do it in the therapy room. You're so confused you don't know what you can or cannot do. You have to trust others to make these decisions for you, trust them to be right." He laughed and shook his head, saying, "I've never trusted anyone in my life."

That was probably true. As a German-American Jew, he was born into paranoia and fear confirmed by Nazi Germany and its death camps in World War II. Although he did not believe in God, he believed in ethnic identity. When I had asked him years before how an atheist could consider himself Jewish he had replied that "it doesn't matter what you believe. It's what people call you." Religion to him had always been the general case of society's fickle and unfaithful ways. One's beliefs bowed to the group's vision, defined in turn by society's prejudice, and within it all the individual could do nothing but accept, go along and bitch. If religion, governments, and the greater society had proved to be untrustworthy, his faith in individuals was equally low. Politicians were, to Norm, individuals distrusted on principle ("What are they getting out of it?"), while religion was filled with "schnoorers and clods." This distrust of humanity and its institutions grew through years of depression and business, flowered among the examples of duplicity he saw as a rule of political affairs.

The countless acts of individual kindness that others see as a counterbalance—as proof that people are good—were for my father anomalies, spikes on some fever chart of human duplicity, examples of abnormal behavior. From this came, at least in part, his fears that I would spend all his money, not merely from incompetence but also from some flaw of cupidity born, he insisted, to every soul but not always given field to flower. Trust the paper on which stocks are written, he believed. They were born in the ledgers of business audited by accountants who lived for the balance sheet. But trust no man or son or friend beyond necessity, and if you must put your faith in another, prepare for disappointment. That was the credo of his life and the one by which he would die. Were the nurse employees accountable to him, their "human nature" would be restrained by his threats of discharge and thus their own financial self-interest. That was, after all, the primary force he and my brothers recognized as ruling most individuals. But these women had been hired by me, and thus he had no power over them. They had become metaphors for his loss of financial control and diminishing personal power. The more clearly one or another had relations with his sister or me, the more clearly he disliked them.

The day I returned to Buffalo, Dr. Pangless's office called to say the hospital's utilization committee had met and my father would be released that week. They had decided that acute bed care was no longer needed and that other arrangements for Norm would have to be made. At the hospital the next day, I found Father back from therapy and showing off for Sara, the nurse he said he disliked so much. His hair was combed and his head held high. He walked to the bathroom and back with spastic determination to demonstrate his new powers to me. I had talked with Sara before driving to the hospital, and we had decided how to handle the news, to inform Father he was about to begin the next phase of his life. "You're going home, Dad," I said with a smile. "Your house is waiting for you."

When I broke the news he was not pleased. In fact, he was visibly terrified. "Let's go for a walk," he said, and on his walker lurched down the hall and into the visitors' lounge where, six weeks before, Aunt Janice and I had waited for him to die. In the lounge he insisted we talk abut other things until I grabbed the conversation and steered it towards the present concern. With Sara present, I explained the program we had worked out for his safe return to what Paula called "civilian life in that old house." Sara would work a morning shift five days a week, from 8:30 a.m. until four o'clock, with Sundays and Mondays off. Those days would be covered by aides from the homemaker agency, which also promised to provide around-the-clock service when Sara was not on duty. Father was appalled. The idea of a constant, alien presence in his house upset him more than the expense, I think, and he immediately began to protest.

I told him there was no choice. He could not get out of bed or walk without supervision and needed people to give medications and help him to the bathroom. He was still too frequently confused to be trusted alone for long periods, I said, and needed the type of medical care which only home nursing could provide. Finally, I told him I did not want to work any more eighteen-hour days when there was a reasonable alternative. He hated this but knew he had no choice. Hadn't he given me power of attorney and hadn't I been spending his money? The question that must have burned in him was this: were he to refuse the arrangement would anyone have listened? It was the crucial issue but, fearing the answer, one he dared not raise. Instead, Norm shrugged and said that if that was how I wished to bankrupt him there was nothing he could do.

And so as the leaves began to color and fall, Father returned to the house on East Street that he loved but not, in his mind, to home. He was in constant rage at the presence of aides and refused whenever possible to acknowledge their assistance. Sara's daily ministrations were bad enough, but what galled Father most were the overnight people who waited in the kitchen or living room until he needed a urinal emptied, help getting out of bed, or something to drink. At all other times he prohibited their presence in his room. Why, he asked, couldn't I take over as I'd done the year before? When told it was "because I want to sleep, too," he said I was being unreasonable. After a few days he exploded in tears, shouting at me that all these extra people were an unnecessary expense he could not afford. "I'm not supposed to get upset, but look at me," he cried, holding up his hands, which shook violently in agitation. "I wanted to come home to my house but with all these people bossing me about, I might as well have stayed in the hospital."

Poor Norm—he mistook the symptoms for the disease, focused his anger on the aides and nurses who had allowed him, were he only able to accept it, a measure of independence. To be like before meant the ability to order and arrange his world, to think and act as he always had, and it was the year's succession of illnesses that made that an impossibility. For months he had not paid his bills because he lacked the strength, the will, and the cognitive power to order his own affairs. Unable to walk without help, he had accepted the hospital as a halfway house from which he would be able to leave when the world was "as before." But now a new and possibly endless phase had begun in which independence itself was what had been lost. The presence of professional strangers—nurses and aides—emphasized for Norm reality's distance both from times past and from his current dreams. Impotent, he fought a valiant, if for us, frustrating, rear-guard action. For days he refused to talk to any aide or ask for help whatever the need. At night he forced the aides to sit out of sight and in another room until they heard him trying to rise from bed. Then they would rush in to find Father struggling to stand erect, insisting he could do it alone. Like mother hens they would nudge him straight on his walker or four-pronged cane before shuffling behind him, steadying his balance as he lurched in anger to the bathroom. There they would have to stand at the door ("What? Do you want to watch this, too?" he would say), breathless and worried, until he rose from his toilet seat and began the wobbling run back to bed.

His official discharge papers arrived one day by mail from General Taylor Hospital. Father opened the letter, gave it a glance, and then told Sara and me that he was tired and would read it after a nap. But for days we had watched as he would pick up and then reject newspapers, magazines, get-well cards, and letters. It was not that he was tired but rather that he was unable. A cognitive dysfunction was left as a legacy of that summer's illness, and reading, the understanding of symbols on paper that make ideas, had become a difficult if not impossible task for him. Father could barely look up and read a telephone number. So Norm and I read the letter together. He held it and I read aloud the words in which the hospital had catalogued his myriad, chronic illnesses. "I'm a very sick man," Father said in surprise to Sara and me. When she replied gently that this was something we already knew, Father asked what these diseases were. Patiently, she explained them one by one: necrotic cirrhosis, chronic lymphocytic leukemia, osteoarthritis, osteoporosis, collapsed vertebra, chronic hepatitis, hypothyroidism, and a history of gastric bleeds. As we three talked, Sara explained how each illness related to his drug regime. She brought in bottles of pills and held them up, remarking on their color and coding each one to a specific disease. It reminded me of Show and Tell as we had learned it once in primary school. Then Sara and I emphasized how powerful the drugs were, the possible side effects each had, and why we were so concerned about Father's health.

Each day that week he would question us about the letter, asking again and again, "What's wrong with me?" as if his mind would not accept the judgment of his body. I wondered if he remembered anything at all of the previous months, and when I asked, he said with a laugh, "I can still see the pink elephant." But almost everything else that had occurred since June had vanished from his memory. He refused to accept that the endoscopy had been his choice, for example, or that he had greeted Paula with a concern over her hourly wage. He had forgotten the dates of entering the hospital or the day of his return. Almost everything was dismissed from memory with a shrug. "I was too sick to know what I was doing," he would say. "You can't hold me to it."

I had to go to Toronto for a few days, and when I told my father, he complained that in my absence Sara's presence would be even more dominant. "It just bothers me to see a thing like that paid $100 a day," he said of her. "She thinks she's one of the family. She's always in here, waiting around. When she wants to take my socks off she doesn't ask, she just reaches down and does it." It was not just Sara, but the situation itself which oppressed him. She was only one of a litany of complaints he flung at me for an hour, but all amounted to his anguish at dependency on expensive, professional help. "Just leave me alone like I was before," he pleaded.

That was the crux of his problem and of mine. Norm wanted a past remembered, one in which life held to his time-honored vision, a time when my presence in Buffalo was an extraordinary gift brought on by the bad luck of the hepatic retrovirus that had invaded his very blood. Now that he was home, the place itself locked hope into a place, and only the unfamiliar faces of professional aides disturbed the memories from which he drew support. Every piece of furniture spoke to him of the Norm Koch who had raised a family and loved a wife while being independent and, in his way, content. Perhaps each mocked him with the truth of his need, which was juxtaposed against those memories of strength. The future was more crucial to me—his mirror and his opposite. I could see what he refused to know, that the certitude that had informed his world was now forever gone. But I did not tell him that. We left the chimera of future independence as a carrot dangling on time's progressive stick. To him I said only that he needed the aides so he would not fall and injure himself as he had the year before. "I never did," he said angrily. This he had forgotten as well.

I returned from Toronto to learn that Father had injured himself in my absence while trying to do exercises alone in bed and thus prove that he didn't need Sara's help. In the attempt he had pulled a back muscle, and as a result walking again became an ordeal. Now at night he asked the aides to carry his urinal or bring a glass of water because the pulled muscle hurt and "you know, Tom, I don't like pain." He had said the same thing a year before. I told him that he had been warned, and he replied, "If you only came back to gloat, why don't you leave tomorrow?" Sara, however, had won his good graces, and that was a singular triumph. She had baked him a pan of brownies and brought it to work as a "special treat." A few days later she made chocolate chip cookies and brought a dozen for him. Alarmed by the muscle pain and pleased by the gifts, he decided Sara was "different now. She's really not a bad person, you know." Baked goods had been the perfect approach, one that he understood. His mother and later his wife and sister had all baked for him. A woman bringing brownies fit into his view of the world. She was a penitent seeking his approval with material gifts. It gave him the chimera of control.

One day that week while I was shopping he called the homemaker service and cut down the work hours of evening aides. When he told me what he had done, I lost my temper, and as he tried to explain how it had seemed a reasonable economy, I shouted over his voice. I hurled abuse and called him names I never before had used in his presence and nobody had said to his face in years. Grabbing his collar, I raised my arm to hit him, as months of worry and resentment spilled forth. His eyes were wide and watering with the wet, darkened look of a trusting but elderly pet's. He would spend me, but not money, take my time but not spend a dime unless it was dragged from him like blood, I spit. When he began to cry, I started the downswing at his face but stopped when I heard the sound of Sara at the bedroom door. She had come to Norm's room from the kitchen while he and I were arguing. When I looked at her she silently turned and walked away. I dropped my arm, walked past the bed, and kicked a wall with all my might. The scuff mark remains there still. "If you get out of bed alone tonight, I will break you in two. If you cry in my presence or make one more complaint, I will send you to a nursing home and never come to visit. Now I am going out. I will be back later. If for any reason you make me come downstairs to-night, or if the aide has any problem at all—I will leave this house and never return." Then I stomped out of his room without a back-ward glance, slammed the front door as I ran down the stoop, rushed to a neighborhood bar, and drank steadily, silently, furiously, until closing time.

For several days Father was too terrified to do more than cower in my presence. He did not remember my raised fist but felt my anger, and that persistent, unforgiving silence that I put up as a wall between us was more cruel and violent than any blow could have been. He appealed to Sara to help make me forgive him, and having gone to her once for support, afterwards accepted her assistance without reservation. Eventually she came to me and said that they had struck a deal. Father would use a urinal at night and had promised to not get out of bed if left alone. The overnight aides were to be discontinued. She was to be given a house key with which to open the door herself each morning. I protested, but Sara insisted that the possibility of his getting into trouble was offset by the confidence and sense of well being the change might bring to his life.

"You've done everything anyone could do, and now it's time for me to take over," she said gently. "It's time you returned to Van-couver." Sara said nothing about what she had seen, and for my part, I lacked the courage to bring it up. That day I apologized to Father, who said he had forgotten the incident, and he in fact seemed puzzled, as if he really didn't know what I was talking about. Perhaps that was true and the specter of an attacking son had slipped into the disappearing abyss of memory loss. He knew something unpleasant had occurred, but like a young child disci-plined two days before, he had forgotten its specifics. But it had terrified and sobered me, demonstrating how easy it is, with some-one so demanding and so defenseless, to slide from frustration to anger and then into violence. Only Sara's presence had saved us from becoming another statistic in the catalogues of elderly abuse. For months the memory of that moment haunted me, and in my dreams I would feel the slightness of Father's weight as one hand lifted at his collar and the other traveled down, down towards his face. I wanted to blame Norm for his nastiness, to say he deserved to be hit for his ingratitude and intransigence. Not only was he ungrateful to those who offered help but he in fact obstructed and criticized everything done by us all—sister, sons, and nurses—to guard his health. His cutting down on home aides—a testing, questing search for independence—was only the most recent example. But it was not simply that my father had become a Nasty Old Man, but that, as M. F. K. Fisher suggests, the unpleasantness of the elderly is a hidden nature come finally to flower.

I have formed a strong theory that there is no such thing as "turning into" a Nasty Old Man or an Old Witch. I believe that such people, and of course they are legion, were born nasty and witch-like, and that by the time they were about five years old they had hidden their rotten bitchiness and lived fairly decent lives until they no longer had to conform to rules of social behavior, and could revert to their original horrid selves.

We are all selfish until socialized, all demanding until peer pressure and ambition teach the balancing act of cooperation and accommodation against desire. Shorn of that necessity and robbed of a future in which reciprocity counts, some may revert to a private world in which the face in the mirror each morning is shaved or rouged only for one's self. The unbelievable frustration of a world proscribed, in which the simplest acts of communal life become difficult feats done in isolation is, to me, a better explanation. Nastiness is anger without love and hope as balances. Roland Blythe offered a better explanation, one in which Norm's actions made sense and one that made of my frustration a pettiness of which I was ashamed and frightened: "Modern geriatric psychiatry speaks of the aged as being wounded in their narcissism—a poignant term and one which eloquently compresses the whole business of what we once were and what we must inevitably become."

Unpleasant elderly are odious to themselves and behave badly to those who would like to wish them well because, I think, of the isolation each feels. Friends may pay duty calls and visit on an irregular basis, but the lack of reciprocal, communal relations based on recurring activities is something the disabled and homebound geriatric feels as the central insult of a deprived life. Unable to walk (or speak or hear) and often with seriously impaired mental faculties, people like my father find themselves alone. The community that had sustained their lives becomes a memory and caretakers the only individuals they meet. It is no secret soul come to the fore, but frustration, anger, and disease that turn these studied, stately Vermeer-like humans into angular, twisting Cubist souls as time and solitude truncate their world, and the image seen in the morning mirror becomes one patched from old nightmares and forgotten fears. That, at least, was how it was with Norm.

Only by fighting me and the necessities of his care could Father glimpse the edges of his own self-respect. It was as if when Norm looked in the mirror, Sara holding him steady before it each day, then the familiar face once known so well had been a mental, emotional construct made of social roles now dissolved. He shaved under a watchful father's brow, pulled the razor along a smiling salesman's cheeks, and moved with care above the ridge of a husband and lover's lips. The neck he saw and along which his Remington razor ran (steadied now by Sara's professional hand) was that of a worried businessman to be soothed after work by a wife's caress. And the Adam's apple that bobbed as he swallowed was made to chant the Kaddish prayer each year at the anniversary of his father's death. Each part of his persona once had a purpose, but none answered to them anymore. There was a nurse to massage him and a hospital bed to lie upon. Soon, he thought, we would say Kaddish for him, but on Yom Kippur, were he to go to temple now, Father would be unable to stand for the service or remember the words to the prayers for the dead that he had chanted for a lifetime. Even his savings, the financial legacy that had been his most secure bridge between past and future, was becoming a resource for the vast but amorphous, eternal present to which disease and failing memory condemned him. The very progression of time—orderly past and harried present to a hoped for and calmer future—had been altered, and with it's diminution came a revulsion of the self. No wonder he had become a figure of distaste and pity to others. That was how my father had come to view himself.

That week I said good-bye to the Buffalo I had grown to know again. Cycling to my favorite places, I called or visited everyone who had given Father and me assistance. They had been his friends and were now mine, as if in assuming responsibility for him I had taken on the reciprocity of his relationships. Aunt Janice and I had dinner one night, and Mrs. Bee—my father's friend—wished me God's speed and good luck. Brook Samuelson recommended I rest up after my ordeal, and the accountant, Leo Stein, congratulated me on a job well done.

Finally I visited my oldest friend, a seventy-nine-year-old man known to the neighborhood simply as Old Phil or, sometimes, Mark the Shoemaker because the store he had purchased years before had first been opened by a man named Mark. Phil Bonavillio's shop was next to my father's old store, and as a child, I had spent hours by his work bench, watching as he transformed worn, beaten shoes into ones that looked new and comfortable. "He's an artist," his son and partner said proudly that day. "I've worked with him all these years and still, each week he teaches me something new." His son, "Young Phil," was now in his forties, but we had known each other since early adolescence when both of us hung out at a local music store. We were friends, and it helped me to see a father and son who lived and worked together; their mutual respect revived my faith in how things could be.

Young Phil told me his father would be eighty years old the coming March, when my father would turn seventy-seven. I promised to return for the occasion and, that day, invited Old Phil to lunch. He protested mightily that their backlog of work demanded he stay, but neither his son nor I took his protests seriously. "Go ahead," Young Phil laughed, "I'll get along without you for an hour." As we ate, Old Phil told me in his still-accented English about his trip to America from Sicily at the age of nine, seventy years before. He said he could still hear the men with mandolins singing on pleasant nights as the boat rocked at sea. He had not forgotten the pains of steerage class or the fears of being a new immigrant who knew neither the language or customs of his future home. But the sound of men singing and the faces of the women who watched their men was what he remembered best after all those many years.

I left Buffalo as the days shortened and autumn matured towards early winter. When I left Father's house, it was with relief, and as the taxi waited, Sara saw me to the door. She kissed me good-bye and for a moment it seemed as if I was just leaving on a quick business trip—as Norm used to do—and that she was not nurse but wife and mother, staying home with our child. I tried hard not to think about that as the cab traveled through Delaware Park, carrying me to the airport.

7

The Deprived Time

How a person feels at the end of his life will tell you what he feels to have been the quality of it all. Who would have believed that a time might come when a man like me would regard the day of his death as better than the day of his birth? Nothing fails like success.

Joseph Heller, *God Knows*

I have come to the conclusion that there is one essential, profound, underlying problem and that is that the old are not loved. They do not feel themselves to be loved, and too many people treat them with indifference and seek no contact with them.

Paul Tournier

There are some boxers, men with more endurance than skill, who come to expect a professional beating whenever they enter the ring. I have known a few who lived not for the raised hand of victory but instead for the feel of an opponent's blow. These were men whose careers were founded not merely on the combination of jab, cross, and uppercut but on an elemental need to be hit once again. It is a type of masochism, an expectation of punishment that becomes a pride in endurance and, ultimately, a stock in trade. These are the punch drunk fighters, future bar brawlers ultimately to be vanquished only when a large chair or heavy bottle is cracked over their head. Emergency ward intimates know the type well. They're wheeled into the hospital—battered, bones broken, and eyes swollen into a discolored squint—by ambulance attendants who stare at the smiles that curl at the edge of a crippled face: the ecstasy of the survivor.

That was how I felt, and perhaps it was a sense that Father knew as well. From Vancouver I stayed in touch with Buffalo by phone while wondering when the next crisis would unite us again. Like Norm, I had lost the economic purpose that previously had confirmed my life. He had no furniture store whose stock demanded arrangement or sale, while I was without a newspaper or broadcast station expecting a story to fill pages or airtime. The people I had worked for in the past had new free-lancers to fill their needs and, like Norm coming home from the hospital, I found myself returning to a limbo I did not know how to break. The responsibilities that had tied me to my place had been severed by the months away from Vancouver just as his physical absence from both hospital work and local friends had made of my father a living memory within his still extant world. Dislocations in time break the order of daily life, and this we suffered together, each in his own sphere. Both of us waited for the final crippling blow and were surprised when it did not come.

Norm did not think of these things. The hepatitis and gastric bleeds had robbed him of his ability to live and plan in time. Like a Zen adept, he simply was. His immediate world had shrunk to the sickroom of his house, where a hospital bed had replaced the box spring and mattress set my parents had slept on for years. His time frame, the sense of a fourth dimension that gives depth to human lives, had flattened to the immediate present. And as Norm lost the ability to order his world, the physical geography of Buffalo disappeared for him as well. Even work became a distant dream, while the location of sons whom he once loved to visit receded from real knowledge into the realm of memory. The very street on which my father lived, East Street, was transformed into a strange and far-away world that he now saw infrequently and that, in turn, rarely thought of him. Those who lived on East Street would ask occasionally, "How's Norm? I never see him anymore," as he became an afterimage, a neighbor whose presence had become so rare he was excluded despite clear residency.

Neighbors no longer visited during the cocktail hour, and in summer, Father did not survey the street from the height of his porch. His was the "old Koch house," a landmark without tenanted definition. This was inevitable, because proximity and familiarity breed not contempt but acceptance. All but the newest of families on any block fit into a pattern, a rhythm of communal lives. On East Street, the Fogel kids' bicycles continued to clutter their driveway across the street from Norm's, and next door to them, Nancy-Ann's dog still barked at night. Father's neighbor, Sam Elaine, rarely shoveled the sidewalk in winter, making it difficult for the Patrick kids from down the street to walk past his house on their way to school. It all balanced, however, when Sam hired a Fogel kid to clear his sidewalk of winter snows, and Nancy-Ann's dog, whose bark announced every stranger, became a vocal security alarm for us all. In the daily, yearly rhythm one learns to accept, then ignore, and finally forget the deficits of one's allies and to acknowledge instead their strengths. A Fogel child walked Sam's dog and he, for his part, had always helped Norm remove the storm doors and insert the screens each spring; Norm gave young Jerry Patrick candy on Halloween, and Jerry then visited Norm when he was ill. These qualities of warmth, help, and neighborliness create a vision of trust and friendship that make single life endurable.

The same thing happened with Father's more general Buffalo circle of friends, who were still mobile and able and well. He could no longer go to the Bees each Sunday or out to dinner on Friday night with his sister Janice; Father did not have the strength or will to go to the theater, and for the first time in thirty years, forgot to buy tickets to the symphony. Leo Stein, the old family friend, dined now with other old men, and it was me, not Father, who visited the stockbroker's office where Norm for years had invested in memories. To his sister and old friends he became an aggravation; his illness allowed us all to forget his better qualities for his deficits. Each of us in our respective worlds became like the old college friend one meets at a dinner party. "I didn't remember him as being so aggravating," one says of the person who was once a "best friend in the world." That old friend is really no more or less irritating than before. It is simply that the things that once made him charming—proximity, reciprocity, and daily contact—have been lost, and so he becomes a contemporary stranger whose deficits are not balanced by virtues.

Even his own house became unfamiliar and distant territory to my father, who could no longer climb its stairs or walk unaided into the living room. When I was in Buffalo a year after the gastric bleed,

Norm asked where I would be staying on that trip. 'Upstairs, in my room," I said with surprise. "Where I've always been." His face had a look first of puzzled concentration and then of blank incomprehension. "What's upstairs?" he asked. "I can't picture it anymore." The world had shrunk to his immediate bedroom, and even upstairs, where he had lived for thirty-nine years, had become strangely foreign territory.

Father became a member of the battalion of invisible ill, a soldier in the forgotten, geriatric legions. He was alone and isolated from his interests, his friends, his world, and himself. The community to which he had belonged was diminished, its members said, by his absence, and some did call on occasion or, more rarely, stop by. But first they called Sara to ask if he was well enough and awake, if he wanted company, and whether it was the right time or was he too ill. The calls became more infrequent as the years went on, and then even when someone called, she would have to answer regretfully, "No, not today. Not now." On those rare occasions when someone did come to chat, some old friend or acquaintance, Father would feel himself dull and with little to say. What was to others distant memory was to Norm a reality, and the doings of their world were, in turn, as far away for Father as the terra incognita of his early youth. Only the most loyal could endure to sit in companionable silence as Father stared out the window, waiting for Sara to remind him it was time to eat or to nap.

The only exception throughout this time was the small boy Jerry Patrick, who, along with his terrier dog, had been Norm's "pal" since the boy was three. Before Norm's decline, Jerry had stopped by once a day for a piece of candy, which Father kept in the front hall in anticipation of Jerry's demands. It began, I think, after a Halloween when Norm had more candy than there were neighborhood children and told Jerry in his devil's costume to come back again. He loved Jerry's assurance and push and liked the company of someone so young, and as Norm slipped slowly away from his world, the schoolboy Jerry continued to visit. I would answer the door as Father slept or bitched, and there would be Jerry (now five, six, or seven years old) with his dog, asking, "Is Mr. Koch awake? Can I come in?" Norm was always thrilled to see this friend, who asked for nothing but a cheerful hello, and as the dog sat politely by Father's bed, the two would talk of school, East Street, and clothes. When it began, my father was a giant and Jerry a little boy, but by this point in Norm's tale, they existed at an equal emotional level, balanced in some strange simpatico.

Sara became the most important person in Father's life, the single, loving individual who five days out of seven greeted him in the morning. As the nurse in charge, she supervised far more than his medication and his meals. Paula and Bruce Foster worked on her days off, but it was Sara who organized the shopping, handled problems with the homemaker aides, called the physicians when physical problems arose, and remembered to buy cards and gifts for the children and grandchildren, whose ages and birthdays Norm would now always forget. She was his all, and nobody was prouder than he when she became pregnant with twins. "For goodness sakes, Norm," Paula said one day with exasperation. "You'd think these babies were yours!" The idea of twins, of birth and children and babies and life, thrilled Norm, who for once did not worry about the cost but immediately agreed when I suggested that Sara be paid her normal rates when she had to stop working and take pregnancy leave.

Paula and Bruce took over for that period and, with Aunt Janice, were scandalized when Sara insisted on returning to work six weeks after her daughters' births. Norm, however, was relieved and excited. Sara returned so quickly in part because she did not want to abuse the luxury of paid maternity leave but, I think, also because she missed Norm and did not want to stay away. But Sara did not return alone. Her new children came as well, and each day they cried, slept, ate, and dozed through Sara's shift in small, portable bassinets of the type used today to hold babies safely in a car's back seat. Norm's greatest joy was to hold one or the other of the twins, and when he was strong enough and as a "special treat," sometimes he was allowed to feed them. His life took on if not new meaning, at least new richness. He called them "my girls," greatly offending Brian, who insisted that his daughters should have that title. But Norm's grandchildren were in Atlanta, inconceivably distant both in time and space from his world; these babies were with him in Buffalo. They would awaken as Father sat up in bed for breakfast. When it was time for his nap, a child would be placed at the foot of his bed, and Father would smile at the baby who, he insisted, always smiled back at him. Then Sara's child and Norm would nap together, Father's head shrunk into the pillows at the head of his bed, the child sleeping peacefully at his feet. Of all the memories of all these years, none is more poignant or more powerful to me than the image of my father and Sara Donatello's children all sleeping peacefully together. This, I thought, is how it is supposed to be: a little peace and future's hope. It was what I'd wanted for Norm but had despaired of ever giving to him, and the rightness of the scene—old man and young, young children—somehow justified for me the fury, frustration and angers of the past few years.

I was a frequent flyer between Vancouver and Buffalo, unable to stay in Buffalo and unwilling to stay away. Each new medical crisis returned me to Norm's house, and as he grew weaker, each new responsibility—for nurses, aides, house repair, taxes, and financial planning—tied me closer to the world that Norm progressively relinquished. Rebecca wrote and, angry at my delay, said I should either fly to Japan or give up our dreams. I made reservations and cancelled them, booked and then cancelled again. A part of me knew this was foolishness, but I could not leave; it was impossible for me to fly that far knowing how tenuous was the balance in our Buffalo world. Finally I wrote her a letter saying I could not go anywhere, even to be with her: "I cannot come, although a large part of me wants to. I cannot leave here now." She replied that perhaps we should stop writing and hoping, cease a long-distance love that had lost its immediacy for me and had become a burden to her. "How long are you going to let your father's illness infect your health?" she asked. To that I had no answer. Perhaps she was right, but it was a measure of my confusion that her letter had come as something of a relief, as an excuse and a reprieve for me.

The next several years are a blur of memories, of periodic medical crises and minor episodes. It was in October of 1987 when I was in Vancouver, for example, that my workbooks record a morning call from Sara. It woke me from a dream in which she and I were pushing Father in a pram down East Street on a pleasant Sunday afternoon. In the dream he was our child, Sara's and mine, although his face was still yellow, wrinkled, and old. We three paraded in the day's late sun as autumn leaves gently fell, stopping to talk with others whose children were as tiny and young but whose faces were similarly ancient and spent. It was a Mexican paseo, with everyone determined to enjoy autumn's freedom before hard winter set in.

Then the dream segued to my parents' old bedroom where Norm lay in his crib and stared at the bed that Sara and I now inhabited. His old-child's face was interested and a bit bemused. That was when the telephone rang, and at first it was confusing to talk to her by phone, so real had been the dream.

She told me that Norm had fired a new aide from the previous night, preferring to be alone, and then, on his own initiative, cut back the homemaker agency's service hours at night. I protested that he could not afford independence, but she insisted that it was worth a try and urged me to accept her judgment. "After all, that's what you hired me for." Norm had to try self-sufficiency one more time and had promised her not to leave his bed until she arrived the next morning.

The conversation was strangely like that of the dream's, with talk about how well the baby could walk and how well it got along with its friends. Had he fallen in the last day or two, and was the child able to make friends? Early childhood and infirm old age share the characteristics of fragility and dependence within an all-consuming present. But in the former there is a future to plan, and in the latter, a past to dwell upon. For Norm there would be no more plans such as his immigrant parents had wished upon him, and the looking glass by which we all measure hope had become for him a clouded vision in which prior events were dominant. For us—for Sara, Janice, and me as well—his future held no allure. Like parents of a colic-plagued child, we were intent on immediate change. Had he slept well the night before, and was he able to walk on his own? Did he fight with other children, and was he able to socialize well? The long ago that he remembered so clearly had been mislaid by us, just as most young mothers displace the memories of childbirth's messy pain for the new and more triumphant events in the life of a six-month-old.

A few days later Father called to tell me that he had "an accident." Alone at night, he was getting into bed and "somehow landed on the floor." For what seemed to him like hours, he tried to pull himself erect and succeeded in merely bruising his body against the night table he tried to use for support. Finally, he gave up, clawed a blanket from his bed, and used it all night as a coverlet. The next morning Sara found him on the floor, and his first words were "I know what you're thinking, but it wasn't my fault." Her husband, Ralph, had driven Sara to work, and she asked him to help lift Father back from the floor into bed. "This was the first time he'd ever met Ralph," she laughed over the telephone lines in a separate call. "He came in and stood over Norm, who looked up and said, 'Hi, I'm Norm Koch. Boy! You look tall from here.' " After this she forced Father to again accept overnight aides from the homemaker agency, and Norm agreed, telling me that it was "fair punishment. I know that's what it is." "Have you learned anything from this?" I asked, and he said yes, he had: "I've learned that I'm still old and weak."

But two weeks later, after his bruises healed, Norm had forgotten the incident and again pleaded to be left alone at night. When I reminded him of this and other falls, of his weakness and forgetfulness, he insisted I was making it up and complained to my brothers that "Tom is getting bossy." My brothers believed his frustration was due not to geriatric decline but rather to my strictness. Walter insisted that Norm had the right to choose what level of care he would have, and I, for my part, insisted that he had abdicated that choice when he chose to live and that I would make these decisions for him.

That was the pattern, a gradual diminishment and a series of small incidents, as we waited for calamity to strike. Portents passed in a blur, telltales in the wind reported over the phone by Sara or by Father. He complained to Sara that paying both his father-in-law's and his own heating bills was more than he could afford. Janice and I were paying his, however, through the custodial account I had set up to handle his money. His father-in-law had been dead for fifteen years. He told others I was spending his money "like water" and that he was going to "take over" his own affairs again. On another occasion he called to remonstrate with me for something I'd done but forgot, in the time it took for my number to be dialed, what it was that had aggravated him. Each March he would call me repeatedly to worry that he had yet to do his taxes, and each time I told him not to worry because that was now my job. Valiantly he tried to write to me, but his letters were now a few lines scrawled in a shaky, uneven hand. The firm, strong penmanship in which he once took pride had become a nearly indecipherable flicker of letters bunched together or stranded alone as his ballpoint skittered out of control and across the note pad's page. Each letter said the same thing. He was "better," hoped to return to work and was looking forward to the day when I (or someone) might visit again.

There were pleasant moments throughout these years, I do not mean to deny them. There were days in Buffalo when nothing untoward happened and we would chat about the old times and events that Norm remembered so clearly. Sara would bring his lunch, make his bed, change his clothes, and tell him when it was time to nap. Her son, who visited Father on occasion, became a favorite of Norm's. Like Jerry Patrick, Sara's Richard was a young and strong-willed boy. "Oh, she's going to have her hands filled with that youngster," Father would say with relish to me. "I know just how it will be." Sara would tell us of her son's transgressions, and Norm would laugh with delight because it was precisely for this companionable, essential distillation of life's youth that he lived.

In 1988 Brian's wife, Prudence, visited with Norm's grandchildren for a day. Before their arrival, he fretted and worried to Sara and me over what he could do to entertain the children—then aged eight and twelve. "They're young," he said. "They don't want to just sit around here with me." Did I think he should take them to Niagara Falls? Perhaps they should all go to Buffalo's zoo or Delaware Park, if not the go-cart track where Norm and I had raced with glee twenty-five years before. All these things he once had done with us, and in his excitement, forgot that he could do them no longer. When the children finally came, the day went quickly, and the children were content to spend it with him at his house. They needed nothing further, and for Norm, just being in their presence was exhausting excitement. Walter visited once or twice a year, and after one visit, while I was in Vancouver, Father asked me, "maybe when you're not too busy you could visit me?" He did not remember I had been there two weeks before. While some strength and will had returned, his memory now ran on a narrow trail whose total vista was measured in days. Time had become a valley in perpetual shadow where the back trail, the twist of paths walked long before, was all that could be seen.

What had begun as disagreements over our father became pitched battles between Walter, Brian, and me. They insisted I had no right to take over what our father told them he did not wish to relinquish. To my oldest brother it should have been Norm's choice to have home aides or not, and if injured while alone, Walter said, that was Norm's responsibility. If he called when an aide Father disliked was present, Father would complain to him, and because Norm insisted,

"I don't need all these people," my brothers blamed me for spending their father's money on unnecessary and unwanted precautions. Walt believed—had to believe—that his parent had the capacity to weigh immediate pride against possible injury and to know the difference. I knew from my tenure in Buffalo that my father needed to remain safe, and the wealth of evidence showed that he needed care. Norm could not make these decisions any more, and I could not bear the thought of him lying alone on the floor as he had that night without Sara. Norm went through two psychiatric and neurologic assessments, and the reports confirmed my belief that his "cognitive deficits" were moderately severe. But my brothers, who read the reports as well, continued to insist that I overstated the case. "Father sounded just fine," one or another would say to me after having talked to him by telephone. The man was good at hiding his problems, at playing his other sons (to whom he was "Father" or "Dad") against me, his caretaker, jailer, confidant and friend. They would ask him what he thought about the stock market, and he would reply, "What goes up, comes down"; Brian or Walt would ask by telephone how Norm felt, and their father would reply, "Well, I'm coming along." During these invalided years, he had become adept at using innocuous, stock phrases—he had a base of no more than eleven—to hide the hollow center behind his fragile persona's shell.

The real issue was between what he needed and what he was entitled to. To Aunt Janice and me, Norm's health and safety were paramount. We paid his bills through a custodial account I supported with Father's checking account, from which my powers of attorney let me draw. It was our job to assure his bills were paid and that the necessities of his life—food, shelter, housing, and medical care—were provided. What Father said he wanted did not matter to us when what he needed was so evident. Like King Lear's daughter, Regan, we said:

> O, Sir, you are old;
> Nature in you stands on the very verge
> Of her confine. You should be rul'd and led
> By Some discretion that discerns your state
> Better than yourself.

Like Lear himself, my father and my brothers were concerned that the shell of power be maintained and that Father's emotional needs—

the feelings of control, independence, and self-sufficient purpose—
be met whatever the danger or cost. In the play, Lear demanded his
own guard and retinue, but for Norm power meant the chimera of
financial control. His desires dovetailed with my brothers' wish to
see Norm as an aging but still forceful parent able to make judgments,
dispense wisdom, and handle life as it came. It was a luxury I did
not believe we could afford, because clearly Norm could not add,
subtract, understand analogies, or make associations in his declining
state.

"He really doesn't want to do these things," Sara said to me one
day. "He knows he can't and it frightens him. Norm just doesn't
want to be reminded of that. Keep doing what you do." That was
all the encouragement I needed, because of us all it was Sara Donatello
who perhaps understood Norm best. She had become his best friend.
It was to her he increasingly turned for the love and affection we all
need. Quietly, his sister Janice and I paid her bills, because for Norm
to write the checks each week would mean his companion was a
hireling, and that Father could not accept. We paid his electric and
local tax bills as well, so he did not have the shame of his inability
or the worry over the cost of existence, which Father still was convinced he could ill afford. Like King Lear, who despite abdication
wanted both unconditional love and the chimera of control, Father
desired the best of all worlds. The stalemate in the battle between
my brothers and I assured that he would get it.

Norm grew to hate his sister, to detest her health and ascendancy
after a lifetime of her being "just a girl." It galled him that while he
was bedridden, she could still travel to see her sons, who in their
turn visited Buffalo with some frequency. She came to Norm's house
almost daily to visit, assist with the shopping, pay the nurses, and
watch over him. When the roof leaked it was she who ordered the
repairs. The more she did to help her brother, the angrier he became,
and she never understood that his fury, aimed at her, was really
targeted at his own impotence. So when she would stop by, he would
not talk, and pretended to read the newspaper. If he did speak, his
voice was so low that Janice could never hear it. He told us, Sara
and me, he wished his sons would visit more, but each time he added
that he understood and was proud of the fact that my brothers were
busy men.

We were Norm's sons and that was the problem; we were four

individuals separated by geography, philosophy, and personal mor-
alities, individuals joined only by a receding past, and even there we
were distanced, one from the other. Time had ensured there would
be no unanimity of memory, no surety of community on which a
new and present time could be built. Our childhood and mutual
adolescences had become for each of us a unique vision of grievance
or pleasure, a duty or burden against which each measured and measures his individual world. We were islands on opposite sides of
some temporal, experiental, tectonic plate that had shifted our lives,
once anchored so closely, finally and forever apart. The unconsi-
dered, communal past that only Norm still truly inhabited had become our greatest barrier, a wall against which our lives clashed with
the echo of old battles and early memories.

Another year, when he was in the hospital again, doctors again
predicted his death. My notebook records the day when he lay in
bed, face covered by an oxygen mask, unable to swallow, speak, or
move. Fed through a nasal tube, his arms were mottled by collapsed
veins into which plasma and blood slowly dripped. Only his hands
seemed alive. They were constantly flexing and gripping the sheet,
pulling it nervously or tugging reflexively on the oxygen tube that
assured life's support. Father was unable to speak or understand what
was said by Janice and I, who sat by his bed for hours, waiting for
him to die. But he didn't, and returned a few months later to his
home again, but never, really, to full sentience. For months he was
rarely coherent. His short-term memory grew even worse, and during my visit, Father would be surprised each morning to see me
come through the door to his room. "Who is that?" he would ask
of Sara if I shouted good morning on my way to the kitchen. "It's
Tom," she would explain, and he would say, "Tom? Tom! Is he on
the phone?"

"If I ever get to be like Father," Brian said to me one day, "please
kill me as an act of love." Walter had said the same thing several
times before. His injunction was phrased as an assertion preceding
the request. "If I ever lose my ability to live alone, I'll blow out my
brains. But if I can't—you'll do it for me as a brother, won't you?"
They, like Norm, saw life as a solitary challenge in which disability
was the ultimate failure. Father for years had secreted lethal doses of
prescription pills in his house. Brian had hopes for a brother's eu-

thanasia, and Walter kept guns primed against the event. Both brothers saw their father as time's mirror, a horror at the end of the road. My preadolescent nieces, however, who had reveled in Norm's company on their brief Buffalo visit, were less fearful than their elders. Norm's feebleness held no fear for them, and if Sara needed help getting Norm to bath or cleaned after incontinence, it bothered them not at all. They were willing to accept us, their elders, for what we were alone. Norm's grandchildren were too young to list love in a ledger book or count worth on a balance sheet—this column's human success chalked against one where business failed. Father's greatest gift to us was, perhaps, these years of half-life in which we could see both his diminution and yet feel the tugs of mutual history and time that whispered, You too, will reach the day when you cannot be alone.

As Father slept one day, I remembered an incident from long before and marveled that it was associated with the fragile person I now watched over. I was eight or nine, and we were on our way to Yom Kippur services. A man was pummeling a teenaged boy near the temple as hundreds of worshipers walked past with eyes averted, not wishing to become involved. He had the boy pinned to the hood of a car and a choke hold on his collar. No one said or did anything. no one even looked, until my father turned as we walked past and spun the man around, flinging him against the car's fender and ordering him to "leave that boy alone." The man was too stunned to move or react, and the teenager stood rigid in surprise. Then my father shook his head and rejoined us in our march. "That was very stupid, Norm," was all my mother said. When later I asked her why, she said we did not know the reasons for the assault and had no need to become involved. I had been thrilled by my father's action and told him so the next day. He said it had been a dumb thing and an act that he instantly had regretted. It was an impulse, I think, a spark of the once confident football hero, a moral reflex that he had not known he had.

When his body fought to stay alive, that was reflex too. His fight against all physical odds and hope were the last bit of his former, best self flickering to dominance. But the rest of him, the Norm Koch who had sold furniture to suckers and paid his taxes without a whisper of complaint, the man who was a model citizen, was the one who worried about the price of continuance and the drain of his dotage and infirmities upon the world he'd loved.

Perhaps Paul Tournier is right when he says that "there is one essential, profound, underlying problem and that is that the old are not loved." But it is not that they are unlovable. Most of us respect age as an abstract concept. At the least we admire the ability to survive that it represents. The underlying problem is that too many elderly do not love themselves. Bitterly resentful of the changes that age settles upon them, their anger is a barrier to us all. My elderly Vancouver neighbor Mrs. McPhee was one of these. She held aloof not because no one was interested in her but, more sadly, because she was unable to accept the physical limits that were for her longevity's price. Old Phil the shoemaker was free of this in part because he retained his trade but more importantly, I think, because he worked with a son who admired and respected him. If I had stayed in Buffalo and been with my father through the previous years, his illness would have been easier for us both.

The real existential question is not Who am I, but the geographic What brings me to this point, here and now? My father had known who he was, a German Jew and a furniture man, but when circumstances changed, his definition didn't. He refused to accommodate to a new life and, proud to the very end, lost through that stubborn intransigence most of the friends who had once wished him well. "They don't care about me," he would say. But they did, they missed and hungered for the man each had known for a lifetime. That man died in a hospital bed in the fall of 1984 and was replaced with another who resembled him in many ways but who could not accept infirmity as the price of life.

I have planned a funeral speech countless times, imagined a few old acquaintances at his house, where Sara will help serve punch or tea because so few of his friends can drink alcohol now. Then a glass is raised in toast, not to Father but to the people who remember him and to the help they offered us. Uncle Jules is there, and Julia Shea as well. With us with be Paula Debillio and the physiotherapists who taught Father to walk again and again. Do not be sad, I'll say. We've come to comfort ourselves at the death of a man who lived too long and spent his last years waiting to die, a foolish man who denied with every breath the ultimate joy of being alive. You were his friends and knew him perhaps better than I, knew his strengths as well as his failings in the years when he was strong and clever. Remember there was indeed such a time. My memories, now, are of his dotage, but, I'll say, I do know this: he died without any real regrets and lived his life as best he could. In the end, there is nothing else. Learn from his mistakes and don't let age or infirmity rob your existence of joy. That warning was his final gift, and if we heed it, that will be my father's final victory.

Sometimes I sleep with the light on all night, and often I still dream of my father. The nightmares have disappeared, but one dream persists, and I have it in various versions. It is like an old friend in the early morning, the thing I remember when the alarm clock sounds and I stumble from bed into the kitchen to fumble and wait while the boiling water transforms itself into coffee. To understand it, first this background is necessary.

As a news reporter I once covered a marathon, stood at the starting line and watched two thousand eager people run through the streets at a very respectable pace along a circular course whose finish line was, in truth, the place from which they started. Along the way were water stations manned by volunteers, who passed wet sponges and juice containers to the runners speeding by proudly, heads high and backs slightly arched. For over two hours I watched the procession and the gradual deterioration of some who, towards the end, shambled slowly and could barely lift a drink to their lips or a sponge above their heads. My assignment, of course, was to interview the winners as they crossed the finish line. They were the story, unless a cardiac arrest fouled up the day's pleasure. Then one hustled to find out whose anatomy had failed, asked if it was a preexisting condition, and if so, questioned why someone balanced so precariously on the diastolic side would choose to run a marathon at all. But such drama is rare in the running world, and the day was spent primarily in pleasant waiting until an Australian popped by after two hours and eighteen minutes. The best are almost always dull, semi-professional athletes who cross the line, sip a Coke, and speak as if they had been out for a five-minute stroll. Only a touch of sweat gripping their foreheads betrays the fact that effort has been expended at all.

Then I waited to watch the stragglers fight to end a race that was for each a feat of endurance and drive. I worried with the medical team as runners who hours before had been so confident and proud stumbled through the final yards, spent, their heart's arrhythmic, trying to focus on the finish amidst the sounds of sympathetic watchers who waited with me for this moment. A few stopped within thirty feet of the finish line knowing they were close, the destination just past their present, but also knowing even one more yard was too far. The pains and that pulsing burst of wavering vision demanded from each of these runners immediate rest. Their certitude crumbled, they walked the last few feet to sit humbled on the curb. The present had overtaken the images that had sustained their training and practice runs. Some would finally rise and walk the remaining distance, shuffling and limping into the arms of medics and friends who knew that endurance is the only victory and who remained to offer comfort, praise, and assistance.

In my dreams my father is young and we are running, heads high, along the same marathon course. As we run, we age dramatically, step-by-step, stumbling along an asphalt road and helping each other up the hills. Some nights we finish, panting and walking arm in arm across the final yards, and sometimes one of us drops out, stopping to wave the other on. In the dream's final form, Norm becomes the reporter, standing on the sidelines, and I am running alone. He smiles as I approach the finish line, and in his hand is my steno pad filled with notes about others who had passed by before. As I collapse into the doctors' arms, while an oxygen mask is being fitted to my mouth, he bends forward to ask his urgent question, whose answer, I know, will immortalize me forever. "Isn't the cost prohibitive?" Father asks, face filled with interest and concern, body supported by his cane. His look never changes as I am placed on a stretcher and wheeled to the waiting ambulance. It is the last thing ever seen in the dream as the siren of the ambulance begins to wail and everything dissolves into morning.

Afterword

What We Learned

In the people whom we love there is, immanent, a certain dream which we cannot always discern but which we pursue.

Marcel Proust, *Time Regained*

On the evening of February 15, 1989, Norm Koch slipped into a coma and was taken once more to General Taylor Hospital, where he died peacefully the next morning. After his death I immediately began to drink and remember nothing of the next several days except an impression of rum-filled glasses first appearing before me and then standing sadly empty. I think I was sad for the glasses, for their rapid depletion, but proud to have been the agent of their demise. It was all very confused. The only clear memory I retain is of Aunt Janice watching in some surprise as I drank my rum with beer chasers and stating definitively that "you're going to be drunk in no time at all." People have told me I spent that first evening berating my brothers for their absences over the years, castigating my father for being old and sick, and running up a $120 telephone bill to tell everyone I knew that Norm had died. I behaved, in short, like a drunk: with freedom but without responsibility. I did not drink to lament my Father's passing but rather out of fear for my future and anger at the lack of definition that the present held. My real anguish, in the days following Norm's death, was for myself. "I'm out of a job," I told my aunt the day my father died. "I feel like I've been fired. He's been my life and now I'm out of work." It was as if I went to the office after years at a job to discover my desk had suddenly disappeared. "I feel like an actor who has been in the same Broadway role for years," I lamented to a friend. "Now I'm back here in Buffalo—on stage—and a new play with different actors has opened." Not noble sentiments, to be sure.

Since Norm's death I have tried to understand where we went wrong in Norman Koch's care and how my father's decline could have been made easier for us all. The conclusion I have returned to again and again is that none of us—Father, brothers, physicians, relatives, or friends—were prepared. At each step in this tale everyone reacted to the press of events rather than planning and thinking ahead. We had no personal understanding of a geriatric decline and no way to prepare for the course Father's illnesses would take. This is not uncommon. Few people plan for the worst or think about their deepest fears, and certainly the idea of a geriatric decline with cognitive and physical impairments is something few choose to consider before the fact. One can learn from others, but there are degrees of difficulty in that study. Easiest to learn from are the practical mistakes Norman Koch and his family made. This chapter attempts to describe specific areas of planning and action that, had we thought about and considered them early in this tale, might have made the five years of my father's decline easier.

Norm's misery—and ours—came in large part from his progressive isolation, the distancing of his reality from our family history and his community during a period of illness and decline. Living with age is not necessarily an individual's solitary humiliation. Bitterness, anger, and firm denial in the face of a handicap are social and communal phenomena wreaked on the patient's world. They are not inevitable effects of any specific disease. As counterbalance we needed a program of involvement and association rather than a perspective treating enfeeblement as a crisis separate from Norm's life and prior relations. We needed a program of integration and mutuality before the siege began. This would have required talking, sharing, considering, and planning for certain contingencies before the fact. One idealized paradigm that would have answered our needs is set forth in this section. It identifies areas crucial to the maintenance of an elderly or infirm relation and a method by which both patient and family can work together to minimize the deficits of a physical decline. The first section describes how we could have planned before the event for a potential illness, and the next two sections describe some of the things we perhaps could have done better when illness struck. Where appropriate, I have illustrated various points with information gained in interviews recorded by me with other individuals, families, or professionals as well as with the elements of this story.

PRIOR PLANNING

Early Discussions

Conspicuous in this story is the refusal to accept the possibility of a protracted geriatric illness. We were not prepared because we refused to consider ahead of time the fact that Norman was getting old and might reach a stage of chronic illness or decline. In the years before 1984, when Walter, Norm, and I would join Brian and his family in Atlanta for Christmas, the conversation was usually about family history and family events. We enjoyed the type of reminiscence that those who have spent long periods of their lives together typically indulge in at reunions. But at no time, either before or after my mother's death, did we discuss with Norm how he felt and how we felt about the issues of illness, death, and the potential of physical handicaps. It was a topic odious to Norm and one we dared not broach. If at any time in those years we had taken an hour to discuss what would happen if—if he could no longer care for himself, if he needed help looking after his finances, if he required someone's presence in a difficult medical crisis—then everyone would have been able to face those events with a bit more understanding. Instead, Father simply insisted he would "just die of a heart attack," and we were pleased to let the matter rest with this assertion and hope. Certainly there are better ways than this.

In 1986 I talked to a friend worried that his family was at the beginning of a similar geriatric tale. A Vancouver therapist, Paul C. worried because his parents, who lived nearby, were advancing in age and his only brother resided in Toronto. My problems, Paul said, could easily be his. The components of failing parents and distant siblings is not uncommon. When we talked, Paul's brother was visiting in British Columbia, and Paul was determined to speak with him privately about the possibility of a parent becoming ill. "After all, he lives in Toronto, so it's going to me here with them," Paul said. "I want to find out if my brother's thought about that possibility and what he'd do to help. I mean, [my parents] don't have a lot of money, and I don't want it to be all my responsibility."

That was a reasonable fear. The closest family member often does bear the brunt of elderly care simply because of proximity. I suggested to Paul that he broach the subject with both his brother and his parents, that he inform them all of his fears. A few weeks later he told me he had in fact raised his concerns at a Sunday dinner and was both surprised and relieved at the results: "I was kind of nervous at first, but my father said he and Mother had thought about these issues a lot and knew what they wanted. My brother said how he felt and what he'd do, and I said what if one parent gets sick and the other can't take care? We talked for hours, and at the end I knew I wasn't alone [in my fears] and wouldn't be alone if something happened."

It is important to remember that most elderly—individuals and couples—think about the possibility of traumatic illness, cognitive impairment, or chronic infirmity. They know it is a possibility and in fact may be relieved to discuss it with other family members or friends. Some, of course, may not. Had I had the courage to raise such issues before Norm's illness, he almost certainly would have shied from the topic. In such a situation I could have said, Well, you know how you used to tell us to plan for "just in case," or I just want to make sure I know where you stand and what you'll want. Often individuals will agree to discuss the possibility of infirm age in principle but insist that "this just isn't the time." The best response in that type of situation is, Because you're still healthy and able to care for yourself, it's the best time of all. The idea is to make sure everyone understands before the fact an elderly person's feelings on specific areas of care and concern.

These discussions need not be nebulous or aggressive. For example, it would have been self-defeating to ask my father, When you can't take care of yourself, which of us should look after you? The question would have been too broad and too terrifying. His response would probably have been simple: If I get to that point I don't want to live. But at that point he did want to live, and the issue of dignity within his care, of the value of even proscribed life, is really the issue that needs to be addressed. Had we gently raised the topic, it would have been possible to have a discussion of specific, practical issues in which family members could make suggestions and think a bit about how best to share responsibility when and if it were necessary. For example, I could have said, We're worried, Father, that if you at some point need medical help in the home you won't be able to afford it. Is that a real concern? Discussion would have been possible in the benign areas of home organization, financial planning, Norm's feelings about use of extraordinary medical measures—indeed, many of the elements of practical planning that follow in this chapter.

Such discussions serve three purposes. One is to make sure as many family members as possible are informed and involved. Basic disagreements can be identified before the fact and compromises hammered out, in principle. For example, Walter's insistence that a person with cognitive deficits is not worthwhile and my belief in the value of being, whatever the physical problem, would have stood in stark contrast. Norm would have known the positions of his potential care givers and been able to chose between them. Secondly, any such meeting and conversation means a dialog is begun. Once issues are raised and positions announced, people can start thinking about the problem. The dialog transforms individual fears from something to be denied to ideas already met. Finally, it ensures that the most crucial individual—the elderly relative—feels that he or she is being consulted and not simply taken over by well-meaning family members. In the same way that some parents attempt to involve their children in discussions of financial, business, or family matters, so should the families of elderly individuals make sure their elderly are part of the plans and considerations made on their behalf.

Designated Caretakers

A family is not necessarily a community. Prior history offers no guarantee that when a problem arises it can be dealt with by individuals whose recent decades have been spent in disparate pursuits. But assuming, as most experts do, that community is important and family care a critical part of that support, then the elderly are best served by having family and friends work together to ensure an individual's maintenance. The following model is based in part on academic studies of elderly care as well as on ad hoc programs organized in families I have known in which a member was ill. It is in many ways an idealized paradigm, but to the extent that it can be implemented, several obvious advantages will result. First and foremost is the involvement of the patient in his own care and condition. To the extent that this is possible, it ensures that he or she is recognized as a distinct human being with rights, interests, and responsibilities. The growing alienation of individuals from control of their life is one of the most difficult side effects of infirmity. Second, the model allows for the division of care tasks between family members with different strengths and abilities. Not everyone is a good caretaker or financial manager, and the strengths of each person can be recognized and assigned before the fact, providing an opportunity for everyone to work together in relation to a single patient. Also built in is a structure of emotional support for the care giver himself, for the person who finds himself in the role of daily maintenance during a geriatric decline. Finally, this planning model identifies the broad areas where difficulties are likely to arise and thus divides a huge a problem into clear categories.

In Norm's case there were four areas of serious disagreement between his sons, and from my father's point of view, these were the areas in which he felt diminished and enfeebled: home care, financial planning, legal arrangements, and liaison with medical practitioners. In planning for or in the event of a geriatric crisis, a person can and should be recognized—by the elderly individual and the family—as the elderly individual's designate in each area. One individual can fulfill all roles, or the tasks can be split between several different people. Care givers can be spouses, close friends, relatives—whoever is willing to take on the responsibility of mutual care and concern. The idea is to identify a person willing and able to assist the parent or relative when and if that help is needed. This choice of surrogate should not be imposed on the elderly individual but must, wherever possible, be made in consultation with the "client-relative." Typically family members assume such roles, but they can be taken by close friends as well.

Primary Care Giver

Hugh Carter and his brother have divided responsibilities for the care of two elderly aunts in such a way that all four individuals—

the elderly ladies and the men themselves—feel comfortable with the arrangement: "My brother lives with one and visits the other regularly in the nursing home. We decided long ago that he would handle the 'blue collar' people and I would take on the 'white collars.' In fact, today I have to write a letter to the physicians defining exactly what we do not want in terms of heroic measures in the case of an illness."

This system maximizes the skills and locations of both middle-aged men who, while equally concerned about their elderly relations, are in very different positions in regards to them. Hugh's brother works for the electric company in the family's home town and is comfortable with elements of home care for the one aunt and visits the other with regularity. Hugh, on the other hand, teaches at a university five hundred miles from their home and acknowledges that he could not handle the day-to-day aspects of geriatric care as well as "that dear, sweet man, my brother." But the sibling is uncomfortable talking with "professional people"—nursing home directors, physicians, financial experts—and has given those tasks to Hugh. The one is a primary care giver to whom the other defers on questions of daily maintenance and health. The other oversees "professional" problems and, for example, fields problems with the nursing home, taxes, legal matters, and physician relations. The system allows both brothers to share their concern and, to some extent, the responsibility for their "aunties'" care. Further, Hugh asserts that when the aunts do die that a part of his job will be to help ease his brother through the transition from primary caregiver to unattached individual.

It makes sense to designate one individual as the primary care giver, the individual whose task is the daily medical and home maintenance of the elderly relative. Whether that person is at home or in a nursing home, he or she still needs supervision, human contact, and evidence of the concern of others for his or her continuance. Others involved in this type of care-sharing arrangement will normally, as does Hugh, defer to the primary caretaker's judgment in general matters and function in a supportive role to both the care giver and the client. The surrogate roles may be broken down into financial, legal, and medical posts.

Financial Surrogate

Whoever is designated as financial caretaker should discuss with the client-relative the broad outline of that person's financial picture and, before illness strikes, outline possible ways in which he or she would be able to help. For me to have begun this affair with no idea of my father's resources was a serious mistake. I resented his "cheapness," and he, for his part, didn't understand my anger. A bit of prior knowledge and planning could have avoided much of that misunderstanding.

It would have been intelligent if I—or whoever was to be my father's financial second—had met with Norm and his stockbroker in the years before this tale began. The three of us could have discussed, in general terms, issues of income, finance, and plans for contingencies in which medical expenses would be significant. After a business relationship of more than thirty years, the broker knew my father's perspective on stocks, bonds, and monies better than anyone else. When I received the power of attorney it was this man who could say definitively that "your father always did 'x' or 'y' " and ensure that I acted in accord with Norm's preferences as well as his needs. Since these powers grant an individual the right to act in another's stead "as he would were he able," such guidance from a broker, accountant, or other source is legally important.

It is the financial surrogate's job to make sure that the client-relative is as protected as possible, and that means reviewing, before the fact, aspects of an elderly individual's health insurance. There are excellent programs offered, for example, by the American Association of Retired Persons, that supplement Medicare and, for a nominal sum, can cushion the mountain of medical bills that accompany an illness in the United States. If care beyond a person's means is needed, it would also be this surrogate's job to work with family members to find ways to raise the necessary capital.

Legal Surrogate

Either the same person or another working closely with the financial surrogate would be ready to stand in to oversee the relative's legal affairs. The legal surrogate should know where a person's legal documents are kept: mortgage paper, house deeds, birth certificates, stock certificates, insurance policies, will, and personal papers. In what banks does a person keep his or her accounts? Is there a will (and if not, one should be drawn up), and who has a copy? If there are life insurance policies, who wrote them and are they up to date? If additional medical insurance has been purchased, it is critical that someone know what agencies hold those policies so, in the event of serious illness, claims can be submitted. These are all legal issues pertinent to financial matters, and the legal and financial surrogates, if they are separate individuals, would need to work closely together to make sure everything is in order.

In some cases, and especially those where religious convictions are strong, it makes increasing sense for adults of any age to discuss with their lawyers the concept of a living will in which they can state precisely their feelings about prolonging life by artificial means. This is a medicolegal gray area, but in the latter years of the 1980s, cases coming to court made increasingly clear that an individual's wishes would be honored by the courts where those wishes were clearly known. Those who are opposed to being kept alive on a respirator or through feeding tubes when their brain's function has ceased, for example, should discuss with the legal surrogate and a lawyer that belief. Similarly, those who wish to donate organs in the event of their death need to make that clear as well. The more clearly a client-relative has stated, in health, his views on debilitating illness, the easier it is for those who have chosen to assist during a medical crisis.

Most lawyers agree that appointment of an attorney of fact is good insurance for all adults—not simply those who are elderly—to ensure that a person's needs will be met in the case of sudden illness or accident. This is especially important in planning for a geriatric de-cline, and the legal surrogate should have a valid power of attorney for his client-relative. This is a legal document in which an individual makes of the designate an "attorney of fact," giving the surrogate the right to act on the grantor's behalf until or unless the power is withdrawn. This is not a right to be taken lightly, and both the designate and the relative should discuss its meaning with an attor-ney. It is important to remember that a power of attorney is a legal document certified by the courts. A personal letter or "do it yourself" document will not serve.

Often elderly individuals will insist that their spouse can take over if necessary. But if that wife or husband has never handled the family accounts and has no experience with financial affairs, the result can be a disaster. In other cases, although previously able, the spouse may have illnesses or deficits that would disqualify him or her as well. Here the legal and financial surrogates, working with that spouse, can assist the healthier of two aging relatives to plan and make appropriate decisions.

Another form of surrogate relation is the guardianship in which a court determines that an individual is not legally capable of making his or her own judgments and, if necessary, appoints someone to act in the patient's stead. Laws vary from state to state on the level of diminished capacity required before such action can be taken. Unlike the power of attorney, appointment of a guardian limits the rights of an individual to act on his or her own behalf. Therefore, many states set stringent qualifications for guardianships. Guardianships are used to protect a person who, left alone, might make decisions or take actions that are contrary to reason, history, and that individual's experience.

Insurance, house payments, medical necessities—all this sounds like common sense, but it is these mundane but critical issues that a legal surrogate and his relative can think about and plan before problems arise. It would take, at most, an hour's time for surrogate and relative to make a list of the location of important documents and payment schedules on mortgage and insurance policies and place that list in a very safe place. For those, like Norm, who have more than minimal means it would make equal sense to introduce the legal surrogate to the patient's lawyer and spend a half hour explaining what arrangements the elderly individual has made with his family.

Medical Surrogate

Had I once accompanied my father on a visit to Dr. Pangless's before this tale began, our relations during later medical crises might have been easier. As it was, Dr. Pangless was faced with a patient's relative he did not know and who must, at times, have seemed as troublesome as the patient's disease. I wanted information and believed that as Norm's son I had an absolute right to make demands. But Dr. Pangless (and other medical personnel) who may have known my father for years knew me not at all and saw my demands as excessive and unnecessary. Had Norm and I together visited his physician before this tale began, to inform him that in the case of illness I would be the relative assuming responsibility for Norm's care, some of the disputes that did occur could perhaps have been avoided. This visit would have had the added advantage of giving the physician a family member to call if he or she had concerns about the patient's health.

It is crucial that whoever is to be a medical surrogate for the elderly have, before the fact, as complete a medical history as possible. On his various hospital admissions, General Taylor personnel would try to take my father's medical background, and he would cheerfully insist there were no family history of cancer (his mother died of leukemia), no chronic medical problems (forgetting he had been taking thyroid medication for several years and, for a decade, LuKeran for his chronic leukemia), no allergies (forgetting his sensitive skin); there were no medical problems at all, Norm would say, excepting a "bum hip." My father forgot or did not understand that his history of ulcers, for example, might be a crucial factor in his care. Any chronic condition or major medical trauma in a person's past should be a part of this history. A copy of the history should be kept at the relative's house and taken to the hospital during any admission. Had we done this my father's tape allergy might have been included and the tape burns he suffered after the hip operation avoided.

Had he changed physicians any time during the years chronicled in this book, presumably his medical records would have been transferred with him. But a good, concise patient history—childhood diseases, adult hospitalizations, chronic illnesses, constant medication, and some family background—is one of the best ways there is to introduce oneself or one's relative to a new medical team. Not only does it guard against forgetfulness on the part of an ill and elderly man but, if prepared by that person or his medical surrogate, it states very strongly that people have considered the possibility of medical problems and made intelligent plans against the day when such a history might be needed. Not only does it make things easier for the physician, but if it includes a statement that the surrogate is to act for the patient during his illness on medical affairs, it gives legitimacy to that involvement.

It would be equally helpful if the surrogate, relative, and doctor discussed the issue of heroic measures in their first meeting. My father, for example, felt strongly that at no point did he want to be kept alive by mechanical means, and while I knew this, I am not sure his doctors did. By discussing the issue in abstract before a crisis, family and physician can work together when a crisis occurs. If this issue has been discussed with a family lawyer, then notes or documents from that meeting should be part of the patient history kept ready against a crisis. Certainly on issues like this, those who have accepted medical and legal responsibility should be clear, one to the other, about who will make decisions and where the documents are. Because physicians retire and other doctors come on a case in the hospital, it is sometimes a good idea to have several copies of these documents and to make sure they are available not only to the family physician but, when a crisis occurs, to hospital staff.

Often when a crisis occurs, decisions need to be made quickly, and family relations can be irreparably damaged if one or another relative believes that a surrogate acted without consideration of first the patient's and secondly the family's position. Prior sharing of information on what the elderly patient wants—and acting upon that choice when the time comes—will make all the difference in a future where all live with what has occurred.

Community Surrogate

In 1983 and 1984 my father's Buffalo community—friends, co-workers, and sister—was concerned about him. They worried about his dietary habits and ongoing depression. Although I visited with some frequency, it never occurred to me to ask them how Norm was doing. Nor did it occur to them to speak to me about their concerns. In cases like ours where no child lives in the elderly's immediate community, it would have been intelligent to have one individual designated as community surrogate. In the decade before this story began I visited my father's Buffalo home at least twice a year and on each trip visited my aunt, the Bees, and other members of Norm's circle. But on my visits I always saw these people only in Norm's company. Had I written to them or talked with them individually about my father, we would have been more prepared and certainly more aware of nascent problems as they developed. Where there are longtime ties, it makes sense to have the elderly relative inform his or her friends that if they see health problems developing, "Tom" (or Brian or Walter or Jack or Jill) should be contacted. "I'm sure I'll be all right," Norm would have said to Mrs. Bee, "but if I get, you know, funny some day, well, do me a favor and let my Tommy know."

The community surrogate, working with local friends, also can make temporary convalescence easier for the relative. In his first years of illness, a person's peer group is the ultimate support, and when an elderly individual is ailing, those with whom he or she has been friends for years are often glad to help. But if a younger family member "takes over," they may step away for fear their help will be rejected. Their participation should be encouraged and their suggestions solicited about the care or condition of an elderly client-relative. "I wanted to tell you I was worried about Norm," Mrs. Bee said to me once in 1985. "I knew he wasn't eating and seemed to be, well, just not right. But it didn't seem to be my place." So she talked to Aunt Janice, who also thought of me as a distant son who, until this trial began, did not want to be involved. That was my failure, mine and Norm's, and we paid dearly for that omission.

Often another relative lives in the same city, and children assume that an aunt or uncle will willingly take charge when a problem arises. Frequently that is the case, and certainly in this story my Aunt Janice served her brother (and his sons) well. But it is unfair to expect another elderly relative who may have physical problems of his or her own to shoulder the whole burden of care. Nobody can do it all. A community surrogate would have been sensitive to my aunt's needs much earlier and at the same time better able to gauge the extent of care Norm required.

Surrogate Relations

Those who accept a surrogate's position before the fact must be willing, in the event of debilitating illness or accident, to act upon it. This cannot be done at a distance, and a part of accepting such a post is a willingness to be present should the need arise. If several people are to be involved in the care of another, it is important that information gained by one be shared with the rest. I learned only after my father's death, for example, that years before Norm had given my brother Brian his power of attorney. Brian did not tell me at first because he was convinced it was unnecessary to exercise those powers, and then because Father—who had forgotten that an attorney of fact already had been assigned—signed a new document for me. Had I known about those earlier powers—and had my brother been willing to assume their responsibility—then the organization of support for Norm would have been easier during his gastric bleed.

The surrogate system works best when all the surrogates live in the same city as the elderly relative. When there is physical distance separating involved family members, problems more easily arise. While Hugh and his brother have worked out an acceptable division of labor despite their separation, that arrangement is based, in Hugh's words, on his determination "never to second-guess" the other. Each part of this system must work together and utilize current knowledge. For the person handling finances never to visit the community members or for the medical surrogate only to consult by phone with physicians is an invitation to disaster.

Working together becomes extremely complex when caregivers are geographically separated. The relations between them often degenerate over what seem to be the most innocuous things. Recently, for example, I talked at length with a friend, Heather B., who was beside herself with rage. She had been overseeing the complex care of her mother-in-law, Patricia, who recently had lost the use of one arm in a complex battle with cancer. With the doctor's enthusiastic approval, Heather had Patricia's car modified for one-handed use so the woman could continue to drive. Then Heather's brother-in-law, Harold, came to visit and told his brother that "We can get the county to pay for that type of work. Maybe Heather should give them a call."

Predictably, Heather was furious. "If he thinks something should be done," she shouted at her husband, "let him stay here and do it." To Harold, it was an innocent suggestion but Heather took it as an attack on all she had done (while raising her children, looking after her own mother and holding down a full time job) and relegated her to "servant status." For the rest of the visit, she avoided her brother-in-law and repeated her indignation—vocally and nightly—to her husband. Had Harold treaded more softly, praising the work his sister-in-law had done, and asked how, during the visit, he might be of help, then a suggestion might have been more appropriately received. But by blundering in with the best of intentions, he only alienated the single most critical care giver his mother had in town.

The point is that there has to be at least one surrogate in overall charge, and ideally it will be the person closest to or most willing to be with the aged individual for extended periods. That principal care giver is the one to whom others must come. It can take days or weeks to understand an elderly individual's limits and the complex relations among community, care, finances, and personal choice are difficult to balance. What seems at remove like an extravagance may, to the individual in daily association, be an obvious necessity. Throughout my father's last years of medical decline, for example,

Walter consistently criticized the cost of Norm's home-care arrangements as unnecessarily expensive. "As expensive as any for the Shah of Iran," he sneered, and because he visited rarely, he could criticize from a safe distance. Had finances been left to him in Denver, he would never have authorized monies be spent for the level of home and nursing care I believed to be necessary.

Legally, the individual with the power of attorney or a guardianship will have the right to decide on financial allocations. But where several relatives are involved, it is sensible to set up a fail-safe mechanism to guard against real disagreements. My brothers and I, for example, would all have listened to Leo Stein had we asked him to arbitrate a serious disagreement. Walter would not have accepted Uncle Jules's decision, however, and I would not have listened had my mother's sister, Aunt Agatha, attempted to mediate. Usually all can agree before the fact on a family lawyer, a relative, or an old friend to settle disputes between family members. The mediator needs to be someone not too close to the patient, an individual who can maintain perspective on the emotional roller coaster of illness and geriatric decline.

If a single individual takes on all these roles, other family members should recognize that the caretaker is in many ways as much at risk as the patient. Even when the caring roles are divided, the health of the person who is on site and involved daily is potentially at risk. Caring for an elderly relative is like holding a second job, and in extreme cases it becomes a full-time position. Studies of care givers have found that after a certain period without relief, their health declines as well. To guard against this and to ensure the widest possible involvement, a system of family relief can be instituted in which others—whoever is assigned to specific tasks—visit both care giver and elderly together. Often, the care giver becomes so involved and so caught up in his client-patient's case that he or she does not see the effect that work is having. Time off is necessary, and when the legal or medical surrogate can take over for a week or even a weekend, the caretaker gains a better perspective on the reality of the patient's condition.

If the situation becomes long-term, occasional weekends are not enough to guard the health of all. Increasingly, various communities are starting respite services, which provide daily or at least weekly assistance so the care giver can get out of the client-relative's house.

Often these services are volunteer organizations that will send a trained aide into the house for several hours, ensuring the care giver time to be away and on his or her own. In the past, many have used homemaker services for exactly this function, but the demands on these agencies have grown so fast that, at least in Buffalo, they are no longer able to provide this type of occasional or short-term relief. Physicians, hospital social workers, and members of the clergy are all aware of what resources a community may provide and are usually delighted to provide that information to any who ask.

Caring for an elderly relative is a sacrifice, even when made freely. It means a lack of personal time and sometimes drastically reduced earning power. I estimate, for example, that caring for Norm cost me about $150,000 in lost income. It is usually important that this be recognized in some way. Sometimes a bequest in the client-patient's will is made to compensate the care giver, but where money is available, it makes sense to give the care giver at least a token wage during the caring period. Norm tried and I refused, but had we all discussed the possibility of such a situation earlier, the wisdom of such a "salary" would have been apparent. Even a small salary confirms the care giver's importance, and in many cases money for personal expenses will make the difference between a relative's ability to provide care and a situation in which one has to say, "I'm sorry, Mom (or Dad, or Auntie), but I can't afford to do this anymore."

All of these measures are designed to create a structure that will involve and include family members before a serious or degenerative condition occurs. They have the further aim of ensuring that the elderly relative is involved and recognized as an adult within his or her community. The intention is to prepare for and head off problems that may occur while emphasizing to the aging person that he or she is not isolated and alone, but rather surrounded by individuals who care for and respect the elderly person.

EARLY WARNING SIGNS

The surrogate program can act as an early warning system, alerting families to potential problems before they become critical. Consider one of the most common of geriatric problems, the dangerous driver.

Driving

All elderly individuals suffer a decrease in visual acuity. It is a fact of aging that certain cells within the eye do not regenerate, and as one gets older, sensitivities diminish that are important to eye-hand coordination. Elderly are inevitably more susceptible to night blindness, for example. This is a condition in which the eye adjusts more slowly to rapid changes in light intensity and reflections so, for example, headlights at night can cause momentary blindness. At the same time, reaction times and the ability to concentrate will also diminish in the elderly. These are gradual changes whose threshold occurs at different times for different people. In addition, almost any other sensory loss—such as loss of hearing—or other specific physical impairments can effect a person's ability to handle the thousands of decisions a driver makes unconsciously whenever he or she is behind the wheel.

We had all seen the signs in Norm. In the late 1970s he sometimes drove unthinkingly through stop signs and lights because of a lack of concentration. Each time a brother or I visited, there was a new dent or scrape on his Chevrolet, which he blamed on "parking lot bumps." None of us liked to ride with him, and while in Buffalo each of Norm's sons insisted on driving him. But none of us raised the issue with Norm's friends or sister, who sometimes rode with him as well. Later I learned that they too had recognized that my father's driving abilities were degenerating. But it was nobody's responsibility to broach these issues with us, with Norm, or with his physician. Often changes in driving patterns are a first sign of some organic illness that, if caught early, can be treated.

Driving is a powerful symbol in our society, and it is the rare individual at any age who voluntarily gives up its power. But it is fair neither to the family nor society to remain silent when a clearly substandard driver is allowed to remain on the road. A good physician, alerted to the problem, can often find physiologic reasons for the apparent degeneration. If the patient insists on driving, physicians or concerned relatives can, in many states, ask state officials to revoke an individual's license on medical grounds. More often, however, a physician or specialist may ask the patient to agree to limit his or her driving to fit the emerging pattern of physical limits. If night blindness is a problem, for example, the doctor may extract a promise from the patient to drive only during the day.

The community surrogate in such a situation would not only seek advice from a person's friends (have you driven with Norm lately? Good ride?) but, once the problem was identified, work to assure that limited motor vehicle privileges did not isolate the handicapped individual. Certainly Norm's sister, the Bees, and other friends would have been only too happy to drive their friend had any of us asked. In addition, many communities have organizations for the elderly and the sight impaired that can provide support and training for those with minimal vision problems. In Columbus, Ohio, for example, the state Rehabilitation Services Commission has a bureau of services for the visually impaired. One of its counselors, Marilyn Perrin, says that many of her clients are elderly individuals with vision problems. That city's Riverside Methodist Hospital also runs a large outreach program for elderly citizens with specific handicaps. Unfortunately, that degree of support is the exception, but in most communities an individual's personal physician can recommend support, outreach, and alternative services for the patient-relative.

One simple, practical alternative to risky driving is a charge account with a local taxicab company in the impaired person's name. It is not uncommon for individuals who cannot drive because of disabilities to use taxis as an alternative. In most areas regular use of a cab is in fact less expensive than automobile ownership and upkeep. Often regular users make friends with a few drivers who become "theirs" and take on as part of their daily route the transportation of those individuals. As a Columbus, Ohio, taxicab driver once explained to me, "I had this one client for years who had MS. My cab is big and I can take a wheelchair, so every morning I would pick this man up and take him to work, and my last run in the afternoon would be to bring him home. Sure, I liked it. It was steady work, rides I knew about each day, and the guy had someone he knew and trusted, like a friend and chauffeur."

The community surrogate in this case would help identify the problem. The medical surrogate would ensure that any organic causes were treated or ruled out, while the financial surrogate could arrange alternative transportation with an eye to the patient's budget.

Cognitive Decline

Nothing is more frightening to the individual or the family than growing signs of apparent mental impairment. Nobody wants to admit that a disease or deficit affecting an individual's memory or reason is occurring.

It is frightening when an individual who has always been vibrant and sharp begins to tune out for periods and to find gaps in his or her day. To discover that a person who always looked after his or her own affairs now forgets to fill out tax forms, pay bills, keep appointments, or remember birthdays is scary. These are things the relative-client notices first but often denies (to others and himself) out of fear. Because friends may see the signs more clearly than a son or daughter, the community surrogate should listen carefully if friends say that the elderly relative appears to be undergoing personality changes.

The first thing most people think of today is Alzheimer's disease because it is so much in the news. But many things can cause Alzheimer's-like symptoms of apparent short-term memory loss or decreased attention span. Increased hearing loss, for example—and its attendant isolation—sometimes produces similar symptoms, as do other organic syndromes. By ignoring the symptoms, a problem can only get worse, and that is a pity. If hearing loss makes an individual seem as if he or she is "just spaced out," a hearing aid may bring back that person's previous level of attention. In other cases a dementia may be caused by other problems that are controllable and perhaps reversible. For example, what is called "multi-infarct dementia" affects speech, coordination, and memory following a stroke. Patients and families discouraged by the symptoms of this type of dementia may give up and say that the person is just senile and the situation hopeless. But multi-infarct patients may be kept stable for years or, with good therapy and proper care, actually improve.

The point is that both the individual's community at large and his or her medical surrogates need to be aware of possible problems and treat them for what they are: symptoms and not a death sentence. There are a number of tests that specialists can do to ascertain the degree and the cause of impairments when and if they occur. These range from CAT scans to nonintrusive, simple association quizzes that identify the type of impairment. It is helpful and sometimes critical in cases of personality change if the medical surrogate keeps a list of the incidents that are symptomatic. If a patient is having delusions or acting in a paranoid fashion, write down a brief description of the episodes and discuss them with the family physician or a specialist. If the problem is an inability to handle addition and subtraction in an individual who was an accountant, let the medical experts know. The more information a surrogate can provide, the better the chance for an accurate diagnosis.

If a patient has cognitive difficulties, as Norm did, it is important that patients and family recognize the fact. Alzheimer's, poststroke disorders, and other syndromes that cause personality change and memory loss do not extinguish the history we hold in common with our elderly. Even for those who, like my father, find they are unable to care for themselves, there is a world of emotion, memories, and caring that can still be shared. Support groups for families of patients with Alzheimer's and similar dysfunctions have grown up in recent years, and most good family physicians are knowledgeable enough to urge family members to solicit help, advice, and support from such organizations in their area.

Physical Aids at Home

My parents put in a downstairs bathroom and an invalid's toilet with a raised bowl as preparation for mobility problems in old age. That was certainly a sensible precaution, without which my father could not have lived out his last years in his own home. Mrs. McPhee used her apartment furniture as a makeshift support so she could move through her apartment.

As individuals get older, they or their friends may develop mobility problems that make both visiting and living at home more difficult. Since few homes today and none in the past were designed with the handicapped in mind, changes will likely need to be made. A few hundred dollars' worth of alterations may make the difference between continuance in a treasured residence and dislocation to a nursing home or small apartment. Just as important, those changes will make it easier to entertain friends who may have physical impairments and be unable to use normal doors, entryways, and bathroom facilities.

Especially in areas like Buffalo where snow and ice are factors, a railing near the outside door makes excellent sense. Where there are steps, use of a wheelchair style ramp can be installed "as a precaution" or "so that Mrs. X can still come and visit." For several hundred dollars, a carpenter can build and install a wood ramp for those whose homes may need it. In the house, doorways can be enlarged so that an individual on an ambulatory walker can easily go from room to room. Some builders now design for wheelchair access, although in private residences this is still the exception and not the rule. Nonskid surfaces should be placed in all shower stalls and bathtubs and hand grips need to be placed in those same locations as well as by the toilet and, for some, near a shaving mirror.

For the elderly, these changes are excellent insurance against household accidents and, ideally, should be installed before an incapacitating illness makes them necessary. Had we suggested to Norm in 1982 that a few hundred dollars' worth of home repairs might assure his continuity in the house he loved, I think he would have agreed to the changes. Often, if a relative takes the initiative to make his or her home accessible and safe—"so that you can visit me anytime"—the elderly individual will then decide to modify his own home in a similar way.

A family physician can make excellent suggestions to the medical surrogate about what aids would best be added for an individual patient, and the community surrogate can rally support from friends, who may be as grateful as the patient that such appliances are added. The community surrogate also should, in his talks with the individual's circle, be aware of possible mobility problems within that community. It is as important to ensure that old friends can still visit as it is to make sure that the specific parent or relative is safe at home. If Mrs. Bee had said to Norm that his front step was icy and difficult in the winter and she wished he'd put up a hand rail so she could visit him more often, he would have had it done immediately. When the problems are a result of an operation or illness, then the medical surrogate should ask the physician for referral to an occupational therapist, whose job it is to know what changes can best ensure continuance at home.

A book by J. R. Carey on how to modify rooms for specific handicaps is cited in the bibliography.

WHEN A CRISIS OCCURS

Nursing

When a medical crisis occurs even the best plans or programs may need to be changed. Nobody can plan perfectly for the specific event, although the better the preparation the easier it is to bend and shape oneself to the actual crisis. It does not matter if the problem is a stroke, an infection, a heart attack, a degenerative disease, diabetic complications, or emphysema. Whatever the immediate medical problems, the priorities are clear: To ensure the best chances of recovery while keeping the patient as comfortable as possible. Then, after hospital discharge, to maximize home care and convalescence for the comfort of the patient without totally exhausting the care giver.

Many people have written on the practical problems of patient care in the hospital and practical aspects of home care for individuals with permanent impairments. Mace and Rabins' *The 36-Hour Day* has excellent information on many of these issues. Jo Horn's *Caregiving: Helping an Aged Loved One* is perhaps the best book I've found that deals with practical issues. To their work I would only add that, where financially possible, hiring of a nurse or home aide—in the hospital and during home convalescence—is often a long-term economy.

Practically, home nursing can be an enormously cost-effective and beneficial way to maximize an individual's recovery. In 1985, when Paula Debillio came again to our aid, it was after a hospital case in which the elderly patient refused home care and injured herself as a result. Paula related, "She was doing fine when she went home [from the hospital]. Then she said she didn't need help at home anymore because she had her husband. I told her it was too soon, but they insisted. I heard later that she fell, broke something, and was back in the hospital. They called to see if I could help, but I was already working for your father. She died shortly after."

It is sad that physicians rarely make house calls anymore, because it is in the home that care most needs to be given. Had Dr. Pangless visited his patient in his house in 1984 or 1985, I believe, many of the problems could have been minimized or avoided. Certainly the most important thing we did in August 1984 was ask Paula Debillio to visit Norm at his home and evaluate physical problems in situ. Without her intervention and assistance I doubt if Walter or I— separately or together—could have gotten my father to the physician's office or his treatment begun. In the weeks preceding the hepatitis attack, Paula's periodic visits continued, and throughout the next five years she was a constant source of help and information. I am firmly convinced that both Norm's continuance and the pleasure he got out of life during the years chronicled here was directly attributable to his hiring nurses like Paula, Bruce, and Sara. A hidden benefit of their presence was that these professionals sometimes functioned as informed arbiters when my brothers disagreed with me about Norm's care. Walter, for example, who did not trust my judgment, would listen when Paula told him that something was needed to keep Norm safe and well. For his part, Brian respected Sara's judgment and the way she weighed the risks and constantly attempted to balance my father's needs against his desire for independence.

I relied on them absolutely, knowing that I was too close and not well enough trained to make the judgments (Can he be left alone? Is he too frail to even try? Is a problem developing that needs physician input?) that are a nurse's stock in trade. A skilled professional who knows the patient's home context—and family situation—carries an authority that the primary care giver who is not a medical professional just does not have. Since most physicians have abdicated their in-home, on-site skills, nurses have taken on these tasks. Where conflicts arise between surrogates, it may be the presence of nurses that keeps the surrogates pulling together and working with and for the elderly client-relative.

At the beginning, we also used the local Visiting Nurses Association, which provided occupational and physical therapy following my father's hip operation. Many communities have similar services, and a good family physician or hospital will know how to contact this type of service and be able to judge whether their participation is appropriate. Such organizations have huge caseloads and cannot take on the duties of a private nurse or homemaker service. Their job, in most areas, is to make periodic visits to help change a patient's dressings, assist with medications, check on progress, and teach the family necessary at-home skills. Those who want or need full-time assistance will, in most communities, have to arrange for it themselves.

Another benefit of home nurses and visiting nurses is their ability work with the care givers themselves. It is not simply as a respite from care givers' labors that nurses are of value. Few nonprofessional individuals know how to help an individual use a walker, steady someone on a four-pronged cane, help with specific rehabilitations, change bed linen when the patient is in bed, or do other very basic but necessary services. For those who want to learn—and many people do—most nurses and nursing associations will help a relative or care giver anxious to assist a client or client-relative. Paula, for example, was especially generous in her role as teacher. From her I learned not only the specifics of patient care appropriate to Norm's immediate condition but the general protocols to ensure that his home environment remained safe and hygenic.

How Much is Too Much?

The question is how much can any one person do, and there is no easy answer. My brothers were shocked that I bathed my father and accused me, at times, of "playing doctor." In other cases, relatives have gone to extreme measures because of a determination to take all a patient's physical necessities upon themselves. Here is one example in which that insistence probably was not a service to anyone. Denis Howe is an acquaintance who, with his mother and siblings, helped care for an ill and senile father. At one point Denis wrote to me of his father that

he gets clogged up. It must be hell, because he'll go five days without shitting. When it won't come out my Mom, Dad, or myself has to pick it out. . . . His shit is like petrified loaves of knotted bread with the consistency of half-dried clay. The size of the logs is like half a large hoagie [sandwich]. Because of Dad's weakness, we rarely put him on the usual toilet. Instead, we carry a portable one next to the bed before lifting him over onto it.

A severe constipation like this man suffered can often be the result of diet. It is also sometimes a symptom of other types of serious distress. In mild cases, the use of laxatives, enemas, and other remedies can make the patient (and family) more comfortable. Often, changes in diet can help. Physical removal of patient's stool is not only unpleasant but can be dangerous if done improperly. Eventually, the family did get medical advice, and with a new diet and different medications, the problem ceased. But Denis and his immediate family were, for a period, so determined to take care of the patient without help that they prolonged the problem and certainly the unpleasantness for all parties involved.

Some individuals can and do take over what are commonly considered aspects of trained medical care. This includes the giving of medication—including injections—and other types of treatment. Margaret Nielson, who spent eight years caring for a beloved grandmother during a long-term geriatric decline, was determined to learn every skill necessary to keep the woman at home, as the following anecdote shows.

She developed a decubitus on the front of her leg, an ulceration on the skin the size of a half-dollar. When it finally did crust over and separate from good tissue it was becoming necrotic. I was trying to clean it and remove it myself. My stepmother, who was a nurse, showed me how I could remove some of the tissue and try and keep it clean. It was getting so bad that we ultimately had to take her into the emergency room and have it looked at. We had this one young doctor that cleaned it off a little bit and told me to put on these wet dressings, change it three times a day, and this would clear it up. Well, for a week I did what he told me, and it got worse and worse and worse. It was turning to mush and getting blacker and blacker, and all the tissue around it was turning yellow. So I took her back to the surgeon who did her hip [implant] and he told me not to listen to anyone else. He showed me what to do, and he took off one smaller, black scab, and the bigger one he said was too involved and he wanted to wait a little while. I took her home and I took if off with my stepmother sitting there, and I did it with a tweezers and a razor, a straight-edge razor blade.

Debriding a wound can be a dangerous procedure. But Margaret was supervised by a nurse and instructed by the physician. She was convinced that she could learn to do whatever was needed and insistent on her grandmother's continued residence in her own home. Several years after her grandmother's death, Margaret started to work full-time for Homemakers, Inc., and began to work towards returning to school and earning an M.D.

Few people are able to take on that much responsibility. For many of her years as a care giver, Margaret also employed home aides to assist in the grandmother's care. Nobody can take care of another individual for twenty-four hours a day. In cases where disoriented patients may wander off at all hours—in Alzheimer's disease cases, for example—an overnight home aide can ensure the patient's safety while allowing the resident care giver to sleep without worry. Certainly Norm was well served by his home aide staff. In many cases a combination of relatives, aides, and nursing supervision can maintain an individual in his or her environment indefinitely.

Rules vary widely on the degree to which the expense of home care can be reimbursed by medical insurance policies. In New York state, for example, the cost of my father's aides was not reimbursed, although the cost was a tax-deductible expense. Payment to some agencies can, in some jurisdictions and under some policies, be reimbursed.

WHEN IS HOME CARE NOT ENOUGH?

I have talked to some about nursing-home experiences and read in the technical literature about the pros and cons of placing a relative in a facility for extended periods. But I cannot speak from extensive, firsthand experience, since it is nothing we had to live through, and for that I am proud and grateful. Because I believe the infirm elderly should be a part of our whole, I am opposed to their separation from the existing community except as an absolute, last resort. I considered Norm's removal from his home more out of my own feelings of inadequacy ("How can I care for this wreck?") and anger ("He's nasty so I'll just show him") than out of clear medical need. I suspect that many relatives make the decision for nursing-home care not because it is necessarily in the patient's best interest, but instead because they themselves cannot deal with the issues a geriatric crisis may raise.

Both Paula and Sara worked on a case, for example, in which the patient had suffered a debilitating stroke that left him with partial paralysis and a speech defect. They spent several months helping the man, until his wife and children decided he needed to be placed in a long-term care facility. Paula was furious and said of that decision:

It was criminal! That man didn't need to be put in a home. They just couldn't handle his problems. He was aware and said he could afford home care. But his wife didn't like having him around like that. I was there when they called the doctor, and he agreed with me. But a son-in-law was a lawyer, and he drew up the papers. Stan couldn't speak well, but he did understand, and he wanted to be at home. Sure, there were problems. But he could have improved, and instead they just sent him away.

The decision to place a relative in a nursing home is a difficult one for the family, and the move is traumatic for the relative. Such a decision is never one to be made lightly, and if possible should be a decision in which all affected parties are involved. In this case, the physician resigned from the case rather than approve the institutionalization of the patient. Some physicians have said to me that, knowing his patient's feelings, this doctor was remiss in not blocking the move.

But there are times when home care is not possible. A nursing-home residence is not necessarily a barrier to continued relations with family and friends. If the patient needs that level of care, it is important that care givers work together to make the right choice of residence. The general rules of home care and surrogacy seem to apply equally to the nursing-home setting, with the added legal, financial, and social complications the specific situation may require. The financial surrogate will have to balance the cost of home and institutional alternatives against the individual's financial resources, while the legal surrogate must make sure that the patient-relative's legal rights are protected. Physicians often work with certain residences and can recommend them. The community surrogate can ensure that an elderly individual's friends do not forsake their acquaintance and urge everyone to visit the person once he or she is in the new home.

In nursing homes as in the hospital, patients have rights. It is critical that when a person is moved to a skilled-nursing facility, relatives visit and ensure that those rights are not abused. Some nursing homes have family member associations in which problems can be brought out and aired. In others it is necessary for the patient's relative to speak directly to the institution's administration. To the extent that the relative-client is aware and able, most will encourage relatives and friends to take the patient out for an afternoon—for a meal or a movie—to ensure that he or she remains part of the world.

What is crucial is the knowledge that perhaps nothing is more traumatic for the elderly person than to be removed from his or her own residence and placed in an institution's care. The move may lead to severe adjustment problems and accusations of abandonment by the patient. The critical thing is to assure the relative-client that he or she remains loved and needed. "I'm sorry, Pops. I couldn't care for you alone, but I'll still be here every week and help you as much as I can." If there are grandchildren, bring them to visit.

CONCLUSION

Age is not a firm line, and the disabled elderly are not a single, uniform class. In a very real way, we who stand as mirrors to our elders make of disability either a shameful embarrassment or a livable condition. To the extent that we affirm the broad social rule that human value is tied to self-sufficiency, a precept many of today's aged taught us in our youth, we affirm their fears equating a diminished world with one that may not be worth living. If we see their increased need as a personal burden, we affirm that unproductive age is in fact a deficit both to the elderly and to those who will succeed them. In a society where mobility is a virtue and professional advancement a necessity, it is easy to deny the needs and the postures of family members who remain in towns, cities, and homes that we have left. The temption is to dictate to them and the care givers who have remained behind, to insist at remove on what is needed and what the reality may be without active, personal caring. From a distance it is possible to retain the active memory of the disabled elderly as they once were, to conspire with them in their fears, and to insist that things remain all right, that things are as they were. But there is no shame in change and no dishonor in disability at any age. The fear we have of cognitive deficits that affect the elderly is our fear and fragility, not necessarily theirs. There are worse ways to end one's life than to amble forgetfully through the images of past years. Such a life is often harder for those who care than for those whose lives have slipped from the present tense.

Perhaps the ultimate lesson of my father's tale is that age is a mirror not simply of the elderly soul but, more importantly, of ours. It defines and underlines our values, past memories, and fears for the future, not simply our concern for those who ruled a communal past. The greatest gift is survival, and when those who once seemed so omnipotent now stand frail, that transformation need be neither bewildering nor alienating. To choose to include the elderly in our lives is to affirm not only their value but our own. Ultimately, this gives dignity and hope to us all.

Select Bibliography

The following very short annotated bibliography includes a general selection of materials that I have found helpful and informative. Its emphasis is on broad social perspectives, although several specific how-to books are included as well.

BOOKS

Beauvoir, Simone de. *The Coming of Age.* New York: G. P. Putnam and Sons, 1972. For anyone less talented than Simone de Beauvoir, this encyclopedic review of aging in western society would have been the culminating work of a lifetime. Her importance in feminism, unfortunately, has overshadowed her contribution to gerontology. Written from a profoundly literate and humanist perspective, it is the book that places aging in a Western perspective.

———. *A Very Easy Death.* New York: G. P. Putnam and Sons, 1964. A short, powerfully descriptive book about the death by cancer of the author's mother. Although the context is terminal illness, de Beauvoir's discussion of relations with her mother and physicians, hospital routines, and the accommodations required by the care of an elderly, infirm relative can serve as an introduction to many of the problems faced by patients and relatives in a nonterminal context.

Blythe, Ronald. *The View in Winter: Reflections on Old Age.* New York: Harcourt Brace Jovanovich, 1979. A series of interviews with British elderly preceded by a good introductory essay.

Browne, Colette, and Onzuka-Anderson, Roberta, eds. *Our Aging Parents: A Practical Guide to Eldercare.* Honolulu: University of Hawaii Press,

1985. A series of articles by nurses, social workers, and therapists involved in caring for the elderly. Its chapters on stroke patients and nursing home care are, I think, its strongest.

Brunner, Lillian S. and Suddarth, Doris S. *Textbook of Medical-Surgical Nursing.* 3d edition. New York: J. P. Lippincott, 1975. A concise and clearly written textbook whose focus is not simply the plethora of disease to which we are all at risk but, more importantly, what they mean for the patient. In each chapter, medical tests are explained, patient comfort is assessed, and complications that might arise are discussed.

Carey, J. R. *How to Create Interiors for the Disabled.* New York: Pantheon Books, 1978. A general book with good illustrations describing how to adapt home environments for the impaired individual. Available in some public libraries.

Fisher, M. F. K. *Sister Age.* New York: Vintage Books, 1984. In these fifteen short stories, Fisher manages to describe the social isolation and failing physical powers that are for many elderly the terror of longevity. She embue her subjects with no bitterness and writes with compassion. This is fiction as it was meant to be.

Hellman, Lillian. *Maybe.* Boston: Little, Brown and Co., 1980. To the extent that age manifests as a condition of memory, a tidal wave of the past encroaching on a present, Hellman has described it.

Herzlich, Claudine, and Pierret, Nanine. *Illness and Self in Society.* trans. Elborg Forster. Baltimore: Johns Hopkins University Press, 1987. This is a remarkable statement on the degree to which organic disease is defined socially in society. Based both on historical research and on extensive interviews with French patients, its detailed analysis of illness—any illness—as a social as well as physical phenomenon is a crucial contribution to the understanding of disease in general. Its findings cry out for application in the specifics of gerontology and geriatric decline.

Horne, Jo. *Caregiving: Helping an Aged Loved One.* Des Plaines, Ill.: AARP Books/Scott Foresman, 1985. Perhaps the best single book on all practical aspects of care-giving. It is simply written and comprehensive. Its posture emphasizes home care and clearly describes the potential benefits and emotional pitfalls of the care-giving role.

Ignatieff, Michael. *The Needs of Strangers.* New York: Viking Penguin, 1985. Ignatieff explores the gray area between what individuals need as human beings and what they are entitled to as citizens. His opening chapter, which treats King Lear as a geriatric patient, is valuable and compelling.

Kubler-Ross, Elisabeth, *Living with Death and Dying.* New York: Collier Books, 1981.

————. *On Death and Dying*. New York: Macmillan, 1970. Kubler-Ross has written or co-authored more than twenty books on the subject of death and dying. Surprisingly, none of these deal specifically with the issues of gerontology or geriatric decline. Perhaps her most significant contribution to the field, and certainly to the layperson, has been the clear exposition of the steps all must take in coming to grips with any loss.

Lerner, Gerda. *A Death of One's Own*. Madison, Wis.: University of Wisconsin Press, 1985. This book describes how its author, a historian, took care of her husband during his progressive decline resulting from a brain tumor. Its description of the attendant problems of home care and the changes her husband's illness created for them both is compelling.

Mace, Nancy L., and Rabins, Peter V. *The 36-Hour Day*. Baltimore: Johns Hopkins University Press, 1981. This is a practical, nontechnical book on the care of individuals with Alzheimer's disease or other forms of memory-related illness in later life. It is, simply, the single best guide to the complex of family and interpersonal problems that I have read.

Sacks, Oliver. *The Man Who Mistook His Wife for a Hat*. New York: Summit Books, 1985. A series of twenty-four cases of individuals living with cognitive handicaps, each one chronicled by Sacks not as an abnormality but as a fact to be accepted in the midst of a life. It is included here not primarily for the cases detailed (only several of which are technically geriatric), but rather for the perspective Sacks brings to his treatment of individuals.

Woodward, Kathleen, and Schwartz, Murray M., eds. *Memory and Desire*. Bloomington: Indiana University Press, 1986. A series of twelve essays on aging, literature, and psychoanalysis.

ARTICLES

Biegel, Davie E., et al. "Unmet Needs and Barriers to Service Delivery for the Blind and Visually Impaired Elderly." *The Gerontologist* (1989), pp. 86–87. A review for the professional of the problems of serving the sight-impaired elderly patient. It includes a good bibliography on the topic.

Breslau, Lawrence. "The Faltering Therapeutic Perspective Toward Narcissistically Wounded Institutionalized Aged." *Journal of Geriatric Psychiatry*, 13 (1980), pp. 193–206. We talk of the elderly becoming childlike, but it is for most an impression. Breslau attempts to define the perception in terms of psychiatric stages of development more commonly applied to childhood.

"Coping with Care of the Elderly: A Geriatrics Panel Discussion." *Geriatrics* 44, no. 1 (January 1989), pp. 33–44. A group of doctors discuss what they don't like abut working in the geriatric field. Stresses difficulties of taking a family history. Interesting for its frank statement of the critical issues (time, money, status) from the doctor's perspective.

Gaynor, Sandra. "When the Caregiver Becomes the Patient." *Geriatric Nursing* (May/June 1989), pp. 121–123. A study of care givers of elderly patients over a several-year period. It found that over a period of months and years, care givers' health was adversely affected by the stress of their positions. See Stafford for an article on support groups and relief for care givers.

Hedberg, Augustin. "Caring for Your Aging Parents." *Money* (September 1989), 136–172. A special issue which attempts to survey the issues and provide practical information for the potential care giver. Especially useful is Mary Granfield's "A Source List for Children who Care," which names practical books and gives the addresses of national organizations of potential use to those faced with a geriatric crisis in their family.

Iris, Madelyn Anne. "Guardianship and the Elderly: A Multi-Perspective View of the Decisionmaking Process." *The Gerontologist* 28 (1988), supp. pp. 39–45. This offers in simple terms a clear description of the legal concept of guardianship and the role of courts in making such an appointment.

Silverstone, Barbara, and Miller, Sarah. "The Isolation of the Community Elderly from the Informal Social Structure: Myth or Reality?" *Journal of Geriatric Psychiatry* 13 (1980), pp. 27–47. Surprisingly little has been written on the issue of isolation in the elderly infirm. This 1980 article, which has a reasonable bibliography, is an excellent survey of the topic.

Stafford, Florence. "A Program for Families of the Mentally Impaired Elderly." *Gerontologist* 26, no. 6 (1980), pp. 656–68. This describes an early study of support groups for the families of impaired elderly and the importance of such groups. Although the principle is now accepted by, for example, the Alzheimer's Association, it is a useful review for all those attempting to deal with problems alone.

Weinstein, Barbara E. "Geriatric Hearing Loss: Myths, Realities, Resources for Physicians." *Geriatrics* 44, no. 4 (1989), pp. 42–60. This is a review of symptoms and etiologies of hearing loss that points out how often its symptoms can be mistaken—by family and medical professionals—for other diseases including Alzheimer's. Loss of hearing is so prevalent and can contribute to so many adjustment problems that even this brief introduction to the topic can be of enormous value to the layperson.

About the Author

TOM KOCH is a freelance journalist. He has published widely in magazines and newspapers including *Newsday, Baltimore Sun, Toronto Star* and *Toronto Globe and Mail* and is the author of *The News as Myth* (Greenwood Press, 1990).